iPhone User Interface Design Projects

Dave Mark, Series Editor

David Barnard
Joachim Bondo
Dan Burcaw
David Kaneda
Craig Kemper
Tim Novikoff

Chris Parrish and Brad Ellis
Keith Peters
Jürgen Siebert
Eddie Wilson

Apress®

iPHONE USER INTERFACE DESIGN PROJECTS

ISBN-13 (pbk): 978-1-4302-2359-7

ISBN-13 (electronic): 978-1-4302-2360-3

Printed and bound in the United States of America 9 8 7 6 5 4 3 2 1

Trademarked names may appear in this book. Rather than use a trademark symbol with every occurrence of a trademarked name, we use the names only in an editorial fashion and to the benefit of the trademark owner, with no intention of infringement of the trademark.

President and Publisher: Paul Manning
Lead Editor: Clay Andres Matthew Moodie
Developmental Editor: Matthew Moodie
Lead Author and Technical Reviewer: Joachim Bondo
Editorial Board: Clay Andres, Steve Anglin, Mark Beckner, Ewan Buckingham, Tony Campbell, Gary Cornell, Jonathan Gennick, Michelle Lowman, Matthew Moodie, Jeffrey Pepper, Frank Pohlmann, Ben Renow-Clarke, Dominic Shakeshaft, Matt Wade, Tom Welsh
Coordinating Editor: Kelly Moritz
Copy Editor: Heather Lang
Compositor: MacPS, LLC
Indexer: John Collin
Artist: April Milne
Cover Designer: Anna Ishchenko

Distributed to the book trade worldwide by Springer-Verlag New York, Inc., 233 Spring Street, 6th Floor, New York, NY 10013. Phone 1-800-SPRINGER, fax 201-348-4505, e-mail orders-ny@springer-sbm.com, or visit http://www.springeronline.com.

For information on translations, please e-mail info@apress.com, or visit http://www.apress.com.

Apress and friends of ED books may be purchased in bulk for academic, corporate, or promotional use. eBook versions and licenses are also available for most titles. For more information, reference our Special Bulk Sales–eBook Licensing web page at http://www.apress.com/info/bulksales.

The information in this book is distributed on an "as is" basis, without warranty. Although every precaution has been taken in the preparation of this work, neither the author(s) nor Apress shall have any liability to any person or entity with respect to any loss or damage caused or alleged to be caused directly or indirectly by the information contained in this work.

To my wife and family for being so incredibly supportive
—David Barnard

To my wife, Malena, who once again gave me the support I hadn't earned
—Joachim Bondo

To Mom, Dad, and Zach
—Dan Burcaw

To Lindi and our kids, for being cool, hip, and weird. And to Brandy, for always keeping me on task.
— Craig Kemper

To all the people who helped me get started and to Oana for supporting me all the way.
—Tim Novikoff

To my family, Liz, Sovereignty, and Aidan; thanks for all the patience and support
—Chris Parrish

To all my colleagues of the FontShop network
—Jürgen Siebert

To my wife Jenna and daughters Cana and Mia
—Eddie Wilson

Contents at a Glance

Contents

Foreword

Dear Readers,

When we hatched the idea for a series of project-oriented books featuring the work of leading iPhone developers and their apps, there were very few people we could really turn to as recognized experts in the field. We were all beginners of one sort or another: first using Objective-C, first trying out Xcode, learning to write for a mobile device, or perhaps developing our first app for fun. Whatever differentiating baggage we each brought with us, we were sharing the experience of learning Cocoa Touch, the iPhone OS SDK, and an enthusiasm for this new thing.

About a year later, it's a much more sophisticated iPhone world that is receiving this fourth in the iPhone Projects series published by Apress. Not only are there more and better apps but there are many more experienced, truly creative developers and designers. And since interface design and usability become more important as differentiating factors for the most successful apps, we're featuring some of the most creative designers in this book.

iPhone User Interface Design Projects is unique within the series for being design, rather than code, focused. All of those hard-core developer topics that dominated our earlier books needed to be written, because there really is no other place to start. But the really successful apps, the ones you never get tired of using and remain popular on Apple's iTunes App Store for a long time, have great code and great design.

It's not enough to have a unique feature or great performance. Too many other apps will either be copying your unique feature or came out a week before yours. You've got to make great-looking apps, and this book has some key examples of putting a professional polish on your work. But it's really more than applying a simple shine, because as you'll see in these chapters, good design requires plenty of thought right from the start of the development process. And that may be the most important lesson you'll get from this book. You have to think about every aspect of your app if you expect to be one of the shining lights among over 100,000 apps.

Once again, I have worked with Dave Mark, the series editor and author of several best-selling Apress books, including *Beginning iPhone 3 Development*, to find developers who produce efficient and bug-free code, design usable and attractive interfaces, and push the limits of the technology. Dave's common-man touch, tell-it-like-it-is sense of reality, and delight at apps that look great can be felt throughout the series.

This brings us back to the code, or in the case of user interface design, the lack of code. As developers, we all take comfort in the language of code. This book is about the visual presentation of your code. Most of your users have no idea what beautiful code is, but every user can take pleasure when you present the inner workings of your endeavors as a truly beautiful, useful app. It's something every iPhone developer should show off with pride.

We hope you'll find the apps presented in these chapters and the stories of how they came to be interesting as both human drama and as well-designed as the iPhone and iPod Touch technology. Happy adventuring, and send us a postcard!

Clay Andres
Apress Acquisitions Editor, iPhone and Mac OS X
clayandres@apress.com

About the Technical Reviewer

 Joachim Bondo has developed software for three decades, from programmable calculators in the late '70s before computers were commonly available to now the iPhone.

After releasing Deep Green, his critically acclaimed chess application, on the App Store, Joachim has contributed his excellent taste and insight on good user interface design to several Apress titles: *iPhone Games Projects*, *iPhone Advanced Projects*, and now *iPhone UI Projects*.

Introduction

By the time you read this, the number applications on the App Store will have crossed the 100,000 mark. Chances are that if you come up with an idea for an app, it's already on the Store and in abundance. In order to catch users' interest, you'll have to differentiate yours.

Most developers seem to take the easy route by simply lowering their price. The problem is that it's so easy to do that everybody can do it. And if they do, you've gained nothing. On the contrary, you've lost an income that could possibly motivate you to keep improving and updating your app and thereby sustain your name as a reliable developer users can trust their investment to.

If you choose to take the difficult route, however, and differentiate on quality—the route that not everybody can take—you'll not only become a better developer but also earn the respect from other developers and users who'll be willing to spend real time and money on your app.

The ten authors of this book have all released successful apps and can testify to how going that extra mile, or ten, has paid off in many aspects of their lives as iPhone developers. By reading their takes on how to make an app stand out from the rest, you'll gain some of the inspiration and insight that could make your app the one in its category that users will want.

If you're not going to differentiate your app on quality, this book is probably not for you. Instead, just go to iTunes Connect, and lower your price.

What's in This Book

This is a book about user interface design. As a consequence, you'll find lots of screenshots and only very little code. Several of the authors don't even have a programming background, but they all share the same passion for the iPhone and for developing apps of the highest standards in terms of user experience.

David Barnard of App Cubby is one such person; he has created a suite of essential utilities that enjoy great popularity on the App Store. In Chapter 1, he takes you through the process of perfecting entry views and presenting data, which both play central roles in his apps. And he explains how learning from Apple's UI conventions and usability testing can improve your final result.

In Chapter 2, I make an attempt to enhance the user experience and power of the navigation bar and present a relevant subset of large amounts of data in an exciting way. I bring you along on the same journey I took myself, as I actually came up with the design while I was writing the chapter.

Former Apple employee and Yellow Dog Linux distributor, Dan Burcaw talks on going native with his social networking app, Brightkite, in Chapter 3. He covers how that move made it possible to add the extra umph with CoreLocation, Camera, and Address Book integration that web apps just don't have. And, equally importantly, he explains how he tailored the user interface to match his target group.

Chapter 4 is devoted to Web and iPhone developer, David Kaneda, and the creation of his Basecamp project management client, Outpost. He starts with no idea and a blank piece of paper, continues over various attempts to creating the central dashboard screen, and finally settles on a version that manages to present a lot of information in a clear way.

Craig Kemper doesn't leave out any details when telling the tale about how he created his two award-winning puzzle games, TanZen and Zentomino. After reading Chapter 5, you'll understand why the two apps have been downloaded more than 150,000 times combined.

In Chapter 6 Tim Novikoff, a graduate student in applied math with no prior software programming experience, goes through his methodical process of creating Flash of Genius: SAT Vocab, an app for learning vocabulary words that made it to the Top 20 Paid Educational Apps list. His chapter is a fine example of how much you need to consider even when developing a seemingly simple user interface.

Long-time Mac developer, Chris Parrish, goes into depth on creating the perfect balance between simplicity, beauty, and features. If you dream about being the one on stage at the Apple Design Award one day, be sure to read Chapter 7. Chris must have eaten his own dog food as his app for sending digital postcards, Postage, won the award in 2009.

Keith Peters comes from the Flash world and delivers, in Chapter 8, concrete solutions to real-world challenges when porting games that were designed for the big screen of a desktop computer to our favorite device with no keyboard and a small, touch-sensitive screen. You'll realize that essential code doesn't have to be complicated.

If you're even the least interested in typography, you'll want to jump directly to Jürgen Siebert's Chapter 9 about FontShuffle, the application that lets you browse through 500 years of type design. You'll learn about the anatomy of letters and gain the knowledge to choose the right fonts for your programming projects and how to get maximum readability on screen or paper.

In Chapter 10, you'll see another example of how not having a programming background can pave the way for creating beautiful and well-designed iPhone apps that are so much more joyful to use than their large-screen Web counterparts. Snow Reports is one such app, and it's hard to believe Eddie Wilson first had to climb the Objective-C learning curve he found steeper than the slopes his app is reporting from.

There you have it: an array of interesting user interface projects lined up for you. Go ahead and dig in.

David Barnard

Company: App Cubby

Location: San Marcos, TX

Former Life As a Developer: Recording engineer/producer

I don't actually have any specific skills related to iPhone development. I don't do the programming and learned everything else along the way.

Life as an iPhone Developer:

Gas Cubby – Utilities - Sensible Car Care.

Trip Cubby – Finance – Mileage Log Made Simple

Health Cubby – Health & Fitness – Social Fitness

Chapter 1

App Cubby

Creating amazing iPhone applications is quite a bit more involved than it would seem at first glance. Though many gimmicky applications have made money in the App Store, building an elegant, easy-to-use application that solves a real problem or provides meaningful entertainment is the best way to guarantee long-term success. This chapter explores my journey in founding an iPhone development company and building several well-respected, profitable applications.

From Fanboy to Developer

I came to the iPhone platform not as an experienced developer, seasoned entrepreneur, or even programming hobbyist but as a rabid fan. I happened to be traveling in China in January of 2007 and vividly remember sitting in a Beijing hotel lobby, paying way too much for subpar Internet access and trying desperately to get news on the Macworld keynote. Did Apple actually announce a phone? What does it look like? Is it a real Apple device, not like the terrible ROKR I bought and quickly returned?

Fast-forward six months. I'd been watching and rewatching that keynote, reading every blog post, and listening to every podcast. I couldn't wait to purchase an iPhone. My brother called me up late in the afternoon on June 28 and asks me to meet him at the Apple Store. We waited almost 24 hours in line, and I ended up being the first person in San Antonio, Texas to purchase an iPhone. After just a few minutes using the device, it became quite apparent to me that Apple had delivered on the promise of revolutionizing the mobile phone. Being an intellectually curious person, I started thinking quite a bit about this little touch screen device and what made it so compelling. Why was I grabbing it instead of my laptop for certain tasks? How in the world did my Baby Boomer father take to it like a duck to water when he had struggled for years with computers?

That curiosity and the successes of burgeoning jailbreak development community got me thinking about what I might want to create if I were to develop an application for the iPhone. Web applications for the iPhone were functional, but they lacked the power and finesse of Apple's native applications. Rumors started floating around that Apple might actually be announcing an official SDK for native iPhone application development. My casual ideas about iPhone development slowly started forming into real thoughts of starting a business. I had just gotten married and was quickly realizing that my career as a recording engineer, working late into the night for weeks on end, wasn't congruent with my desire to start a family.

In March 2008, Steve Jobs took the stage and laid out a very compelling opportunity. For a very small fee, anyone could start developing iPhone applications and soon sell those applications to a rapidly growing install base. I was sold. My last scheduled project had just wrapped up in the recording studio, so there was no better time to jump head first into iPhone development.

Having spent the better part of a year casually studying the iPhone and thinking about potential applications, I knew that I would need to start working on this full time if I were going to build anything polished enough to match Apple's default applications. It didn't take much to convince my father and uncle, who are partners in a small business, to help me finance this new venture.

With bootstrap-level funding in the bank and my schedule completely open, I dove into the iPhone SDK. Because I have very little programming experience, the coding was challenging, but I was making progress. After about a week, I had a fully functional, but unpolished, tip calculator! As it turns out, a few tip calculators have made lots of money in the App Store, but at that point, I didn't want to risk my family's money on what I perceived to be a trinket application. My plan was to build a series of highly functional data management applications under the App Cubby brand, starting with a business mileage log called Trip Cubby. I quickly realized that to do this I would need an experienced coder.

Contracting out the coding turned out to be one of the best decisions I made in building App Cubby. Doing so freed me up to focus on the business and, more importantly, designing the applications without having to worry about the code. My informal curiosity about the stellar user experience of the iPhone turned into a systematic study. The multitouch interface we now take for granted was a fundamental shift in the way users interact with computers. Designing an application to fully leverage this amazing new technology was not something I took lightly.

Learning from Apple

As I started thinking about the user interface (UI) for the App Cubby applications and reading various books about UI design, I developed this grand vision of revolutionizing the touch screen interface—until I realized that the iPhone had already done just that. Apple has some of the best UI engineers in the world. Studying how Apple solved various UI challenges in their own applications is the absolute best place for any iPhone developer to start planning a UI.

In an attempt to create a distinct look, many iPhone developers consciously choose to ignore the UI conventions established by Apple in the iPhone's default applications (Phone, Messages Mail, Maps, Photos, etc.). There are definitely some interesting and innovative UI implementations that don't conform to Apple's UI conventions, but for most developers, sticking to Apple's published *iPhone Human Interface Guidelines* will take you a long way in making a more user friendly application. Speaking of the *iPhone Human Interface Guidelines*, I think that every iPhone developer should read that document cover to cover (multiple times even). My copy is the digital equivalent of a well-worn book, complete with highlights and notes all over the PDF.

After a couple times reading through the *iPhone Human Interface Guidelines*, it really sank in that the default applications created by Apple are some of the most frequently used on the iPhone and therefore the most familiar to the average iPhone user. Breaking from Apple's UI conventions forces the user to relearn certain actions and creates a bit of cognitive dissonance as the user switches among various applications with contradictory UI implementation. Apple's applications are not completely consistent, but they do contain certain patterns and methodologies that, if implemented, make it easier and more natural for users to quickly and effectively grasp the functionality of any application.

Let's look at data entry for a minute. Since I was planning to build a series of data management applications, I spent quite a bit of time studying how Apple addressed the challenge of entering lots of data into an iPhone application. The Calendar application provides a great example of Apple's hierarchical data entry paradigm.

The first level is what I'll call the main view (see Figure 1-1). This view aggregates multiple entries into a bird's eye view and allows the user to quickly scan a lot of information and easily find the information of interest.

Figure 1-1. *The main view*

Tapping on a summary row (i.e., the *Farmer's Market* row in Figure 1-1) in the main view takes you to the detail view (see Figure 1-2). Here, all the relevant data is displayed in detail.

Figure 1-2. *The detail view*

Tapping the *Edit* button in the top-right corner (or creating a new record from the main view) takes you to the data entry overview in the *Edit* screen, shown in Figure 1-3.

Figure 1-3. *The data entry overview*

In Figure 1-3, all available fields are presented in a grouped table view. Tapping a field takes you to a data entry view, which is shown in Figure 1-4.

Figure 1-4. *The data entry view*

This is where the magic happens: a keyboard, keypad, picker, or list pops up, and the user actually enters data.

In an attempt to streamline data entry, I've seen a lot of developers skip the view shown in Figure 1-4 in favor of allowing the keyboard to pop up over a long list of fields. Figure 1-5 shows what that shortcut might look like in Gas Cubby.

Figure 1-5. *An alternative, "streamlined" data entry screen*

At first glance, this shortcut might seem more efficient than Apple's approach, but in my experience, it causes quite a few accidental taps. While attempting to scroll, users can quite easily accidentally activate a field or tap a button. Combining the data entry overview and the data entry view in a single view takes focus away from the task of actually entering data and makes the user cognizant of the need to tap and swipe carefully.

Focus is the beauty of Apple's data entry paradigm. Because the keyboard takes up so much space on the screen, it's best to have data entry focused on a single field or small group of fields that fit above the keyboard.

Even the Mail application (see Figure 1-6) doesn't hide data entry fields. The Mail data entry view does scroll, and you can access additional data entry fields by tapping on the *Cc/Bcc, From* row. Even so, when you first create a new mail message, every immediately editable field is contained within the view. None are hidden behind the keyboard.

Figure 1-6. *The data entry view in Mail*

Figures 1-7 through 1-10 show how I implemented what I learned about data entry into Gas Cubby.

Figure 1-7. *The Gas Cubby main view*

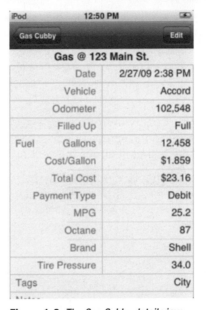

Figure 1-8. *The Gas Cubby detail view*

Figure 1-9. *The Gas Cubby data entry overview*

Figure 1-10. *The Gas Cubby data entry view*

The UI is distinct but also uses the Apple UI conventions any iPhone user will find easy to use.

You may notice that the Gas Cubby data entry view (see Figure 1-10) has an extra toolbar not used in the Calendar application. At times, a user might want to quickly enter data into all available data fields. In this case, navigating back and forth to the data entry overview (see Figure 1-9) wastes time. Rather than breaking from Apple's conventions, I decided to mesh the standard hierarchical data entry model with the shortcut toolbar from Safari, shown in Figure 1-11. This toolbar allows users to quickly fill in every available field using the Previous and Next buttons or use the hierarchical navigation to more efficiently enter data only in certain fields.

Figure 1-11. *The data entry shortcut toolbar in Safari*

Exploring Apple's data entry paradigm and implementing my own version challenged me to think deeply about why Apple chose this particular implementation and what designs may have been left on the cutting room floor. Some people complain about the perceived inefficiency of Apple's data entry paradigm, but for most users an intuitive interface actually outperforms a potentially faster, but more ambiguous interface. Efficiency is defined as "achieving maximum productivity with minimum wasted effort or expense." There are lots of ways for an iPhone UI to waste user effort, but wasting taps seems to be the focus of most left-brained iPhone developers.

To Tap or Not to Tap?

When I first started mocking up UI elements for Trip Cubby, every feature was measured by the number of taps required to accomplish a specific result. My thought was that by minimizing the number of taps, I was creating a more efficient application. But as I continued studying design and started actually using the early builds of Trip Cubby, my initial ideas and assumptions about what makes a truly efficient UI on the iPhone were thrown out the window.

One of the keys to creating great UI on the iPhone is taking a step back and thinking a bit about how users actually interact with the iPhone—with their fingers. Yes, that's incredibly obvious, but something so obvious generally caries significance that few people take the time to explore.

The finger is an incredibly efficient pointing device, far more efficient than the mouse. When the mouse was first introduced, it revolutionized human interaction with computers. I would argue that Apple's multitouch interface will, in time, prove to be even more revolutionary.

A mouse manifests an unnatural disconnect between the motion of the user's hand and the action on screen. Most people these days have used a computer enough to be somewhat accustomed to the mouse, but if you watch someone use a computer for the first time, you'll see a definite learning curve to using a mouse! I've even noticed a bit of a learning curve when using a new mouse or tracking settings with which I'm unfamiliar.

But the human finger, that's something just about every human being in the world is quite accustomed to using. We've learned since birth how to control our fingers with an amazing level of precision and speed. Imagine if you were to attempt playing the piano with a mouse. Your tune would be choppy and unmusical at best. A touch-screen piano, however, would be playable, even if it didn't match a real piano for feel and accuracy.

The more I thought about the finger as a means of interaction the more intrigued I was by how drastic the shift was from the mouse to multitouch. That's when it finally hit me. Taps are cheap!

If the appropriate action is obvious to the user, the time actually required for that user to tap the proper spot on the screen is miniscule. Confusion about where to tap wastes far more time than an extra tap.

Again, this conclusion may seem quite obvious. After all, ambiguity has been a challenge in all human computer interfaces, and reducing ambiguity has been one of the pillars of good interface design. But the iPhone is the first graphical computer interface where the speed and precision of the pointing device makes the physical action of pointing almost irrelevant when considering the time it takes to accomplish a specific result. Let that sink in for a minute—taps are cheap.

Understanding the finger as an input device is key in the process of making good interface decisions for the iPhone.

Here's quick example: Let's say you are designing a simple yes/no questionnaire. Each participant will be asked a series of questions verbally and should respond by selecting "yes" or "no." Some will be responding using a computer and mouse; others will be responding using an iPhone. To make the interface as intuitive as possible, you quickly decide that the *Yes* button should be green and the *No* button red (assuming a US audience and ignoring for a moment other cultural interpretations of color). Both buttons should have very easy-to-read text that is visually isolated from the background. Figure 1-12 shows what these buttons might look like on the iPhone (if you didn't hire a graphic artist).

Figure 1-12. *A sample survey application*

Since the buttons have already been created, it's easy enough to just use the same buttons on the computer. Now, you start administering the survey and observe the action and thought required for users to select an answer.

On the computer, the user first must decide what button corresponds to the correct answer (identification). With clearly labeled, color-coded buttons, the process of identification is quite quick. Next, the user must navigate the mouse to the appropriate position on the screen (positioning). Depending on the size of the button, the time it takes to visually locate the mouse pointer on the screen, the tracking precision and speed of the mouse, the position of the mouse on the tracking surface, and even the experience of the user, getting the mouse to the appropriate position on the screen can actually take significantly longer than the process of identification. Finally, the user has to click the mouse button (action). With a mouse, clicking is generally instinctual, but inexperienced computer users may still need a split second to decide whether to right-click or left-click.

On the iPhone, the user decides which button corresponds to the correct answer (identification) and then moves a finger into contact with the appropriate button on the screen (positioning and action).

In this scenario, the buttons on the iPhone and computer are exactly the same and should both be very easy to properly identify. Positioning and action are where the rubber meets the road. I haven't actually done this test and don't have any hard data, but it should be pretty obvious that moving from a mouse to a finger as a pointing device is a fundamental shift in the use of graphical interfaces.

At this point, some of you may be thinking that this was an unfair comparison, as the keyboard would obviously have been the best way for the computer user to interact with this survey by pressing Y for "yes" and N for "no." That's just the kind of logic-driven, computer-geek thinking that must be put aside when designing UI for the iPhone. Shortcuts are nice, but the average computer user can barely remember the keyboard shortcuts for copy and paste, much less the long list of shortcuts available for most modern applications.

To use the keyboard in the survey scenario, the users would first have to be told to press Y for "yes" and N for "no." Each time a question was asked, they would have to make the proper decision and then think "press Y for 'yes' and N for 'no'" before pressing the proper key. Eventually, the user would be accustomed to the interaction and become more efficient. But that's why the mouse was so revolutionary in its time and why the multitouch interface is an even bigger leap: each smoothes out the learning curve and mitigates steps from thought to outcome.

A physical keyboard can be quite efficient in the positioning and action phase (if the user is a touch typist), but the time it takes to identify the proper action is where the slowdown occurs. The user must first learn the commands and then remember and properly execute them. The mouse and graphical interface have generally made improvements in the speed of identification; it's easier to identify the symbol or actual name of an action than it is to remember a key command for that action, but this improvement in identification came at the expense of having to position the cursor before taking action.

The multitouch interface has the potential to combine the strengths of both traditional forms of user input. As a graphical interface, iPhone UI can use names and symbols to help users quickly identify the appropriate action. As a touch screen, the iPhone benefits from the speed and intuitive nature of using a finger as an input device.

The potential benefits of the multitouch interface are, however, easily squandered with a bad UI. That's where counting taps, which I would imagine is the gut instinct of most developers coming from the world of costly mouse clicks, can be dangerous. If actions are ambiguous, the physical speed of tapping is completely negated by the time it takes the user to identify the proper action. Using a confusing interface to save a few taps is the iPhone equivalent of keyboard shortcuts. Sure, some users will read your 50-page manual and end up a bit more efficient, but the learning curve is steep, and average user will continue to struggle.

Creating a user-friendly iPhone application is about striking a balance between efficiency of identification and efficiency of tapping. Because tapping is quick and intuitive, finding that balance generally leans in the direction of additional taps. There are times when counting taps might help make a great UI a bit more efficient, but starting the design process by counting taps will generally lead you down the wrong path. When designing for the iPhone, ambiguity is far more costly than taps.

Admitting that taps are cheap doesn't help UI design unless you also have a good grasp on ambiguity. Once you've spent much time on a project, the UI becomes so obvious to you it's hard to be objective about the ambiguous aspects of your application. The best way for a developer to get objective feedback about a particular UI implementation is to do usability testing.

Usability Testing on the Cheap

Since most iPhone applications are created by individuals or small teams on tight budgets, I would guess that very few have been subjected to usability testing. And it shows! Just because you don't have a budget or a formal understanding of the theories of usability testing doesn't mean you shouldn't test your application. Usability testing can become very time consuming and expensive if done on a large scale in a traditional way, but there are cheap and free ways to do informal usability testing that will greatly improve any UI.

Finding Users

First, let me clear up the most common misconception: usability testing is not the same thing as beta testing. If you don't test and set a direction for the UI first, beta testers will generally send you into a death spiral of adding unnecessary features and buttons to an interface that has no focus. Beta testers are typically more advanced iPhone users who don't mind taking a few minutes to learn the ins and outs of an application. They will quickly see beyond any usability problems and start brain storming new features and advanced options.

To properly test the usability of an iPhone application, you need to find several "average" iPhone users. I enlisted the help of family and friends, but you might want to put out an ad on craigslist and offer free lunch or an iTunes gift certificate. You're looking for people who know how to use the iPhone but aren't power users. The best way to do usability testing is in person, but it can be done via video conferencing or by having the user just video tape the testing.

Testing Done Right

If you're serious about usability testing, I recommend reading up on the theories and techniques; it's a fascinating field of study. In case you can't be bothered with doing additional research, let me give you a very quick overview to help point you in the right direction.

The first thing to do is to properly condition your test subjects. They need to understand that there are no right and wrong answers. Making mistakes is expected and is actually helpful. Explain that by making a mistake they will actually be helping you find flaws in your application. Don't explain how the application works or give any kind of tutorial on how to use your application. Usability testing is intended to simulate the real-world use of an application, and contrary to the hope of all software developers, most users will never read the manual. You can, however, give a basic description of the intent of your application. In my case, I would say something like, "This is Trip Cubby; it's an application designed to help track and report mileage for taxes or reimbursement."

Ideally, your test subject will be somewhat familiar with the scope of your application. In my case, my wife made the perfect test subject for Trip Cubby. Her job required quite a bit of driving, and she had been tracking her reimbursable mileage with a convoluted combination of sticky notes and scribbles in her calendar. Plus, she had been using an iPhone for a few months but was definitely not a power user.

Next, you need to set up a scenario and ask the test subjects to actually use your application. The first time I had my wife test Trip Cubby, I handed her the iPhone and said, "You just drove 33 miles to give a presentation at 123 Main Street. Try entering that information into Trip Cubby."

Once your test users are in action, it's time for you to observe and resist the urge to intervene. It's best to have the test subjects vocalize their thoughts as they perform the actions. By watching people interact with your application and listening to their thoughts as they walk through various scenarios, you should start seeing potential improvements in the UI. If no one figures out that your cute little disk icon means "save," maybe you should just use the word *Save* onscreen. If the testers keep tapping the wrong button on a cramped toolbar, maybe you should leave a couple buttons off and make the remaining buttons bigger. If users are completely stumped, and you have to intervene with several minutes of explanation, you should consider a complete overhaul of the UI!

Usability testing is sometimes tough for developers who are attached to a particular UI implementation, but being flexible and willing to adjust the application to real world users is incredibly important.

My wife Elizabeth's first use of Trip Cubby is provided in the following section to give you an idea of the sorts of things you might hear from users during this process.

Walking Through a User's Test

Faced with the *Trips* screen shown in Figure 1-13, Elizabeth, my first usability tester, said something along the lines of "OK, I want to add some information."

Figure 1-13. *The Trip Cubby main view*

"Oh, there's a big plus button," she said. "That must be for adding data." She tapped the button as was presented with the data entry overview shown in Figure 1-14.

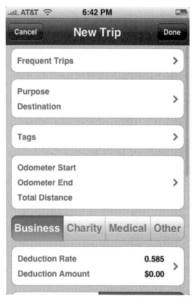

Figure 1-14. *The Trip Cubby data entry overview*

"Hmm, lots of information," Elizabeth said of the *New Trip* screen. "What do I do next? Frequent Trips? Um, I don't really know what that means. Purpose? I suppose the purpose was that I gave a presentation." She tapped the *Purpose* row to open the data entry view shown in Figure 1-15. "OK, I'll just type presentation."

Figure 1-15. The Trip Cubby data entry view

"Well," she wondered, "should I say what type of presentation? I guess my office manager doesn't really care what type of presentation, so I'll just leave it at that. Destination? You said 123 Main Street, right? OK, what do I do now? Looks like there are only two options: *Cancel* and *Save*." She tapped Save, and the testing went on from there.

Ideally, I would have video taped these sessions and studied them at length, but like I said, you can learn a lot from quick, informal testing. I repeated similar scenarios with various friends and family members throughout the testing of Trip Cubby. Having spent so much time studying and mimicking the UIs of Apple's default applications, I didn't run into any major issues while doing my informal usability testing, but I did rename several features and move a few buttons around.

Learning from Usability Testing

One of the most interesting things I learned by watching users interact with my applications is that iPhone users expect tactility. Pretty much every touch of the screen should have some sort of visual reaction, even if it doesn't actually accomplish anything. This is something that I should have learned while studying Apple's own UI interactions, but it didn't occur to me until I watched family and friends interact with my applications for the first time.

I designed the detail view of Trip Cubby to fit quite nicely on a single screen, as shown in Figure 1-16.

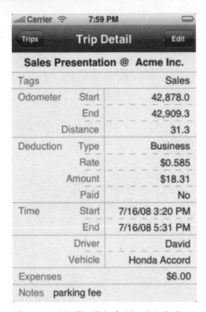

Figure 1-16. *The Trip Cubby detail view*

Because all of the information was visible at once, the screen didn't actually do anything. You could tap the *Edit* button at the top of the screen to update the information or tap the *Trips* button to return to the main screen, but the data section of the detail view was completely static. I noticed that users swiped up and down to see if there was any additional data. Swiping but not seeing motion was disorienting. They didn't necessarily expect more data, but they expected the screen to react to the touch.

The solution to this was twofold. First, I allowed the screen to scroll up and down even if the data didn't run off the page. This change also served a practical purpose in that we allowed the Notes field to expand rather than truncate long notes, but the primary purpose was psychological. When users swipe, the application responds. Next, I implemented swipe navigation for the detail views. Instead of having to navigate back to the main view and select the next record, users can simply swipe to the left or right to reveal the next or previous record.

Fit and Finish

After diligent study of Apple's UI conventions, internal iteration, and informal usability testing, you may think you're ready for release—you're not. iPhone users have a very high expectation for the fit and finish of an application. It's something that's experienced over time, not just shown in screenshots. Users feel and react to subtle details when interacting with your application, so no detail of the UI should be left to chance.

I literally spent weeks obsessing over the background image used in our applications. I started with the idea of a very distinct worn paper look, kind of like an old logbook that had spent a few hot summers in the glove box (see Figure 1-17).

Figure 1-17. *The Trip Cubby detail view prototype*

I quickly realized that a background like this would distract from the data, and data was the focus of my applications. After trying tons of different backgrounds, I finally settled on one with a subtle grainy texture (see Figure 1-18). Even then, I used Photoshop to tone down the texture a bit.

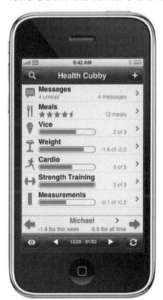

Figure 1-18. *The Health Cubby main view*

If asked, I doubt many users would say that the App Cubby applications have a textured background (it's less obvious on the iPhone than it is in print), but I guarantee the applications would feel less polished if I had just picked a solid-color background.

It may seem like minutia, but getting the little things right goes a long way in how users perceive an application. Users might not be able to explain why, but they can feel a polished application.

Summary

The iPhone is a revolutionary device and requires a thoughtful approach to solving the unique challenges of multitouch UI design. Apple has addressed many of the more obvious challenges in their own apps, but just copying Apple isn't enough to create a beautiful, usable interface. iPhone developers must study existing design patterns, but also innovate, test, and iterate.

Joachim Bondo

Company: *Cocoa Stuff (one man shop)*

Location: *Copenhagen, Denmark, Europe*

Former Life As a Developer: *27 years of experience in starting up and running smaller software development companies and developing software using a wide range of programming languages such as: BASIC, COMAL 80, Pascal, C, C++, Objective-C, SQL, NewtonScript, PHP, JavaScript, Bash*

...in environments such as: THINK C and TCL (Think Class Library), MPW (Macintish Programmer's Workshop), Metrowerks CodeWarrior and PowerPlant, 4th DIMENSION, NTK (Newton Toolkit), Sybase, MySQL, TextMate, Xcode, Cocoa, Cocoa Touch

...on platforms such as: Mac OS 3–8, Newton OS, Palm OS, UNIX (FreeBSD, Mac OS X), Linux, Mac OS X Panther–Leopard, iPhone OS

Life as an iPhone Developer: *Deep Green, chess game, using the official iPhone SDK from Apple since the day it was released. Several apps on the App Store developed for clients.*

What's in This Chapter: *The design of a Google Reader client for the iPhone*

Focusing on two areas of the user interface for my next application, I go through the iterations of creating and improving user interaction designs that will hopefully work better than what's currently available in competing offerings for the iPhone OS.

Key Technologies covered in this chapter:

- *User Interface Design*
- *Navigation Bar*
- *Custom Views*

Chapter 2

Yet Another Google Reader

I'm Joachim Bondo, the developer of Deep Green—"without question the best iPhone chess game" says John Gruber of Daring Fireball.

In this chapter, I'm going to take you through an early design process of my next application on the App Store, yet another Google Reader client. And I'm going to do it as I'm designing it for myself. In other words, at the time of this writing, all I have are a few ideas in my head. I haven't sketched or coded anything. I'll do the sketches here with you, for the first time.

I've chosen two areas of the user experience that I'd like to improve compared to what I've seen on the App Store so far. I'll be racing the book-production process, to see if my application can make it to the App Store before this book makes it to the brick-and-mortar stores, so that you can see the result of the design work I started here.

Ready, set, go!

Choosing to Develop a Newsreader

I'm a heavy user of Google's Reader service (http://reader.google.com). It's where I keep informed on what's going on in my areas of interest, such as technology, programming, photography, watches, and design, as well as the blogs of friends, peers, and competitors.

Instead of jumping from web site to web site to see what's new, I get everything consolidated in one place where it will appear as it becomes available. Despite my attempt to limit my consumption, I average between one and two hours per day on Google Reader.

There are many alternative solutions, on many platforms. Google Reader is just one, but I like that it provides an API (although currently unofficially) and that it tracks what items

I've read regardless of where I access them: it doesn't matter whether I consume the news from my home or work computer or my iPhone; it's all synced.

Another nice feature, from a developer's perspective—and let's face it, I *am* a developer—is that I don't have to mess with the many formats and odd implementations of fetching news feeds. Google has done all that for me and keeps maintaining it even after my application has shipped. I can concentrate on creating a spectacular user experience on top of it.

The iPhone-optimized Google Reader web site is currently the best experience on iPhone operating system—even compared with the many native applications available. It's now my proclaimed goal to make "without question, the best iPhone newsreader."

Identifying Pitfalls of Current Newsreaders

The difficultly in finding an application that could satisfy my newsreader needs on the iPhone has puzzled me. The perfect application may sit there on an App Store shelf somewhere, but of the many ones I've tried, and even paid for, I've not found a suitable one. The one I keep falling back to is Google's iPhone-optimized Reader web site accessed via Mobile Safari (see Figure 2-1). Despite its flaws, I consider it to be the best newsreader experience on the platform.

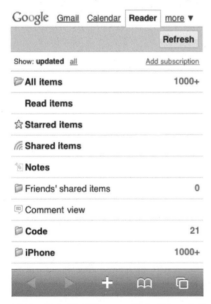

Figure 2-1. *The iPhone-optimized Google Reader web site in Mobile Safari*

I'll be using the Google Reader web site as the benchmark, because it does a fairly good job in pretty much the same way as most other newsreader applications, and because I don't want to pick on any particular application. But before diving into some of the usability problems, let me quickly run through the implementation supported by a few screenshots.

Exploring the Google Reader Experience

At the core, we're dealing with news items. A *news item* is an article or blog post on the Internet. It has a title, date, author, a body of text, and possibly images. The news item is the data part of what you see on a web site. Figure 2-2 shows a blog post from my web site and the corresponding news item in Google Reader on the iPhone.

 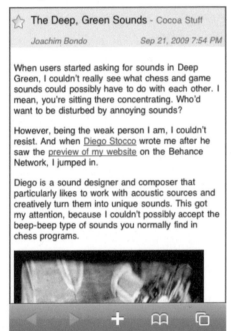

Figure 2-2. *A blog post on my web site and the corresponding Google Reader news item*

This example may not be the best, because my web site has only a little extra stuff, such as logo and navigation, because I took the time to make an iPhone-optimized style sheet. But if you look at the example in Figure 2-3, you'll see how nice it is to be presented with only the item and not all the extra noisy stuff on the web site, especially if you're mostly interested in the news contents.

Figure 2-3. *A busy blog post and the corresponding clean news item*

News items belong to a feed. A *feed* is basically a news stream of a web site. You *subscribe* to feeds. Finally, feeds can be organized in *groups*, which can be regarded as directories in your file system. The Google Reader web site doesn't currently support groups within groups. Figure 2-4 shows some of my feed subscriptions containing unread items at a time where I'm about to subscribe to a new feed.

Figure 2-4. *Groups, feeds, and items in Google Reader on the desktop*

Google's Reader web site is optimized for the iPhone, so there's no horizontal scrolling, and the text is displayed in a comfortable size. The main view looks like Figure 2-1, and in Figure 2-5, I've scrolled down so you can see how groups and feeds can be mixed at the top level.

Figure 2-5. *Google Reader's main view on the iPhone*

When you tap a group, it opens, and you see the feeds therein. Figure 2-6 shows the feeds containing unread items in my iPhone group. Tapping a feed displays its items in a list as shown in Figure 2-7.

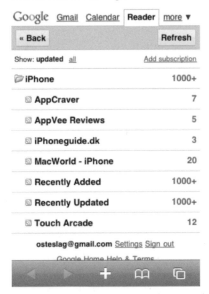

Figure 2-6. *The contents of a group—a list of feeds*

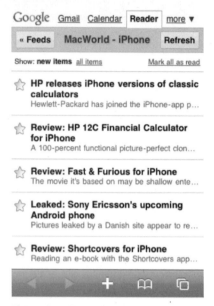

Figure 2-7. *The contents of a feed—a list of items*

Tapping an item in the list displays the full text along with links for sharing, adding a note, e-mailing, toggling the read/unread state, and finally a link to the original article on the web. See Figure 2-8.

Figure 2-8. *Viewing an item*

I'd like to think I can make this experience better in a number of areas. Let me go through a few of the biggest problems. It basically boils down to lack of overview, cumbersome navigation, and lack of data control.

Lack of Overview and Cumbersome Navigation

The cost of the iPhone's portability is obviously screen size, and there's only so much you can show with just 320 × 480 pixels available. This limitation makes it a lot harder to be a UI designer but also a lot more fun.

In my opinion, one of the best UI designs Apple has made with the iPhone OS is the navigation view paradigm. They've obviously felt challenged by the screen size limitation and have come up with a great solution. The way they've designed the table view and navigation bar to present and offer navigation in an indefinitely deep hierarchy of data is simply ingenious. And it's become the obvious choice for presenting large amounts of data. Therefore, it comes as no surprise that pretty much all the newsreader applications I've come across use the table view and navigation bar.

Except for not being able to see more than what fits the screen at a time, there's one problem in particular with this solution: it's very inefficient to step through data sideways (i.e., to go directly to a sibling). Not only do you have to make several taps, you also have to go up a level just to see if there is something else at that level.

Take, for example, the folder hierarchy shown in Figure 2-9. If you've drilled down to the *A/AA* path on the iPhone, and you want to go to *A/AB*, you first have to know there *is* an *A/AB* path, and then you have to go back one step to *A* before you can move into *AB*.

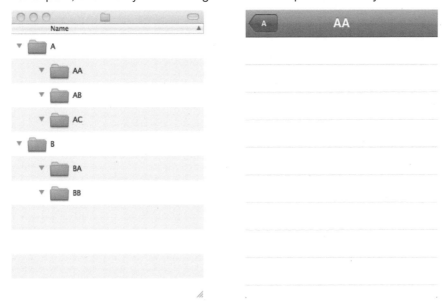

Figure 2-9. *A simple, illustrative folder hierarchy on Mac OS X and the iPhone OS*

"But that's just two quick taps," you say. You're right, but again, it's not just the two seemingly easy taps. It's mainly that you can't see what's in the parent, only its name—if that name fits on the back button, that is.

In other words, when you're in folder *AA* you can't see there's a folder *AB*. Depending on the context, this can cause a feeling of tunnel vision by narrowing the user's perception of the data being presented. An example of this problem is the popular demand for a unified inbox in the Mail application.

The navigation view paradigm is great for looking forward, not so much sideways or upward. All newsreaders that rely exclusively on navigation views will inherit these problems, and Google Reader is no exception.

Google Reader is further taxed by living inside Mobile Safari's chrome. In Figure 2-10, you'll see the worst-case scenario with the address/search bar visible. In real-world usage, this bar is most often not shown, but the toolbar is, and in Mobile Safari, the toolbar's visibility has nothing to do with the Google Reader functionality.

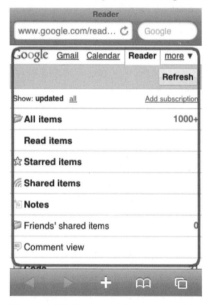

Figure 2-10. *Google Reader confined to the area between address/search bar and toolbar*

In the newsreader applications I've used so far, I've spent a proportionally large portion of my time navigating up and down between groups and feeds. I'd like to do more reading instead.

Lack of Data Control

"Lack of data control" is a very broad term, and I use it as such. So let me dig a little deeper. We're living in the information age, and that doesn't seem likely to change anytime soon. With all the information available to us everywhere, it becomes increasingly important to be able to filter information and to make it available to us when we want to consume, or discard, it.

As the screenshots have revealed, I can have thousands of unread items at any given time. I usually catch up once or twice a month when I have the time for it. When I glance through news items, I may read some right away and save some for later, but I often don't know which I'll save until I view the individual items.

Even what currently seems to be the most polished and popular Google Reader application on the App Store doesn't support all these use cases. If you tap an item, for example, it gets marked as read, and there's no way to mark it back to unread; therefore, you lose track of the item and can't easily find it again if you've chosen not to have read items displayed in the application. With so much information available, I bet many users have chosen this option.

You can star an item and review it later, yes, but you may want to use the star in a different way. When we software developers put these kinds of constraints on our users, we may limit them severely in their productivity.

Google Reader lets you toggle the read status, but it requires you to scroll all the way to the bottom of the article, which can often be quite a travel—especially if you want to read it later because it's a lengthy article.

Another and possibly even more important issue, to which I haven't seen a solution anywhere, is the ability to prioritize your feeds and the items therein. I can make no distinction in the applications between what I must read and what can wait. As you saw in Figure 2-6, I subscribe to various related feeds that I've grouped in the *iPhone* folder (only feeds with unread items are shown). But some of these are more important to me than others.

Instead of grouping my feeds they way I have, I could group them by importance, but I would lose the current grouping and have unrelated feeds mixed together, which is not what I want. That would be like having a newspaper with sports and politics mixed together, and who could even imagine such a thing? Besides, the importance is also likely to change from time to time, depending on the things I'm currently working on or active within.

In other words, neither Google Reader nor any other newsreader application I've used lets me give a hint as to what's important to me and what my reading patterns are, let alone automatically adapting to them. Every feed, every item is treated the same.

Improving the Newsreader Experience

There's no single way of using a newsreader. I'm sure there are countless different ways. When developing a newsreader, or any other application for that matter, the common assumption is that you should have a pretty good idea about how your users work and think in order to be able to give them what they want.

It may be my progressive age or pure arrogance, I don't know, but I've never programmed for other users' expectations. I truly believe in the success of developing applications for oneself, and not for some potential user. You'll end up with a better result for everybody, because you're more likely to put more passion into it if you do it for yourself, and in any case, users are going to look at your application and determine whether it's for them. So the users who end up using your application will be getting a better product.

I once gave a presentation on how I envisaged developing and implementing a fairly large workflow solution for Denmark's then-largest advertising agency. I had been briefed by the man in charge, and during the whole presentation, he was shaking his head and looking rather discontented. When I was done, he said, "This is not at all what we asked for, but it's exactly what we want!"

That doesn't mean you shouldn't listen to your users. On the contrary, you can't think of everything—users see things and come up with ideas you didn't think of yourself, and that's a great resource that you should definitely tap into.

Defining the Application Definition Statement

Here's a thing we *have* to do before starting any application design: formulate the product statement, or the Application Definition Statement as I noticed Apple started calling it at WWDC '09. It will help us making the right design decisions along the way, and it should have the following format:

```
<Your differentiator> <your solution> for <your audience>
```

In my case, I've chosen to formulate it as follows: an effective Google Reader client for the aesthetically aware news consumer.

My differentiator is "effective", the solution is "Google Reader client," and my audience is "the aesthetically aware news consumer."

By stating that the application is effective, I'm addressing all my complaints about the existing applications in one word. It's a little bit generic and very subjective, though. Being effective will mean different things to different users. But I still find "effective" to be the best descriptor, because that's the goal I'm trying to achieve, and it allows *each* user to attach *individual* emotions or values to being effective—and hopefully, I've achieved that too.

The target audience is the news consumer (i.e., people who read news). Online news feeds are implied by the saying this is a Google Reader client. And by targeting the aesthetically aware news consumer, I'm also saying that it's a tasteful and beautiful application.

Cumbersome navigation and lack of overview are the two main areas of problems. To me, those are big productivity killers, and I'd like to make my application more effective by addressing these two issues. That's exactly what I'm going to spend the remainder of this chapter trying to do.

Making the Application Native

Let me first get this out of the way. It really goes without saying, but I am anyway, because the Google Reader client is an iPhone-optimized web site, and making a native application is an important aspect of creating a superb user experience.

A native application allows me to implement features such as animations to help visualize and understand the connection between data and gestures to let the user navigate using the most intuitive user interface imaginable on an electronic device.

Making an application native doesn't necessarily make it faster, however, because I'm getting data over the Internet, and there's quite a lot of it. In fact, a this native application may even be slower, because I'll have to do a lot of local processing on the device, such as parsing and caching, while the web client gets the heavy lifting done by Google's server farm. I can, however, do things to create the perception of increased speed by displaying data as soon as it starts becoming available and other little tricks like that.

Making the Navigation More Effective

I pointed out some of the problems with the navigation view paradigm as Apple has implemented it. I'm not going to totally abandon the paradigm, because it's generally a very good design, and users have come to know it very well.

I'll just see if I can improve on the two aspects that don't work so well: improving the sideways navigation (i.e., going from one feed to a sibling without first having to go one step up) and giving the user a better indication of the current location in the navigation hierarchy.

If I can make a navigation bar on steroids by adding these two features, it sounds like that would make for a more effective navigation.

The navigation bar will be shown in the following four types of views, or screens, and should offer the following navigational options:

- Top (shows list of groups/feeds): There is no navigation.

- Group (shows list of feeds): Navigation can move up and perhaps to neighbors or siblings.

- Feed (shows list of items): Navigation can move up and to neighbors and siblings.

- Item (shows item detail): Navigation can move up and to neighbors.

The Top and Group views are the same, except that Group view will only show feeds because it can't contain other groups. When the user is at the Top view, there won't be any siblings to navigate to, so the navigation bar will contain no such options. When in Group view, the navigation bar might offer direct navigation to other groups, or possibly feeds.

The user will spend the most time in the Feed view when browsing news items and in the Item view when reading the news. When dealing with my navigation bar on steroids, I'll concentrate on the Feed navigation bar, because it will contain the most options.

Here's why: When in Item view, the user should be able to navigate to only the next and previous items, because visualizing several sibling news items in the navigation bar is not viable. News items don't have a clear and simple visual representation, such as an icon. They have only data, such as a date, author, or title, and none of these are suitable for mass representation in the navigation bar. A news item may contain images that I could use, but these are often photos, which don't typically scale well to very small sizes (despite the iPod application's display of the album cover in the navigation bar), and the user wouldn't know what the image represented anyway. Therefore, in Item view, I'll have to provide simple navigational options such as next/previous arrows.

A feed, on the other hand, has an icon that clearly identifies it and distinguishes it from other feeds. The most common thing to use is the site's `favicon.ico` file. This is the icon you see in your web browser's address bar. It's small, most often 16 × 16 pixels, but I don't want it to take up too much space anyway. As an alternative, as the iPhone OS keeps gaining market share on the mobile browser market, more and more sites are providing a higher-resolution icon file, the `apple-touch-icon.png` file, which is typically 57 × 57 pixels in size. This is the icon that's used when you make a home screen bookmark from Mobile Safari on your iPhone or iPod touch.

That said, let's see what kind of steroids I can inject into the navigation bar. If I just used the standard implementation, it would look something like Figure 2-11.

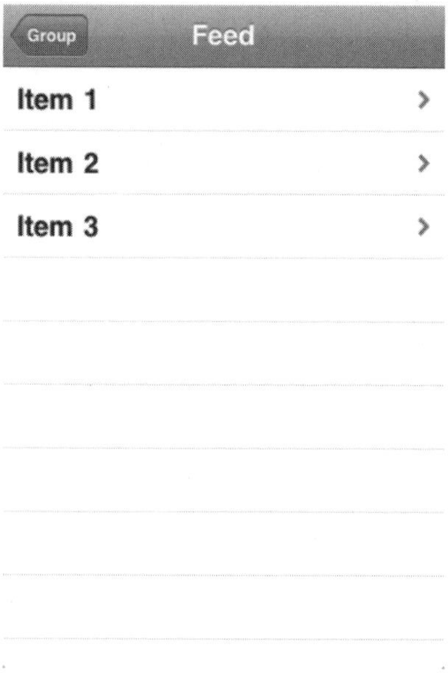

Figure 2-11. *Group/feed navigation bar the standard way*

Again, all you see here is the feed's title and its parent's name, or the portion of it that fits the back button. So if I want to display the siblings, I could simply line them up in the navigation bar as shown in Figure 2-12.

Figure 2-12. *A first attempt at a multifunctional navigation bar*

Tapping the feed icon next to the feed title would take us back to the Feed view, just as if it were a regular back button. This behavior is nice, because that's where the user is accustomed to finding it.

The user would tap an icon in the row to activate that feed or drag horizontally to scroll for more feed icons, and when the finger is lifted, the feed in focus would be loaded. The arrows indicate that there are more icons in both directions. I probably wouldn't want to display them.

While scrolling, I could display the icon and name of the feed in focus in the area below the icons, although the user's finger would obscure that (see Figure 2-13)—not a good solution, but I won't completely write it off either.

The bar looks a little bit busy, which I'm not too keen on, but that might be solved by making the icons grayscale, which could look good in a black header. And the icon for the currently displayed feed could be shown in color. But I'm getting ahead of myself. For now, we're just working on the high-level UI design, not fine-tuning the graphic design.

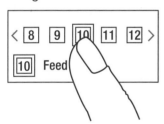

Figure 2-13. *The user's finger obscures the feed name while dragging.*

Swapping the elements, so that the row of feed icons would be displayed underneath the current feed title as shown in Figure 2-14, is not desirable, because this layout would imply that the sibling feeds where children of the current feed.

Figure 2-14. *The wrong way to represent siblings*

A third possibility, shown in Figure 2-15, could be to display the name of the feed in focus above the icon row, much like the dock in Mac OS X. But this layout is a little bit busy, takes up more vertical space, duplicates information, and is perhaps not very pretty. This solution isn't good either.

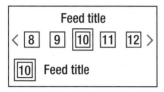

Figure 2-15. *Showing the name of the feed in focus above the icon isn't a good solution either.*

I haven't found a solution I'm happy with yet, but I have a model I can keep improving until I am. The purpose of this chapter isn't to come up with the perfect result but to illustrate my iterative process.

And, even at this early point, I've achieved the goal—deriving a solution that lets us navigate sideways with a single tap and at the same time gives a better indication of where we are in the hierarchy. I've even managed to do it with the same UI elements, icons in this case, by giving them multiple roles: command and display.

Giving a Better Overview

When faced with news items, possibly by the thousands, it becomes increasingly hard to find the ones that are the most important to you at any particular moment. Even though you've subscribed to all feeds yourself, you don't necessarily want to read everything as it becomes available. Sometimes, you may just want to see what's new; other times, just read one or two lengthy items that you marked earlier, and yet other times, perhaps catch up on some of those low-priority items. Ultimately, only you know what's important, but what if the application could assist you along the way?

There are two aspects of this assistance: the logic behind finding out what's important right now and the presentation of it in the user interface. With regard to the latter, the user interface in general should always allow you to quickly find what's the most important. But I'd like to see if there's a way to have the application itself present the news in a way that allows you to discover what you might like to read here and now.

This is much like opening a newspaper and being presented with the news in an exciting, unexpected way. But where the newspaper looks the same for every one of the hundreds of thousands of readers, I'd like my newsreader application to adapt to every single one of *its* hundreds of thousands of users.

In other words, based on the user's reading pattern, and whatever other logic I can come up with, I'd like to be able to figure out what's most important to the user right now and present that in an exciting way.

Studying the User's Reading Pattern

I love applications that successfully adapt to my personal behavior all by themselves. Just as much as I hate when they try and fail (remember Microsoft Office's office assistant, Clippit?) So not only should the user be able to turn this adaptive feature off, it should also be implemented in such a way that it doesn't annoy the user if the logic isn't perfect for the given situation.

In a way, this feature should be invisible. It works under the hood and affects only what data is being shown. It doesn't actually show the information. But it has everything to do with user interface design and user experience.

I'm not going into details with how to implement this feature, first because I don't exactly know at this point, and second because it's a huge subject that deserves much more space than I can give it here. But I'll go through some of the parameters I'll weigh in and, in the next section, talk about how this data could be presented:

- The order in which groups and feeds are visited (15%)

- The order in which feeds are read (25%)

- The `< read items count>` / `<available items count>` ratio per feed (20%)

- An application-provided user feed rating (40%)

The number in parenthesis is the weight I could give each, and these are unsubstantiated figures based on my gut feel. This list will allow me to rank every group and feed. The user's own rating would weigh the most, because it's an explicit rating, but I need to handle a feed that may not be rated at all but is also visited first thing most of the time. Obviously, this feature requires a lot more research, but you get the idea.

You could argue that newer items should weigh more than older ones, but I speculate that this varies from user to user as well as from feed to feed, so I've chosen to leave it out.

The essential thing is to end up with a figure on each feed that is the perceived *importance* of a feed and its items. This importance figure will be used when presenting news items to the user in the overview that I'm going to create next.

Presenting the Information

Independently from the group/feed/item view hierarchy, which the user has set up via Google Reader, I'd like to offer a nice *overview* (a separate UIView) of news items. Just like you don't know what's coming next when you're about to flip a page in a newspaper or what song iTunes will play next when shuffling, I'd like my application to make the decision about what to present—in my case, based on the importance.

So what's a good way of giving an overview? The immediate solution might be to display a table view sorted by importance so that the user, in theory, could just read all items starting from the top. It's not much of an overview, and it's a little bit ordinary.

I'd like something where you could just sit back and let the news scroll by—like a news ticker but a little bit more clever. And if you see something you'd like to read roll past, you just tap it to go to that item, perhaps something like Figure 2-16.

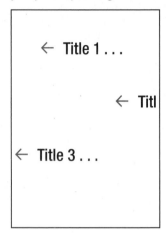

Figure 2-16. *An idea for an overview of random news*

Let's see if the idea in Figure 2-16 works. You'd see the news scrolling in from the right, eventually leaving the screen on the left side, and I'm already getting stressed just imagining this. The biggest problem is that all titles have the same weight and are competing against each other. You'd spend the time trying to catch up with the news stream. Although this might be what's happening in the real world, it's not the experience I want to give.

Somehow, the overview should differentiate the presentation of the items, based on some of the metadata available, so that the user's attention would be directed by whatever his or her mind was open to at the moment. After brief consideration, I've come up with Figure 2-17.

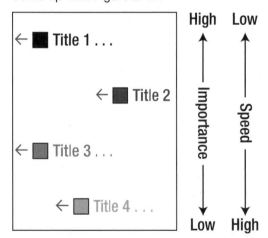

Figure 2-17. *Another idea for an overview of random news—this time using metadata to differentiate them*

In Figure 2-17, I'm using four pieces of information: two are displayed, and two are used to place and highlight the items. The central element is still the news title itself, and the feed icon next to it helps identify where it comes from and what type of news it is.

The importance is used to vertically position the item, so that the more important the item is, the higher in the view it's positioned. I'd also consider adjusting the horizontal scrolling speed, so that less-important items scroll by faster.

Finally, I'll use the date of the item to tint the title so newer items appear brighter. Older items would blend in more with the background. I find this a better way of dealing with the timeliness of an item than using the date in the calculation of the importance.

At this point, I think overview feature will work. I could try to improve it further, but I'm quite happy, so I won't do more at this point. The next obvious thing is to implement it and try it out. This might lead to further iterations. Time will tell.

Outlining the Next Steps

So far, I've concentrated on two specific design elements to which I wanted to create some effective and user-friendly solutions. The navigation bar still needs some work, while the overview could make the cut. But there's obviously much, much more to making an application destined for the top lists on the App Store.

Before leaving it to my fellow authors, I'll just add a few remarks on the work that's ahead of me at this point:

- *Overall UI:* As mentioned, I've only treated two specific user interface elements. Before even being able to do that, I should have settled on the overall user interface. And I have, even though I haven't shared it explicitly here, because it's going to be very similar to that of Google Reader and many of the other newsreader applications.

- *Architecting the application:* I also need to figure out how the model layer should be built and what API it should expose to the controller layer. With this type of application, I need to put extra care into designing it so that everything takes place asynchronously.

- *User testing:* As you've seen, a lot of iterations are involved in coming up with a good design. That's not to say my design is good, but bringing in users as you modify your design can provide you with valuable input and save you a lot of time.

- *Graphic design:* Once the user interface design is finalized, I'll go ahead and engage the graphics designers. Because this is such a text-heavy application, I'll probably hire a person with experience within newspaper or magazine design. I'd like to draw strong references to the newspaper world.

Summary

In this chapter, I've treated two design elements: the navigation bar and the overview for my next application, *an effective Google Reader client for the aesthetically aware news consumer*. If done right, these elements will help differentiate my application a little bit from the rest. Being different might not be a quality by itself, but in this case, I choose to see it as an improvement over the competition.

The overview seems like a simple, almost screensaver-like view, but underneath it lies some complicated logic that could turn out to be a great feature not seen anywhere else.

By the time you read this, I hope you can find my application on the App Store, download it, and enjoy the result. I don't even have a name for it yet, but you should be able to find it on my home page at http://cocoastuff.com/products/.

Dan Burcaw

Company: Founder and CEO of Double Encore, Inc.
Co-Founder of Push IO LLC

Location: Denver, CO

Former Life As a Developer: Development background primarily focused in Linux and open source in the 1990s. Co-founded Terra Soft Solutions, the developers of Yellow Dog Linux for Apple's PowerPC product line. While at Terra Soft I led all development efforts from python based apps to Linux kernel enhancements.

Life as an iPhone Developer: Double Encore was an early mover in the iPhone consulting spacing as I founded the company on the eve of the App Store launch. Since then we have shipped more than 20 app releases including:

- 91st PGA Championship (Sports)
- Brightkite (Social Networking)
- PencilBot ESL 1 Green (Education)
- PencilBot ESL 1 Blue (Education)
- PencilBot ESL 1 Red (Education)
- PencilBot ESL 2 Green (Education)
- PencilBot Test 1 Green (Education)
- PencilBot Test 1 Blue (Education)
- PencilBot Test 1 Red (Education)
- Tango Card (Lifestyle)
- PublicEarth (Navigation)

- **Bad Decision Blocker (Utilities)**
- **Tint Color (Productivity)**
- **Pirate Glossary (Entertainment)**

What's in This Chapter:

- **Brightkite: A Location-based Social Network**
- **Double Encore: An iPhone Development Agency**
- **Why Build a Native Application?**
- **Using TabBar Navigation for Complex Apps**
- **The Importance of First Use**
- **Virtually Infinite Drill-Down with Navigation Controllers**
- **Best Practices for Address Book Integration**

Key Technologies:

- **Navigation Controller and Tab Bar Controller**
- **Address Book**
- **Core Location**
- **Memory Management**

Chapter 3

Brightkite for the iPhone

"We don't want to release something that's not rock solid. And, by rock solid, we don't mean crashing, but rock solid from a usability standpoint," said Martin May, cofounder of Brightkite. "The app should be as easy to use as possible. We have some very ambitious goals concerning the user interface, but getting it just right takes time." So began my company's first major iPhone project—building Brightkite's native iPhone application. This challenging and energizing project set a bar for quality that, while still rare on the App Store, is one we strive to emulate or exceed with every application to which we lend our name. The Brightkite iPhone project was successful because of not only unprecedented focus on design and usability but the close collaboration between Brightkite and my company, Double Encore, Inc. There were many challenges during the process, but the lessons learned during that first major project contributed to Double Encore's continued presence in this niche industry.

Introducing the Brightkite Location-Aware Social Network

Brightkite, a location-aware social network founded by Martin May and Brady Becker in 2007, was for a member of the inaugural class of TechStars, a seed capital and mentorship program for start-ups. Brightkite can be used to locate friends and find out what they are doing in real time and to meet new people nearby.

Here's a simple explanation of the service: Brightkite users post geotagged notes and photos for others to see. Depending on user-selected privacy settings, a location may be as specific as "Brightkite HQ, 2911 Walnut Street, Denver, CO 80205" or as approximate as "Denver, CO." Brightkite offers a variety of activity streams that show posts from nearby users, people you are following, or even the entire Brightkite community.

The Brightkite web site went into private beta in April 2008, and an invitation into the service was a hot ticket throughout the summer. Martin and Brady understood that mobile was vitally important to the success of their service. Even the first release in April had SMS support, which allowed mobile phone users to interact with the service through simple text messages.

Introducing Double Encore

A conviction that iPhone SDK would profoundly change the mobile space compelled my resignation, in June 2008, from a nearly four-year tenure at Apple, Inc. I then launched Double Encore, one of the first iPhone development agencies, in anticipation of a shift that would place powerful software at the center of the mobile universe. I had witnessed such a shift in the 1990s, during my involvement in the Linux space, when I experienced the nascent and eventual domination of software technology in the enterprise computing space.

In 1999, I cofounded Terra Soft Solutions, the company that developed Yellow Dog, a commercial flavor of Linux, for Apple's PowerPC product. Terra Soft Solutions also developed software that allowed scientists to harness the collective computing power of many Apple machines clustered together to accelerate research. Terra Soft's products were at the core of mission critical systems, including a sonar platform that shipped onboard each vessel in the U.S. Navy submarine fleet.

Martin May contacted me shortly after I founded Double Encore. I knew of Brightkite from the buzz generated earlier that spring when it launched a private beta release of its location-aware social networking service. May was familiar with Yellow Dog Linux and asked if my team would be interested in building the Brightkite native iPhone application. While we had started working on a few smaller iPhone applications, the opportunity to build Brightkite's native application was a welcome challenge that I believed would lead to a more significant Double Encore presence in the application development market.

Moving From Web to Mobile

Released in the spring of 2008, Brightkite's iPhone-optimized web application met with great enthusiasm. Yet, with the launch of the iPhone App Store looming, a native Brightkite application could obviously offer a significantly more remarkable experience. To put the native application in perspective, it is important to understand both the feature set and user interface of the web application (see Figure 3-1).

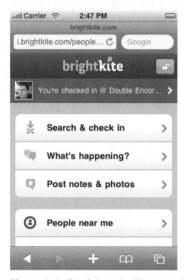

Figure 3-1. *The Brightkite iPhone-optimized web application*

The Brightkite web application incorporates three fundamental activities: checking in, viewing activity streams, and posting notes or photos. Let's explore each of these activities further.

First, a user can search for a place and check in at that place. "Checking in" is Brightkite parlance for associating oneself with a particular place. Second, activity streams offer a real-time view of check-ins, notes, or photos from friends or from anyone using the service. Third, posts (of notes or photos) are geotagged to a user's check-in location. For example, I could post a note about writing this chapter at my current location, "Double Encore, Inc." (see Figure 3-2).

Figure 3-2. *Posting a note via the Brightkite iPhone-optimized web application*

The Brightkite iPhone-optimized web application was well received by Brightkite users as a superior way to utilize the service via a touch interface versus sending SMS commands. The simple, iPhone-like interface offered many features found on the standard Brightkite web site. However, despite being impressed by the web application, users noted a few shortcomings with two of the major functions of the service: checking in and posting a photo.

For example, the process of location selection could be time consuming. Although placemarks (one of Brightkite's shortcuts) enabled users to bookmark places for future posting, the initial process of searching for and choosing a place to check in or post a note was a lengthy affair. Posting a photo was even more difficult and involved multiple iPhone applications plus the Brightkite web application. A user would first take a picture with the Camera application and then use Mail to send the photo to a special e-mail address provided by Brightkite (via the web application), where the Brightkite backend would associate it with a specific post.

Earlier, I mentioned another major activity on Brightkite: the activity streams. From a user experience perspective, activity streams worked fairly well with the web application. There were a few tricks and challenges to overcome in implementing the streams in the native application, but I'll explain more about that later.

In March 2008, Apple announced the iPhone SDK, which allowed developers to build native iPhone applications with the same tools and frameworks that Apple used with their built-in ones. The SDK's feature set provided Brightkite with the means to improve the overall experience of core functionality, such as checking in and posting photos, as well as to develop further innovations to drive the service forward.

The Rise of Native Applications, to the Web's Despair

The iPhone SDK was providential to iPhone users and developers. Following the launch of the iPhone in 2007, developers hungrily pursued a vision of creating applications as speedy and powerful as Apple's built-in iPhone applications. With the arrival of iPhone SDK, their dream was realized. SDK provided the tools to build stunning applications with major access to iPhone functionality. For example, developers could include the Camera or Safari browser in their applications and utilize most of the user interface elements found in Apple's built-in applications.

At Double Encore, the iPhone SDK was eagerly anticipated and welcomed as the impetus to enhance the Brightkite application and, consequently, the user experience. Certain key features of the SDK appeared ideal for improving a few of the quirky aspects of the web application.

For example, reverse geocoding, provided by Core Location, converts the latitude and longitude pair into a list of human-readable intersections, addresses, or even specific places. Therefore, Core Location made it possible to use reverse geocoding to suggest check-in or post-to locations based on the latitude and longitude reported by the iPhone.

Moreover, a native Brightkite application could eliminate the tedious workflow involved in photo posting by offering built-in Camera functionality.

Address Book was another SDK feature used in the initial App Store release of the Brightkite iPhone application. We decided to use Address Book to simplify inviting friends to the Brightkite service via email or SMS. Address Book integration also allows users to discover friends already using the service. We did have some special concerns about integrating Address Book, which will be discussed later in this chapter.

With all of the rich capabilities afforded by the iPhone SDK, we anticipated the complexity of developing the Brightkite application. We also welcomed the challenge, because we understood that optimizing user experience was key to the application's success.

IT'S ALL ABOUT LOCATION

Core Location is a framework included in the iPhone SDK that gives developers access to the device's current location. Before discussing how we used Core Location in Brightkite, it is worth discussing how a location fix may differ depending on what type of device is being used.

An iPod Touch has only Wi-Fi network connectivity, so the device determines a location fix by querying a database of Wi-Fi access points, which are mapped to physical locations. I wouldn't want to drive around the world mapping Wi-Fi access points, but it has been done, and the database is impressively accurate. On the original iPhone, Wi-Fi can be supplemented with cellular telephone tower triangulation data. Triangulation is less precise than Wi-Fi, but it's adequate when Wi-Fi data is not available. A GPS radio integrated with the iPhone 3G lets Core Location provide a much more accurate location fix.

Core Location is now widely used in thousands of iPhone applications. Typically, you might find the framework used in an applications such as an ATM finder, which offers a sorted list of ATMs with the closest location displayed at the top and the rest in descending order.

Brightkite's use of location is a bit more sophisticated because the service revolves around a specific place, rather than geographical coordinates. To provide the precision expected by users, the correct place is displayed on the *I am* screen shown in the following illustration, which is the main tab used to perform check-ins or posts.

In experimenting with Core Location, we discovered some interesting challenges. First, because Core Location's data comes from a system-level process, it sometimes reports old or stale location data. This anomaly was particularly frustrating for early Brightkite iPhone application beta testers, as a location across town might show briefly before the application updated to a more accurate value. We found that we had to check the time of the Core Location value and establish that it came after the Brightkite iPhone application launched.

Additionally, on iPhones with built-in GPS modules, the time necessary for Core Location to determine an accurate location fix could be as long as 5-10 seconds. This necessitated an engineering decision to leave the GPS radio on for the duration of the Brightkite application launch, therefore ensuring a constant stream of location data and optimum accuracy. Although this approach does affect battery performance, the typical mobile application user jumps in and out of an application rather than leaving it running for a significant period of time.

Once we were getting fresh, accurate location data, we added a snap feature that unquestionably improved the overall Brightkite experience. On the service side, Brightkite not only links geographical coordinates to a specific check-in place but it also recognizes the frequency of visits to that particular location. This allows the Brightkite native application to automatically snap to a frequently visited place as the user approaches. This place-snapping functionality is one of the most widely touted, user-gratifying features of the native iPhone application. This snap feature just wouldn't have been possible in the web application.

It should be noted that, in iPhone OS 3.0, a web application can request Core Location data via a JavaScript call. Had this been available a year earlier, Brightkite may have not moved as aggressively into native iPhone application development.

A Creative Paradigm Shift

Initially, the wireframes for the Brightkite native iPhone application mirrored the look and feel of the web application but with the addition of the Camera and Core Location integration previously discussed. The web application mimicked aspects of the iPhone user interface design but ultimately flowed much like web applications in which users drill down into content and navigate to and from pages with back and forward arrows and hyperlinks.

Shortly before Double Encore was brought onboard to develop the native application, Martin and Brady began to have second thoughts about the native application user interface strategy. They wanted to design a user interface that would include most of the features available on the Brightkite service, with room to add more in the future. However, it was vital that the application be simple for first-time users to learn.

We also needed to respect the diverse Brightkite community, whose members use the service in a variety of ways. For example, some use Brightkite as their main social networking tool, while others use it to post to their Twitter or Facebook accounts. Options and customization had to be critical design considerations.

Our analysis indicated that a tab bar interface would allow scaling as features were added to the iPhone application, handle the first time use case, streamline the check-in and posting process, and provide a way for users to customize the application (the alternative was to use the drill-down navigation approach that Brightkite had already utilized with the iPhone-optimized web application). The tab bar, shown in Figure 3-3, is a user interface element in the Phone and iPod applications. However, at that time, the tab bar was not widely used outside of Apple's applications, and very little sample code existed with an implementation.

Figure 3-3. *The tab bar user interface element*

Moving to a tab bar meant replacing the drill-down menu system found in the iPhone-optimized web application with top level functionality that was only a tap away, regardless of how deep the user navigated through the interface of a given top level function.

The iPhone SDK's tab bar controller offers a nice benefit that gave us a way to scale the application's features over time. When a tab bar has more than five items, a *More* tab is provided on the right most side of the tab bar. Tapping *More* provides a standard UITableView of other tabs (presented in a list) that the user can navigate to. In version 1.0 of the Brightkite native application, we ended up having nine tabs in addition to *More*: *I am*, *Friends*, *Nearby*, *Universe*, *Messages*, *Placemarks*, *Requests*, *Search*, and *Settings*. Brightkite users love to customize their experience, so we turned on the tab bar controller's edit mode, which allows a user to rearrange what tabs go where in an application's tab bar. The only exception to this was *I am*. We didn't allow users to move *I am* from its location as the first (leftmost) tab of the tab bar, since checking-in is vital to participation on Brightkite.

BRIGHTKITE SHARES

Brightkite is a great Twitter client. Say what? It turns out that Brightkite check-ins, notes, and photos can be cross-posted to a variety of other services. For example, Brightkite posts often show up in Twitter streams. Since Brightkite notes are limited to 140 characters, there is an intuitive correspondence between the two services. With Twitter integration turned on under **Account Settings ➤ Sharing** at www.Brightkite.com, the Brightkite iPhone application is a handy way to post to Brightkite and Twitter at the same time (see the following screenshot).

What's more, this feature doesn't stop with Twitter. Brightkite also integrates with other services such as Facebook, and users can post photos to Flickr, an easy way to publish pictures to the Web. As a bonus, since Brightkite is location-based, photos are geotagged before they are sent to Flickr by the Brightkite service.

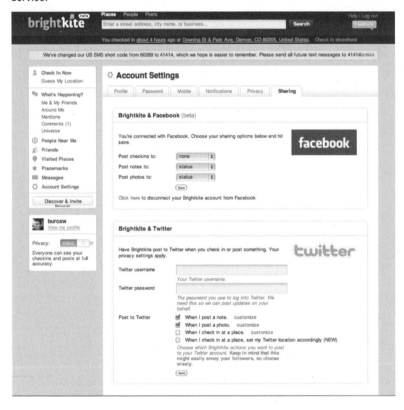

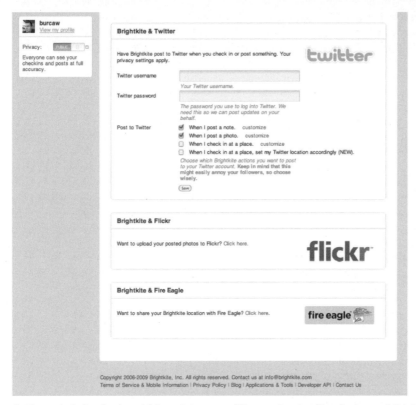

Geotagged photos (and posts) have been one of the most compelling features of Brightkite. In fact, the company has been covered in the mainstream media because of the citizen journalism coming from Brightkite users. For example, Brightkite users were on the scene posting photos at President Obama's Inauguration. They also posted some of the first photos of the US Airways crash into the Hudson River in New York. Be sure to read Brightkite's blog post on citizen journalism at http://blog.brightkite.com/2009/01/17/citizen-journalism-at-the-presidential-inauguration/.

Designing for the First-Time User

Throughout the development of the Brightkite native application, the first-time user experience was an unwavering consideration. From a business perspective, a native iPhone application offered Brightkite an opportunity to grow and expand. Critical to this objective were the first-time users who would ultimately download the Brightkite iPhone application but had no previous exposure to the service. Our job was to ensure the fewest possible entry barriers for first timers.

The sign-up process represents the greatest hurdle for a successful first-time user experience, and we erroneously began engineering a cumbersome, multiscreen process. After selecting a username and password, the user would be stepped through the various configuration options of Brightkite—everything from setting up a user profile to turning on mobile notifications to deliver SMS messages for Brightkite activity, such as a nearby check-in.

Late one night at Brightkite headquarters, we tested the first prototype of this sign-up flow. I remember handing Martin May my iPhone and the latest build. Martin ran through the sign-up process by creating a test account. We looked at each other, and I got the feeling plans were about to change.

A moment later, Martin firmly stated, "This is too complex." With that, the sign-up process quickly changed to the final shipping implementation (see Figure 3-4), which launched a first time user right into the application after completing a very simple one-page screen. The new sign-up process minimized the number of fields requiring data input to the bare necessities needed for authentication purposes, such as username and password. Helpful text hints inform the user about the information we are asking for, and the text content and color changes if necessary as the user types, for example, if the provided e-mail address is not a valid format or the password is too short. By reducing the number of screens, keeping data input to a minimum, and adapting the sign-up screen's messaging as the user interacts with the application, the shipping implementation vastly reduced the barriers preventing someone from trying Brightkite.

We still exposed all of the original features of the initial signup process in the application's *Settings* tab. This was very easy to do because of a technical design decision we made in building the *Settings* tab. Brightkite's web site is full of customization options and settings. Martin and Brady wanted to expose as many of these as possible via the iPhone application, with a simple means to add more over time. We built the *Settings* tab to construct itself from a hierarchy defined in a property list similar to an iPhone application's `Info.plist` file. From a code maintenance perspective, this gave Brightkite the ability to add or remove items from the *Settings* tab with relative ease.

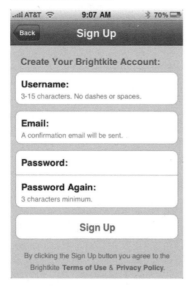

Figure 3-4. *Sign-up made easy*

Now that we'd reduced the sign-up impediment, what came next? Brightkite is a social network, which implies a collaborative experience. A first-time user doesn't have any friends in the friend's list, so we had to find a way to encourage first-timers to explore Brightkite anyway. The solution was to show a new user the *Nearby* tab, expanded out to a 100 kilometer radius. This meant that many first timers would see a busy activity stream of Brightkite user posts within their general geographic location (see Figure 3-5). A sample of the Brightkite experience might entice them to participate and to invite their friends to join too.

What about checking in, you might ask? After all, wouldn't a first-time user be encouraged to check in first? The *I am* tab in the Brightkite application is the first tab all users are brought to after sign-up. On this screen, they are shown their current locations and given the opportunity to check in or post a note. Many first-time users will do this first thing. Others will tap around the application and see what Brightkite is all about before getting involved—hence the importance of providing a good first-time user experience in the various activity streams, any one of which may be the reason a user decided whether or not to check in. Moreover, just getting someone to check in doesn't mean we suddenly have an active Brightkite user. In my experience, if there is a lot of activity in the streams—among friends, people nearby, and the universe—I am more likely to want to check in and post a note or photo.

In some areas of the country, Brightkite isn't as widely used. I have had friends come to Denver that weren't active Brightkite users in their hometowns but really enjoyed Brightkite in Denver because of the amount of activity. Making the *I am* tab the first screen the user sees after sign-up (and subsequent application launches) is important given the typical smart phone application usage patterns of quick in-and-out behavior. Yet, usage is really driven by the streams.

Since, again, the first-time user doesn't have any friends in the *Friends* stream, so we also encourage making friends. In this case, the placeholder graphic on the *Friends* tab has two action buttons: one to discover friends who are already on the service and another to invite friends to the service via their Address Book (more on this can be found in the "Best Practices for Address Book Integration" sidebar).

Figure 3-5. *The expansive Brightkite is a whole universe.*

Creating Virtually Infinite Drill-Down

The Brightkite service has three types of pages accessible through the activity streams: posts, places, and people. Posts are check-ins, notes, or photos from a person at a specific place. From a post, a user may navigate to a place or person. From that place or person, a user may navigate to another post, and, thus, to another place or person, and so on.

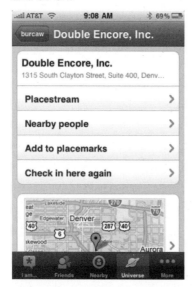

Figure 3-6. *From a place, users can choose to add a placemark, navigate to another place, find people nearby, or check in; drill-down is essentially infinite.*

Navigation controllers for our tab-bar-controller–based user interface represented another critical design component. We realized that the interconnectedness of posts, people, and places would potentially allow users to drill down, virtually forever, but would require a careful implementation to avoid excess memory consumption.

In simple terms, my team needed to create a drill-down function. In a typical navigation controller, each view controller is retained in memory. In Instruments, the performance and memory optimization tool that ships as part of Xcode, a navigation controller drill-down typically shows an increase in memory usage over time. As a user backtracks the navigation stack, memory usage declines in proportion to freed, unneeded view controllers.

Managing memory so well that the iPhone's memory watchdog process would never kill the application presented an ambitious goal, considering the resource-constrained nature of the iPhone and the watchdog's aggressive tendencies. For those not familiar, the iPhone operating system has a background watchdog process that looks for memory use by sampling the system at frequent intervals. Among other tasks, the watchdog is intended to protect the system's core phone functionality from third-party applications. Should the watchdog identify a problem, the offending application receives several warnings before the system ultimately performs a shutdown.

The Brightkite drill-down among posts, people, and places signaled that our design would excessively consume memory. Initially, we brainstormed ways to avoid the problem altogether. For example, we considered limiting the allowable drill-down. We finally decided that any artificial limit was not intuitive to the user and, therefore, unacceptable in our product.

In an infinite drill-down scenario, the memory curve continually increases until the iPhone operating system issues one or more memory warnings. Our testing revealed that freeing unused application data at the time of the warning, through the didReceiveMemoryWarning method, failed to prevent memory shutdowns. This is a key user experience point: a user can't tell the difference between a crash caused by a code defect and one that occurred at the hand of the memory watchdog. We concluded that preventing the system from issuing an initial memory warning would substantially decrease the possibility of a memory shutdown.

We readily solved the memory problem by implementing a grandfather strategy. In other words, as the user drills down, the tab bar controller frees the view controller on the grandparent stack rather than on the previous (parent stack) view controller. Essentially, our tab bar controller must retain just enough data about the freed view controllers to rebuild the state, as the user taps the back button and traverses back up the stack. After implementation, the memory graph in Instruments revealed a static memory footprint instead of a steady climb. Memory was allocated for a new view as the user tapped on a post, person, or place and, concurrently, the tab bar freed the grandparent view controller.

You might wonder why we went to such lengths for the Brightkite application. As noted, we believed that any artificial limit intended to reduce the memory footprint would confuse the user. We also discovered that, given the iPhone environmental conditions, in some cases, even minimum drill-down could trip the operating system's watchdog. Our solution to virtually infinite drill-down also proved serviceable in our tab bar controller for switching between tabs. When we realized that the memory patterns of the tab bar were similar to the navigation controller, we implemented the grandparent strategy for tab switching as well.

BEST PRACTICES FOR ADDRESS BOOK INTEGRATION

The Brightkite native application included Address Book integration as the basis for the Discover and Invite feature. The feature allows users to easily locate existing friends on the Brightkite service and to invite friends to the service as well. Unlike using Core Location, accessing the Address Book from a native iPhone application does not require user permission. However, to protect potentially sensitive information in a user's Address Book, we made several design choices to better inform the user.

First, Discover and Invite contains complex descriptive text (see the following illustration), which details the exact process to the user. Additionally, the Discover and Invite workflow requires the user to conduct several actions, such as selecting specific Brightkite-serviced friends to locate or inviting specific friends to join the service. The workflow includes button labels, such as *Next* and *Send*, which precisely describe immanent activity to the user.

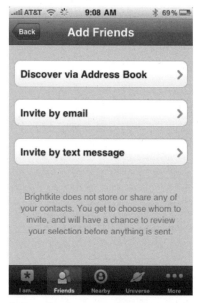

From a development perspective, be sure to test Address Book integration with large address books that contain contacts from Outlook, Gmail, and other services. We had to do a fair amount of optimization to speed up the process, and we discovered several crashes after running the code against Address Book data populated from mail programs other than Apple's Mail. In particular, Outlook and Gmail appear to structure some information a bit differently, for which our code was originally not prepared.

Summary

The Brightkite iPhone application resulted from an intense collaboration between Brightkite and Double Encore. The joint team collectively designed and delivered a world-class iPhone application by paying meticulous attention to detail and considering the user experience above all else. As a result, the application received an enthusiastic reception from Brightkite users as well as from the media when it premiered in October 2008.

Of course, with any large-scale project, we might have done things differently if we could go back and do them again. In particular, the visual design iteration of the native application required major effort to get just right, compared to the original Brightkite web application that achieved a similar visual design with less effort due to the power of HTML, CSS, and JavaScript.

With over a year creating of native applications under our belt, we've begun to apply a hybrid approach to our current efforts. Native applications are important for their access to iPhone's unique features and the general performance versus a pure web application. Yet, designing certain elements with web technology and embedding into a `UIWebView` is a pragmatic way to achieve the power of a native application, with the rapid design iteration that is possible via HTML/CSS. This hybrid approach isn't ideal for everything, as web technology is typically slower to render and not as smooth on the iPhone as native code, though it makes a lot of sense for read-only content where the user is not interacting with the application.

David Kaneda

Company: *Morfunk*

Location: *Philadelphia, PA*

Former Life As a Developer: *Frontend web design and development*

Blogger, www.webkitbits.com, www.davidkaneda.com,

Open source developer, www.jqtouch.com.

Life as an iPhone Developer: *Outpost, productivity*

What's in This Chapter: *Outpost:*

Wireframing, designing complex structures, creating graphics within context, working with a small team.

Chapter 4

Outpost

In this chapter, I'll introduce you to my process for designing an intuitive project management interface application within a small team. I created my iPhone development company, Morfunk, shortly after attending SEED 3, a conference in Chicago about design and entrepreneurship. The theme of the conference was taking control of your work, doing what you love, and other general inspiration. Coincidentally, this event took place just a few months before Apple announced the first iPhone beta SDK. Flush with confidence and inspiration from the conference, I concluded that an iPhone application would be the most logical, and most fun, way to get into the business of designing software.

Up until that point, I had always been a web designer and developer. At the time, I was working as senior web designer at a local design office that focused on educational and architectural web sites. I also had a fair amount of experience creating web applications and was very curious about native Mac software, but I was too intimidated to dive into Objective-C and Cocoa. I was particularly excited to design the user interface within the context of the operating system. I knew I wanted to make the application—now, I just needed to know what it did.

In this chapter, I'll take you through my process of figuring out what my application should do and how it was designed to match the context of the iPhone.

Establishing Outpost

I spent a few days thinking about what kind of application I would make. I'm a big productivity and *Getting Things Done* (GTD) enthusiast, so I wanted to create something useful, especially to small businesses and professionals. I considered time-trackers, invoicing tools, and similar applications (most of which have since been made in one way or another). Then, I remembered—my primary tool for managing projects, Basecamp, had a public API that I could use to work with their data from an iPhone application.

Basecamp is a web application by 37signals, coincidentally, one of the primary speakers and organizers of SEED. 37signals has written extensively on the subject of productivity, design, and building software. One of my favorite books when learning web design was *Defensive Design for the Web*, written by them about five years ago. Basecamp, their flagship application, has been acclaimed by publications like Newsweek for its simplicity and usability. Basecamp is a simple project management application built specifically to ease collaboration. Its primary features revolve around creating and sharing messages, milestones, to-do lists, and files. Users can leave comments throughout the application. Additionally, Basecamp can help manage time tracking, copy writing, and online discussions. Creating a Basecamp iPhone application seemed perfect, and my only fear was that 37signals already had similar plans underway.

I remember being nervous the first time I e-mailed Jason Fried, founder of 37signals and the one I saw speak at SEED. I asked if he was planning an application and, if not, if he would mind me making one. I also ran the name "Outpost" by him. He wrote me back fairly soon, saying he heard a few were in the works, but they had no immediate plans to do one. He concluded, "We'd love to see you put one together." That was all the go-ahead I needed.

I wanted the application to be fairly comprehensive. This wasn't entirely possible due to limitations of the API offered by Basecamp, but there was still a lot of information to show. We needed to incorporate the ability to add, edit, view, and delete things like messages, to-do lists, and milestones. I was also very concerned with giving users dashboard screens, which Basecamp provided as a means to traverse specific types of data across all projects.

I was less concerned with allowing comments and was unsure if this feature would make it into the application. Similarly, I was not very concerned at all with features like time tracking (typically offered on higher-level Basecamp plans).

At first, I had hoped to create the application on my own. Three books on Objective-C and two very long days later, I quickly realized I was spinning my wheels. One of the biggest lessons I took away from SEED was to not get in your own way. I wanted to make this application quickly, and I realized my primary interest was planning and designing an iPhone application, not necessarily programming it.

I took two days off of work from my day job and started making calls. My basic approach was simple: I Googled, texted, and searched jobs sites. In those two days, I talked with developers in India, the Czech Republic, Kentucky, California, and Canada. Ultimately, it was Jim Dovey, in Toronto, who expressed the most enthusiasm for the project and was willing to work in a relaxed, equity-based environment. I offered him a small advance to help him clear time for the application, and he declined it, telling me to save it for the lawyers when we formed the company and trademarked the name. Thankfully, I listened.

Wireframing Outpost

I wanted to get the ball rolling quickly. The first, basic thing I needed to get to Jim was an overall concept of how the application would work. Though excited about the application, he wasn't a Basecamp user himself. I developed the initial concept over about a week, creating countless sketches by pen and notebook. I treated it like a puzzle: Sometimes, I sketched a deep-level screen, like the screen used for editing a message and then worked my way up. Sometimes, I started with the dashboard and worked down. This process gave me a clear idea of problem spots and areas where I would have to compromise. I created a sketch in a matter of seconds and quickly compiled those ideas that had potential and trashed the rest.

I considered scanning these sketches to send to Jim, but they were very loose, and I didn't know for certain that they would really work on-screen. I was also eager to get designing. I decided that making wireframes would ensure the designs were practical, allow me to start seeing the design challenges, and provide the clearest direction for Jim.

I tried quite a few wireframing tools. A wide set of tools is available to assist in designing or laying out an iPhone application; some of the most common I saw were template kits for OmniGraffle and Illustrator. Aside from this, I saw a few people working by hand with pen, stencil, and watercolor. I found OmniGraffle helpful in creating quick outlines of what screens could be, but these images lacked any sort of polish or refinement. I had an Illustrator stencil set, as well, with a few great elements, but I didn't know the best way for incorporating it with the OmniGraffle sets. Likewise, the native Developer Tools Interface Builder was helpful in quickly creating elements like tab bars and table rows. I came to the conclusion that Photoshop would provide the best means for bringing all of the pieces together and providing a pixel-accurate preview of what we were making, and it is still my choice in iPhone UI design and wireframing. Photoshop makes it easy to pull elements from a variety of sources, combine them, and refine with as much or as little detail as I'd like. A side benefit of the Photoshop wireframes is that elements are easy to export and implement in the final design.

Figures 4-1 and 4-2 are my initial Photoshop mockups for the *Settings*, *Dashboard*, *Projects*, and global *To-do* screens. The *Dashboard* screen in Figure 4-2 shows buttons to refresh the view and change settings, though these were later moved.

Figure 4-1. *The early Outpost startup screen*

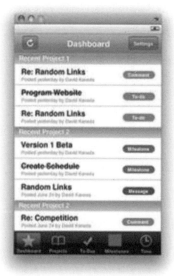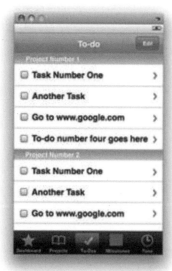

Figure 4-2. *Early Outpost Dashboard, Projects, and To-do screens*

Some would argue that these aren't true wireframes, because they are in color and certainly contain more detail than traditional wireframes—and they're probably right. They were not perfectly designed, however, and Jim knew it. We had several discussions leading up to this point about what was possible in regard to customization for iPhone applications. I knew we would have control over color in various places, like the title bar and row headers, and I knew certain graphics, like the arrows, could be easily replaced.

Certain structural elements shifted. For example, the original primary dashboard had a refresh icon at the top-left corner to represent syncing with Basecamp. Later, we wanted to add more information and control over the sync process, so we gave the sync operation its own tab and removed the time-tracking feature for the first version.

These wireframes were also extremely easy to make. Being a web designer, sketching in Photoshop becomes second nature. While still rough, the Photoshop sketches communicated loads of information that would have been impossible to describe over the phone or with a basic visual outline. The primary dashboard, for example, had a specific layout for primary and secondary information and labels. Completed to-do items were presented in a strike-through font, to mimic Basecamp and provide a quick visual cue for the row.

I wanted to send notes along with the screenshots. I thought this was a particularly important point to effectively communicate certain ideas, some not even visual, so I ended up throwing together a web page with everything on it. After sketching everything in Photoshop, I rendered all of the screens as JPEGs, and took down as many notes, questions, and ideas as I could think of.

Figure 4-3 shows a series of shots from a single screen for viewing a message. I wanted to replicate the look of Mail in the way it displayed metainformation (the *Title*, *From*, *Date* and *Category* fields) and a styled message. I also found it important to show comments directly beneath the messages, as they were so closely related, and to provide a quick mechanism for adding a comment. One detail that I stressed in my notes was to show the most recent comment when adding a new one; this way, users had a reminder of the most recent context of the discussion.

Figure 4-3. *Early Outpost Message screens*

Designing Outpost

The Outpost application had to contain a *lot* of information. Basecamp is a project management system that people use in very different ways, to hold different amounts of data. At its core, though, the web application provides users the ability to track messages, milestones, and to-do items. Therefore, our application had to preserve this basic functionality, and we had to accommodate for a variety of usage possibilities.

Two Screens, One Application

One of the main features that Basecamp offers is the ability to view project data in a granular, project-specific, way, as well in a comprehensive dashboard view. As Figure 4-4 shows, Basecamp's dashboard view allows users to view a stream of recent activity across their projects, as well as a global to-do list and milestone calendar. It allows users to quickly see what's going on across all projects.

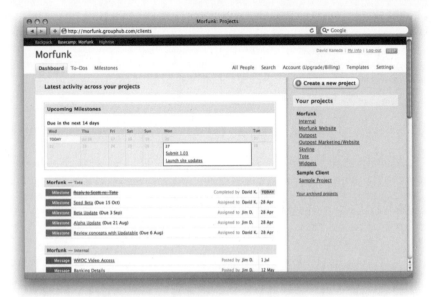

Figure 4-4. *Basecamp's dashboard view*

Clicking a project name or specific item from the *Dashboard* tab takes the user to the project view, which has tabs specifically for that project. In Figure 4-5, you can see the project-side *Overview* screen. This shows primarily shows upcoming milestones and, below that, recent activity. The user can then select *Return to Dashboard* or switch to a different project (both options are in the top-left of Figure 4-5).

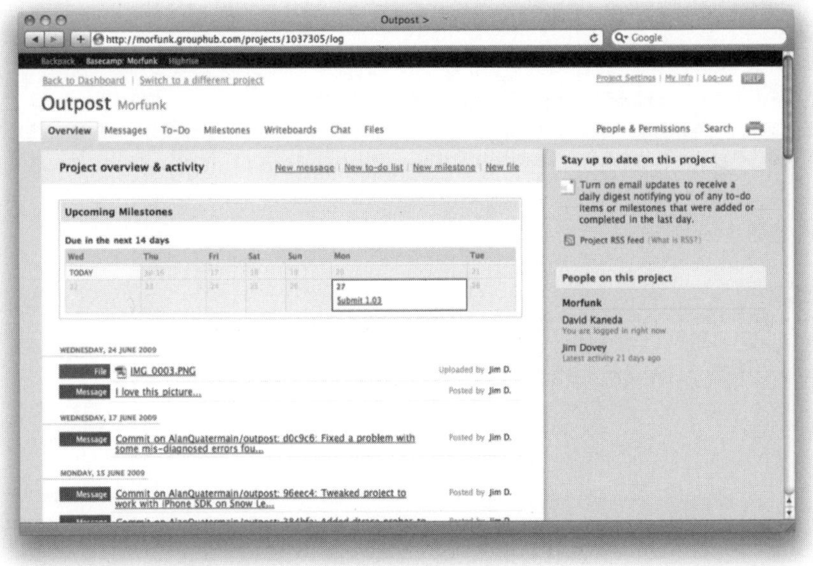

Figure 4-5. *Basecamp's project view*

I thought it was extremely important to include both of these views in the iPhone application, but doing so presented a huge challenge. With limited screen real estate, we had to be careful not to overwhelm the user with buttons and links and, at the same time, make the distinction between the two interfaces clear. As you can see from Figures 4-4 and 4-5, both screens share similar language for referencing to-do items and milestones.

First Attempt

My first idea was to have a tab bar across the bottom of the application on both screens and differentiate them by adding a row above that of the project view with the project's name and client (see Figure 4-6). I figured we could switch the view away from the dashboard when someone tapped a project name or specific item, akin to Basecamp's interface, and then provide a new tab bar on the project side that had a button for switching back.

Figure 4-6. *The original dual-screen tab bar concept*

After giving this some consideration, though, we decided against this design for two reasons. First, having a tab bar in both states made them look too similar, even with the extra client and project labels appended on the project side. Second, we were using a tab bar button for switching between states (including the tab bar itself). This was the real deal breaker for me. Visually, tabs indicate multiple views that are quickly switched between. Using a tab to alter the overall state of the application just didn't make sense.

I went back to the drawing board.

Second Attempt

Ultimately, we realized we didn't need the tab bar on the project view at all (see Figure 4-7). This side of the application could simply be a series of hierarchical list views, with the top-tier menu consisting of just the parts of the project (messages, milestones, and to-do lists).

Figure 4-7. *Project-side screens without toolbar*

We still needed a way to quickly get back to the dashboard side, so we created a full-width button at the bottom of these screens for switching back. While a back button is typically placed top-left within an application's design, this back button was different. The user wasn't moving back within the structural flow but was navigating between the two sides of the application. Another reason for my decision to place the button at the bottom of the screen was that it corresponded with the tab bar on its alternate side (see Figure 4-8).

I designed the button to look very different from the default tab bar by using a light blue. I found this color difference important, because my button was functionally different than a typical tab bar and better suited to be a custom UI element. I also used this area to show the project and client name, in that order. There were extra benefits from the switch as well, which we soon discovered. As the tab bar is restricted to five items, our custom element meant projects could hold more than five items, which was useful when we added project-specific *Recent Items* and began considering to add time tracking (a feature of higher level Basecamp plans).

To polish off the button, we also added a flip animation when going between the two states. In regard to user experience, I think this animation really helped explain the alternating state of the application. We also modified the header color for projects to be a tinge lighter than that of dashboard screens.

Figure 4-8. *Final Outpost dashboard-side Milestones screen*

Fitting In

As our application was business-centric, I thought it was important to create as clean a design as possible and adhere strictly to Apple's Human Interface Guidelines (HIG). Because I wanted Outpost to be as straightforward and native-feeling as possible, I looked for much of my inspiration in native applications. I spent many hours reviewing applications like iPod and Mail to look for trends and design patterns to apply to Outpost.

While the majority of the application uses default iPhone styles, with elements like navigation lists and tab bars, many elements were created specifically for Outpost. By doing this, we ensured Outpost had a clear, unique style in a very subtle way. This would help us eventually differentiate ourselves from the competition for being distinct while still having a native feel. For example, I wanted to make buttons throughout the application, like the arrow within a circle that denotes jumping to a specific item, as custom UI element, as this button was a common user interface element. Using screenshots from the application, I made the drop shadow and stroke to match the native element but altered the color to teal blue to match the rest of our theme, and slightly modified the arrow to be a bit bolder (to match our brand and web site design). Likewise, row labels, like those denoting the types of items on the dashboard, were created as custom elements and color-coded to match Basecamp's conventions. Traditionally, information capsules like this are shown in a light blue bar with rounded sides, but we wanted to embellish with a slight bevel and drop shadow, so they related to the arrow button. The colors were taken directly from Basecamp, so users would have an immediate association with each row. You can see an example of these custom IU elements in Figure 4-9.

I believe details like this went a long way in establishing recognition in the Basecamp user base. We originally posted an early promotional site, to start an e-mail list of potential customers, and posted some of the early concepts as a sample—the response was fantastic.

Figure 4-9. *The final Outpost Dashboard screen*

Technically, to create certain elements, I took several screenshots of buttons from native applications that I would be emulating. I then brought these into Photoshop and re-created them using purely vector shapes and layer effects, like drop shadows, strokes, beveling, and embossing. The result was a set of reusable looks that could be transferred to new elements, if necessary, or further customized. You can see some of these styles in Figure 4-10.

Figure 4-10. *Custom buttons used throughout Outpost*

Certain areas that held limited functionality had a stronger opportunity for branding and design. The sync screen, for example, required a very simple interface, so we strengthened it with our icon's image, a tent.

Working in a Small Team

One of the biggest benefits of working in a two-person team with one designer and one developer is how facile we can be in implementing and modifying the design. If Jim needed me to revise a graphic, he would leave me a message (on Basecamp, of course), and I would reply within a few hours with the graphic. Certain elements could not be built in Xcode (the primary iPhone development environment) the same way I would craft them in Photoshop. We wanted to use a custom header color, for example, but the gloss is applied automatically in Xcode. For this situation, Jim quickly came up with something close, and I helped refine, through iChat, using requests like, "Could it be just a tad more saturated and a little lighter?" Altogether, we were able to get the right look in about 10 minutes.

Designing with HTML

One of the components which I particularly enjoyed creating was the Message view screen (see Figure 4-11). Messages in Basecamp are processed with a small script called Textile, which essentially gives users certain shortcuts to basic HTML. For example, to italicize text, you can put underscores around it: _like this_. I thought it was important to show the text in its styled form, so we embedded the HTML form of the message in a WebView. This allowed us to style the text directly with traditional web Cascading Style Sheets (CSS). Being a web designer, I jumped at the chance to help with the application's development and programmed the style sheet for this view myself.

Figure 4-11. *Final Outpost project-specific Message screen*

All That Glitters. . .

As a platform, the iPhone is still incredibly young, and certain elements lack predefined standards. This was the case when we began to design the check boxes for to-do lists within the application. At the time (in the original iPhone operating system), no native application included a check box mechanism. The closest item, functionally, was the on/off switch in settings panes, which wasn't appropriate.

We ended up taking the look of the check box in Mobile Safari and customizing that to match the height of our rows and to add a bit more texture and definition. While this was still stylized, we felt using a Safari check box would also improve the association with the Basecamp web application.

Since then, the iPhone OS has changed significantly, one difference being the ability to select multiple e-mail messages for editing or deleting. Now, we have a standard defined by Apple of what check boxes should look like: a gray outlined circle that changes to be filled with red and a checkmark once selected (see Figure 4-12). We have yet to modify the check boxes in Outpost, though, as I remain unconvinced.

Figure 4-12. *The check box style used in Mail, which connotes multiple selections*

Technically, within Mail (and a few other places these checkmarks are used), these check boxes represent the selection of a row, semantically very different than toggling or editing the state of the row. When this element is available in other applications, for example, the user can click the entire row to alter the state. In ours, I believe the user should be specifically clicking the check box to mark a to-do list item as complete or incomplete, whereas clicking the row itself leads to a window with more information. For these reasons, I'm leaving our square little boxes (shown in Figure 4-13) in place until the right inspiration comes along.

Figure 4-13. *To-do check boxes in Outpost*

Summary

Ultimately, designers have the luxury of making iPhone applications look however they choose. The challenge of this is finding a balance between using default controls, like navigation lists, and completely customized designs that can alienate the user. As illustrated in this chapter, we created many conventions within Outpost. Some were structural, like using a flip transition to switch between two exclusive modes of the application. Some were purely cosmetic, like changing the button styles. Throughout our application design process, though, our primary goal was very straightforward—create an application that felt native and custom at the same time, had the features we wanted, and stayed out of the way of the user.

Craig Kemper

Company: *Little White Bear Studios*

Location: **Oregon**

Former Life As a Developer: **Tens years of experience creating educational desktop software in C and C++, using Microsoft Visual Studio, CodeWarrior, and Xcode.**

Life as an iPhone Developer:

TanZen   **Category: Games-Puzzle**   **Toolset: Xcode and Photoshop**

Zentomino   **Category: Games-Puzzle**   **Toolset: Xcode and Photoshop**

What's in This Chapter:

- ■ *Finding the Elusive App Idea*
- ■ *Creating a Design Document*
- ■ *Diving Into the Code*
- ■ *When is a Game Not a Game?*
- ■ *The Heaven and Hell of Finally Getting on a Device*
- ■ *The App Store Arrives!*

Chapter 5

TanZen and Zentomino

I'm Craig Kemper, the developer behind Little White Bear Studios, which makes the popular games TanZen and Zentomino (see Figures 5-1 and 5-2). At the time of this writing, these two games have been bought over 150,000 times combined and have received rave reviews by users, peers, and professional review sites.

Figure 5-1. *The TanZen icon*

Figure 5-2. *The Zentomino icon*

In this chapter, you'll learn how I along with the help of my talented wife, Lindi, designed a successful user interface (UI) that takes advantage of the unique size and feature set of the iPhone. By focusing on UI design, I hope to convey the importance of creating an immersive user experience with your app. The UI may determine if you have a life-changing runaway hit, or a complete flop, so concentrating on a good presentation is just as important as how great your code is. I am neither a master programmer nor any sort of artist, so please don't feel like this chapter couldn't possibly apply to you. I'm an average software developer with a day job, a wife, and three kids. I just took a chance on the iPhone, by investing many late nights for a few months, with the hope of improving the life of my family. And about a year and a half ago, I was just starting out with iPhone programming—like you.

Finding the Elusive Application Idea

 In March of 2008, Apple opened the door to you and I, by introducing the iPhone software development kit (SDK). We've been granted access to a device that offers a wealth of possibilities. The iPhone is a miniature computer in your pocket. It's a blank canvas, with the potential to be a useful tool and entertainment device to millions of people around the world. That kind of compact power is *Star Trek* stuff. And thanks to

Apple's App Store, we get those keys to the kingdom at nearly zero cost. All you have to do is come up with the idea for your application.

If you're not sure where to start, consider how my wife, Lindi, and I came up with our applications: As soon as the SDK was announced, I signed up for the developer program. Although, I was immediately put on a wait list, Apple did allow us to download the SDK and give it a go on the simulator. I played around with the SDK for a couple weeks and learned a lot about Objective C and the iPhone operating system (OS). I didn't own an iPhone at that time, but fortunately, through my masterful powers of persuasion, I managed to convince Lindi that I needed one for development. Since I was on the waiting list, I could not put applications on the phone, but at least I could use it on a daily basis and hopefully come up with a winning application idea.

Finding the perfect application idea was the next step. I decided quickly that I wanted to try my hand at creating a game. Coming up empty on an idea for days, the idea found me one day in the form of a tangram puzzle game, which was sitting on a large meeting table at my day job.

Tangrams are Chinese puzzles, where you have the task of using the seven geometric shapes shown in Figure 5-3 to reproduce a larger shape. The puzzle game has been popular for hundreds of years, and schools around the world use tangrams to teach spatial reasoning to young children. Every aspect of the game was suited for a touch screen device, and the sheer number of puzzles involved guaranteed an ever-expanding game that could keep players involved for a very long time.

Figure 5-3. *The seven tangram shapes*

I researched tangrams obsessively and studied what made the game a joy to play. I noted all the different ways the computer versions of the game chose to implement their UIs. Some were better than others, but most failed in one way or another to capture the joy of the physical version of the game. Mouse clicks, shift keys, arrow buttons, and a lot of computer-assisted shape placement permeated these games. Most of them used plainly colored pieces that made me feel like I was stuck in geometry class learning about angles. Real tangrams involve touching pieces and spinning them with your fingers; they're all about tactile feedback and being free to move pieces wherever you want. The computer tangram games felt nothing like this. They felt, well, like computer games. And that's the moment I decided to buck the trend and try to create a computer version of the game that felt more like the real thing. The iPhone seemed like a perfect platform to do just that. The average iPhone user isn't a gaming expert. It's our job as developers to make them feel at home, even though the playing surface is completely void of physical feedback.

Creating a Design Document

I'm a big supporter of the theory that you should spend a great deal of time designing an application before you ever write a single line of code. If you just start coding away, you're going to discover things that are wrong and then have to recode, or worse, you'll code yourself into a corner that hurts you down the line. A good design is the backbone of your application and will help you make vital decisions quickly and cheaply, before they become too expensive to fix later.

The design document for my tangram game (see Figure 5-4 for excerpts) started very simply. I began by creating an outline of all the things I wanted the game to include, and the things I absolutely didn't want. It's important to know the personality of a game, as strange as that idea may sound. What is the goal, and how should the players feel when they play it? Is this a quick, pick-up-and-play sort of game? Or is it an involved, multihour experience? You need to know the answers to these questions before you start, or you'll run into feature creep, in which your game slowly gains features that really aren't needed.

I created several sections about the various interface elements needed in the game and detailed many scenarios, even those I knew I didn't want. I also gathered several ideas from Lindi, who served as a sounding board, idea editor, and therapist throughout the entire development process. With her assistance, I created lists of advantages and disadvantages for each feature, noting the various strengths and weaknesses, and how a decision would affect game play. These lists helped to eliminate the obvious poor choices before I ever started coding. Be careful not to go into too much detail at this point in the design, however, as things that sound good on paper will sometimes fall apart completely once they're actually tried in the real world.

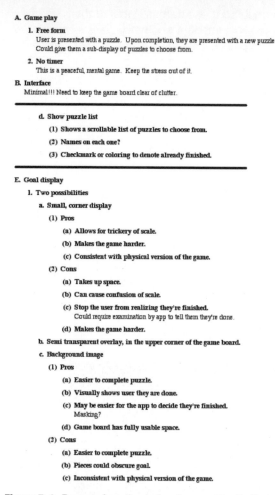

A. Game play

  1. Free form
    User is presented with a puzzle. Upon completion, they are presented with a new puzzle.
    Could give them a sub-display of puzzles to choose from.

  2. No timer
    This is a peaceful, mental game. Keep the stress out of it.

B. Interface
  Minimal!!! Need to keep the game board clear of clutter.

    d. Show puzzle list

      (1) Shows a scrollable list of puzzles to choose from.

      (2) Names on each one?

      (3) Checkmark or coloring to denote already finished.

E. Goal display

  1. Two possibilities

    a. Small, corner display

      (1) Pros

        (a) Allows for trickery of scale.

        (b) Makes the game harder.

        (c) Consistent with physical version of the game.

      (2) Cons

        (a) Takes up space.

        (b) Can cause confusion of scale.

        (c) Stop the user from realizing they're finished.
          Could require examination by app to tell them they're done.

        (d) Makes the game harder.

    b. Semi transparent overlay, in the upper corner of the game board.

    c. Background image

      (1) Pros

        (a) Easier to complete puzzle.

        (b) Visually shows user they are done.

        (c) May be easier for the app to decide they're finished.
          Masking?

        (d) Game board has fully usable space.

      (2) Cons

        (a) Easier to complete puzzle.

        (b) Pieces could obscure goal.

        (c) Inconsistent with physical version of the game.

Figure 5-4. *Excerpts from the design document for TanZen*

The design document shown in Figure 5-4 became the go-to guide for TanZen development and acted as a reminder of what was important when decisions needed to be made. The design document is not law, as you're always free to add to it or modify it at any time. But overall, it provides the information necessary to get started and helps guide you through to the very end of the project.

Diving into the Code

After coding up a very quick proof-of-concept application, where I drew simple tangram shapes on the screen and moved them around with my finger, I was ready to begin the real coding. However, before I began, I wrote yet another small document, this time detailing the object-oriented design structure of the code. This document broke the game into modular pieces, so I could tackle each part individually, without affecting everything else. Each tangram piece became a class, with a general parent class to control common functions. The game board had it's own class, which could contain any number of piece classes. Additionally, each separate view in the game was a class.

Objective-C uses objects, and TanZen is all about moving objects on the screen, so coming up with a generic yet versatile object-oriented design was going to aid in development, as well as make it easy to execute large changes in the interface, without disturbing the basic way the game pieces worked behind the scenes. The more modular the code was at the beginning, the better coding would be in the future. And if you can maintain that modularity through the end of the project, you'll probably even end up with code you could reuse for a future game. This is precisely how my second game was created in one-fifth the time of the first.

Creating the Piece UI

After creating the seven basic pieces in the game (see Figure 5-5), I went to work on implementing the interface design for manipulating those pieces. I wanted to take advantage of the iPhone's features but not overwhelm players with token uses of those features. Since I was trying to emulate physical tangrams, I tried to re-create those movements in the code. Obviously, the most frequent thing done in tangrams is the movement of pieces, and simply tracking finger touches on a particular piece gave the perfect control.

Figure 5-5. *The seven tangram shapes in TanZen*

The second most frequent action in tangrams is turning the pieces. My design document stated that rotation of pieces should be done with a twisting motion, which is what you would do in the real game. By placing one finger on each side of a piece, I could twist them, and the piece would turn in any direction. This took a very long time to get right on the simulator, since I couldn't use actual fingers to test it! As soon as you're able, start working on a real device. There's a bit longer turnaround time to load, but you'll save countless hours in the long run.

Next up was flipping. I had a hard time trying to keep this motion the same as its real life counterpart. There just wasn't a gesture for it, other than a pinching action, which would be much too similar to rotation. Eventually, I decided to implement flipping via a simple double-tap. Flipping isn't used extensively in tangrams, so I decided it wasn't as vital to match the movement of the real-world game. Working with the iPhone, you learn quickly that compromises like this are a daily occurrence. Coming up with the perfect iPhone UI is a blend of inspiration and bitter reality checks.

Pieces, Pieces Everywhere

One of the really head-scratching design challenges involved where the heck to place all these pieces at the start of each puzzle. Various computer tangram games solved this problem in different ways. Some used a hidden tray, while others just threw them all around the puzzle area. I didn't like any of the examples I found. I knew I wanted the pieces to be visible at all times, but I was having trouble visualizing how to place them on the screen. So I spent at least a day with a physical set of tangrams, trying all sorts of combinations, before finally coming up with the simple yet clean placement that ultimately appears in the game (see Figure 5-6). If you find yourself stuck on a UI issue, try moving the problem to a different, and perhaps easier to iterate on, medium.

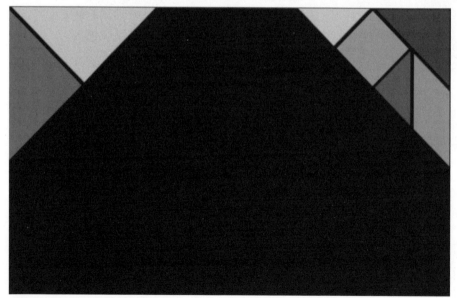

Figure 5-6. *The default piece positions*

Being Deceived by the Simulator

At this point in the game's development, Apple showed no signs of letting new people into the developer's program, which would've allowed me to develop on a device. Now on month two with the simulator, that little tool was my best friend during late nights of programming. It seductively reproduced my designs, asking for nothing in return.

But here's something every new iPhone developer needs to know: The simulator is not your friend. It will lie to you, right in front of your face. What's that you say? "The simulator accurately displays the 320 × 480 iPhone screen." Yes, you are absolutely correct. But, guess what? The iPhone has many more pixels per inch than your average computer screen, so your trusty simulator is displaying everything several times larger than the actual device will (see Figures 5-7 and 5-8). Go ahead; put your iPhone against your screen, and bring up the simulator next to it. Notice anything? All those fancy little doodads you made to control things will be microscopic on the iPhone. Don't feel bad. Many people made the same mistake, including us!

Figure 5-7. *The simulator screen size, as depicted on a 19-inch monitor, is quite large.*

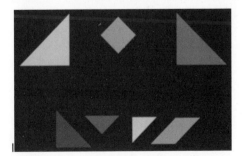

Figure 5-8. *The iPhone screen size is tiny.*

After my terrible moment of realization about screen sizes, I quickly found that my wonderfully simple yet natural method of piece rotation was not going to work at all. Even with the larger pieces, there was simply no way to comfortably get two fingers around a piece and perform a twisting action. What could I do to fix this? At that point, I had no idea. The rather nebulous App Store deadline of June or July was fast approaching, so I did the only thing I had time for: I mapped rotation to a simple tap. Each tap rotated the piece 45 degrees in a clockwise direction. I didn't like the solution. The gesture felt unnatural, and it didn't jive with my concept for the feel of the game. But it solved the problem, and I needed to move on to other coding tasks. Did I mention that you will need to make compromises yet? Luckily, this was one compromise I was able to take back later in development.

Playing to the Emotions of Your Customers

A user interface is not just about widgets and buttons. It's also about the emotions it creates in the player. Most video games are all about getting to the next level. Personally, I stop playing a video game once I can't get past a level after several tries. I put it down and never pick it up again. A tangram game could have thousands of puzzles. Some of them are easy, and some hard. I didn't want people to get stuck and quit my game, so I decided to go with a rather open feel, allowing players to choose any of the puzzles they wanted (see Figure 5-9).

The decision to make a frustration-free game led to other choices geared toward minimizing stress. I decided to record all current piece locations, in every puzzle, so players would never have to worry about losing their progress. Since the piece locations consisted of just a few numbers each, storing tens of thousands of locations would take only a small amount of space on the device. Along with that, I added the minor, yet vital, feature of including the iPhone's status bar in the game. If you're playing a game while waiting for a bus, for example, you'll want to know what time it is or when to stop playing the game because of low battery power. Yes, including the status bar costs you some screen real estate, but you might gain much more in user experience.

Since TanZen was going to give players a vast array of puzzles to choose from, how could you stop them from choosing only the puzzles that fit their perceived skill levels? Remove all difficulty levels from the game! There aren't easy, medium, or hard puzzles; there are just puzzles, with no order to them at all. The player is free to pick any puzzle at random, without the emotional baggage of how hard it's supposed to be, as shown in Figure 5-9. Perhaps if more games broke away from the standard mold of conquering increasingly more difficult levels, they could capture a wider audience of gamers.

Figure 5-9. *The puzzle selection screen allows the player to choose any puzzle to play.*

The final, and probably one of the most emotionally satisfying features of TanZen, was the progress tracking. Every time a player completes a puzzle, the game marks that success in the puzzle selection screen by showing the pieces they used to solve it (see Figure 5-10). This simple feature was designed to play into users' emotions, making them want to complete another puzzle, then a page of puzzles, and ultimately, the entire game. The puzzle-selection screen doubles as a trophy case!

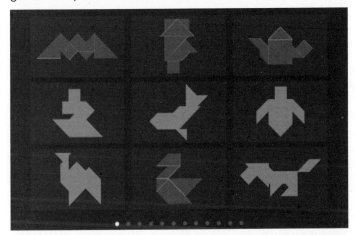

Figure 5-10. *Tracking the player's progress gives a sense of accomplishment.*

Words? We Don't Need No Stinking Words!

TanZen uses very little text for a few reasons. For one thing, text doesn't help players solve puzzles. Also, it takes up space on an already-limited screen. Finally, the App Store is available all over the world. Could I possibly create a game that is universally understood without written language? I decided to try—having no text in the main portions of the game! This decision led to the elimination of puzzle titles and all textual notifications of any kind.

Given the limited space of the device, and the worldwide market it's sold in, are there ways you can simplify your interface, so that it can be attractive to everyone?

How Many Buttons Does It Take?

As I was developing the game, I was coding in a bubble. The App Store didn't exist yet, so I had no idea what the proper interface for an iPhone game should be. Apple's only advice to developers was to make simplified versions of what we'd make on the computer. Well, to me, that meant fewer features. Fewer features meant fewer buttons. For my game, I knew I needed a few options on the game screen. Also, all the standard iPhone applications had an *Info* button to get to settings and such, so that button seemed required. I also needed to offer players a way to get to the puzzle selection screen. Did I need anything else?

My oldest daughter suggested that the game needed a reset button to send the pieces back to the default locations. I nixed the idea, as it didn't seem vital to the game experience, and having three buttons would create an uneven interface. I considered having a single button that brought up a sublist of button choices, as well as mapping the same sort of thing to a double-tap action on the game surface, but both had drawbacks. The single-button version sounded a little complicated, as it would add another subwindow to the screen. I wanted to keep things simple. The double-tap idea ran the risk of being confusing and hidden from the player. When in doubt, keep it simple, and keep it clear. Two buttons it is, one in each lower corner of the screen (see Figure 5-11).

If you're having trouble deciding which features to include in your application, try making a list. Separate the required features from the unnecessary ones. Then decide which required features will be used the most. Those are the features you need to include in the primary interface, so they're always easy to find.

Figure 5-11. *A simple two-button layout*

When Is a Game Not a Game?

By this point, it was about a month before what most people considered the first possible App Store opening date—the week of Apple's Worldwide Developers Conference (WWDC) in the middle of June 2008. I now had the basic workings of the game done. There were buttons, pieces, a puzzle selection screen, and a reasonable, if not perfect, way to manipulate pieces. It was certainly a playable game. To be honest though, the game was not even close to something I would've wanted to present to the public for sale at that point. It just looked like a standard tangram game, similar to what you could play for free on the Web. What would make people pay for this game?

We all know when we're playing a good game. But what makes it a good game? Is it the rules or the obstacles you have to overcome? Yes, but that's only half of it. The other half is the presentation. Think of your favorite World War II shooter game. Would it be nearly as much fun if your weapon were a simple, single colored, stick shape? Would you play the game for hours on end if the goal was to shoot fifty cardboard cutout shapes of people floating around the screen at random? Of course not! Presentation is just as important as the game play itself. Players want to be immersed in the game and forget the world around them. Give them a theme to grab hold of, so they can form an emotional bond and fall in love with your creation.

The Eureka Moment

I took a break from coding and started thinking about a theme for the game. I went back to my design document to see what the goal of the game was. According to the original concept, this game was supposed to be stress free. The goal was to be challenging, yet calming, so Lindi and I started brainstorming ideas for accomplishing that goal. We tossed around a few possibilities but always came back to the notion that we wanted the players to have a calm and enjoyable game that they looked forward to playing every day. We almost wanted players to think of the game as a calming, meditative, Zen escape. That was it! A Zen garden! Rocks! Sand! What could be more calming than that?

We decided to create a sand background and make all the buttons into rocks. And the pieces themselves could resemble chiseled rock shapes. The puzzle game could be a meditative challenge, with each tangram bringing you one step further on your path to enlightenment. TanZen was born!

I'm Not an Artist, But I Play One on the App Store

I now had a catchy name and a great idea for a theme but no graphics to back it up. I had been using Photoshop for years, mainly for simple image editing, a few school projects, and a bit of digital coloring. I had never created actual art with it, let alone a game interface. I am not an artist, but I am a perfectionist and so is my wife. We know when something looks wrong and when it looks right.

I scoured the Web for Photoshop tutorials on how to realize our theme. Within a day, I had the basic game background completed. The idea was to create a subtle sand background that would look good but not distract from the game pieces or the puzzles themselves.

The buttons took a few days to get just right. I used black rocks for the main game screen buttons, so they wouldn't distract from the game pieces. For the Info screen, I used a couple different colored rocks for its buttons. And to reinforce the Zen garden idea on both screens, I added raked circles around the rocks.

The game pieces were a week in the making. I first created some rather plain, stone-looking shapes. They looked cool to me, but Lindi felt they were missing that something special. I tried various kinds of textures and colors, giving each piece its own unique look. While cool looking, that design was much too busy. I needed something peaceful that would fit the theme.

Lindi started researching Zen colors, and we immediately gravitated toward a green color. I tried it with a few of the 3-D textures I'd created and came up with a very organic-looking result. The pieces didn't look like stone anymore; they looked alive, like green bamboo. How Zen! With a little custom shading and a few transparency and layer tricks, I suddenly had seven unique game pieces. All of them were slightly different, but they looked great together. I was extremely happy with the way the pieces turned out. They were downright touchable! Adding them to the rest of the interface created a wonderfully cohesive Zen experience (see Figures 5-12 through 5-14).

Figure 5-12. *The main game screen with buttons and pieces*

Figure 5-13. *A sand-themed puzzle selection screen*

Figure 5-14. *The Info screen, complete with rules*

After many days of constant creating, tweaking, and a little bit of constructive arguing, Lindi and I had created the interface and transformed a simple puzzle game into an immersive experience. We had no idea if this would be good enough for the App Store, but it was our baby, and we loved it.

Vital, Yet Invisible

The look of the TanZen interface is something I am very proud of. But there's one feature of the game that I'm equally thrilled about, and it's something that no player has ever even noticed: the sizes of the pieces change, depending on the overall size of the puzzle. A large triangle in one puzzle may be quite a bit bigger or smaller in a different puzzle, as they are designed to scale proportionally to the size of the given puzzle (see Figures 5-15 and 5-16).

I realized pretty early on in the design process that having enough space to maneuver the pieces was vital to the gaming experience. Since tangram puzzles vary greatly in height and width, and the iPhone has a limited screen area, many of the classic puzzles were not going to fit on the screen. I decided that I wanted every puzzle to look spectacular, fitting perfectly in the given space. And this meant scaling the puzzles, and the pieces, to fit. The solution ended up working flawlessly. And like any truly great design, it solved a huge problem without bringing attention to itself.

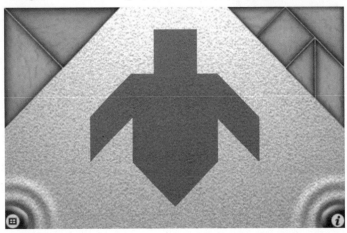

Figure 5-15. *Larger pieces are used for puzzles that are short in height, as these puzzles can be enlarged to fill up the screen space.*

Figure 5-16. *When a puzzle is taller, it must be reduced in size to fit, and the pieces must scale down to match.*

Racing to the Finish Line?

By the time the art was finished, only two weeks were left before WWDC and the possible opening of the App Store. And if the App Store didn't open, I was positive that Apple was finally going to let the rest of the developers into the program, allowing them to finally test on the iPhone, instead of their dubious friend the simulator.

With everything else completed, I spent the next few days adding over a hundred puzzles to the game. This seemed like a reasonable number to include, and completing them all would probably take most people several days or weeks.

With that done, it was finally time for testing. I had been doing a lot of personal testing during the creation of the game, but now I needed outside help. Beyond basic functionality testing, it's always best to get someone else to test for you. You've been in your code for a long time and have unconsciously trained yourself to avoid the sticky areas. A fresh set of eyes will find the stuff you're ignoring. Luckily, my house was filled with testers of all ages! I had testers ranging from age five to thirteen, plus my wife.

My family tested the game for a couple days. Surprisingly, the kids really enjoyed it. And better yet, nobody found any bugs! I had tried to design a very simple game under the hood, so it was nice to know that the plan worked. The only negative feedback I got was that the tap to rotate was consistently causing the pieces to be overrotated. The method was functionally flawless, but in their zeal to complete a rotation, each tester would always tap one too many times. But with no other solution and running out of time, I kept that implementation.

Building a Better Rotation

WWDC had finally arrived, and we found out that the App Store wasn't opening until early July. With about a month left before the store opened, I found myself with some extra time on my hands. For the past month, I had been working until 3 a.m. nearly every night and then heading to my day job a few hours later. I was running on fumes and should've just taken a much-needed break from the whole thing while waiting for Apple to get around to letting me test on a device, but I didn't. I liked TanZen at this point, but the tap-to-rotate problem couldn't be ignored any longer. It was just wrong. I was willing to let it go when WWDC started, as I thought the App Store was opening, but once I had some time to experiment, I was determined to make rotation work better.

I already knew that using a pinch-and-twist motion would not work, due to the size of the screen. And tapping to rotate was just plain annoying, as players would have to tap eight times to make a complete rotation. So, what to do? After a bit of brainstorming, I came up with the idea to create a rotation mode that, once activated, would map finger movement to a rotation. The solution sounded simple enough, so that's what I tried next.

I quickly added some code to enter rotation mode if the player tapped a piece once. Since the player would need to know which piece is in rotation mode, I added a simple outline around the piece (see Figure 5-17). Once in rotation mode, any movement of a finger on the screen would cause a rotation to happen, in the direction the finger moved.

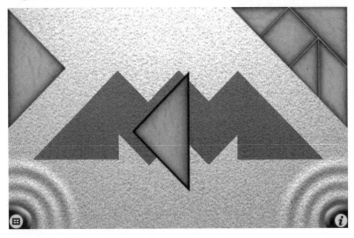

Figure 5-17. *Simple outlined piece selection*

Now, I had a much better form of rotation, which didn't involve constant tapping and allowed use of the entire screen to adjust the angle. But I still wasn't satisfied. The simple outline around the piece, showing which piece was in the rotation mode, just wasn't enough feedback. I needed something that showed the player which piece could be rotated, as well as representing the fact that they could now rotate. Rotation involves making circles in two possible directions, so I put a little circle with arrows on the piece the player was rotating (see Figure 5-18).

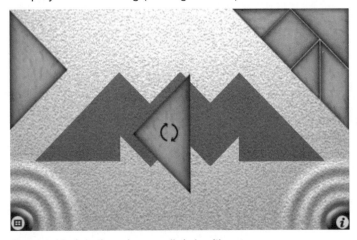

Figure 5-18. *Selection using a small circle with arrows*

That could work, but I actually wanted an image that would make the player move his or her finger in a circle around the piece, not on it. What about a bigger circle, like the one shown in Figure 5-19?

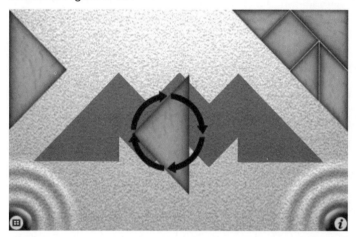

Figure 5-19. *A larger selection circle suggests movement around the piece, instead of on it.*

The circle in Figure 5-19 is not bad but not quite right. It definitely gives the rotation clue, but artistically, it's a bit too harsh. I needed something special that fit the game's Zen theme, so I spent a few hours in Photoshop, trying to find a solution that screamed, "Rotate me!" in a subtle and classy way. After much experimentation, I found it (see Figure 5-20). Add a little translucency for a subtle feel, and there you have it!

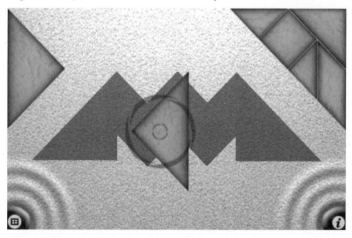

Figure 5-20. *A ring that suggests rotation around the piece, yet is subtle enough to fit the theme of the game.*

Finally Testing on a Device

As chance had it, one of my coworkers had attended WWDC, and when he returned, he revealed that he was actually one of the few thousand people allowed to develop on an actual device! He had no idea the program was so limited, and before the conference, neither of us knew the other one was going to develop applications for the iPhone. For the next thing that happened, I owe him my eternal gratitude: he very kindly offered to compile my code, so I could try it on a device! I was finally going to see how my game played on the touch screen. The very next day, I had TanZen on my iPhone.

Seeing TanZen on a device was an exciting moment after spending months getting to that point. The graphics were crisp, clear, and bright. The pieces moved as expected, and everything worked. I was so relieved. I then took the game home for Lindi to play with it, and that's when everything went to hell.

Lindi immediately found the game unplayable. She moved pieces around, trying to place them, and failed most of the time. She had never really used an iPhone much at all, so she had no experience using her fingers to manipulate small items on the touch screen. After she struggled for a few minutes, we figured out the problem—her fingernails. My wife has completely average-length fingernails for a woman, but the simple fact that she had them meant she had to use the flat part of her finger to move pieces, instead of the tip. This caused her to lose the tangram pieces under her fingers on every move, and she constantly needed to reposition them. Arrrgh! I had never even considered that fingers would cover up the pieces, as I was having zero trouble manipulating pieces with the mouse. The evil simulator strikes again!

When you're designing your interface, always remember that the user's only pointing device is a large blunt instrument, which can easily cover a large portion of your screen. If they need to see what they're manipulating, you need to design around that obstacle.

Going Back to the Drawing Board

Less than a month remained before the App Store opening. And what did I have? A beautiful-looking game rendered nearly unplayable because of the limitations of the device. The first order of business was to figure out how to make the game playable for people with longer fingernails. I mulled the options over in my head.

I couldn't make the pieces bigger, as the puzzles wouldn't fit on the screen. What I needed was a way to grow the control scheme outside the visible piece area. What if I expanded movement to include an invisible area around the piece? Then Lindi would be able to move a piece without actually having her fingertip directly on the piece. Sounds a bit like the rotation scheme, doesn't it? In rotation mode, any movement on the screen would rotate the piece. Could the same solution work for movement? Seemed reasonable, but how would I distinguish between a move and rotation and still allow new pieces to be manipulated? A rotation mode and a movement mode were needed. Yikes, this could get confusing to players. I needed to simplify the situation.

The rotation mode idea needed to morph into something new. Maybe tapping once would now put the piece into selection mode. A selected piece could then have various kinds of manipulations applied to it, without worrying about disturbing other pieces. But how would I allow users to move, rotate, or flip a selected piece?

Flipping was obvious—just double-tap the active piece. And there's no need to see the piece while you're doing that. However, moving and rotating need visibility to work correctly. Maybe it needed screen elements that could be activated, so a player could decide between a move and a rotate. Perhaps the rotation ring could be used for movement, allowing the player to grab the ring instead of the piece. Then additional knobs could be tapped to initiate rotation (see Figure 5-21).

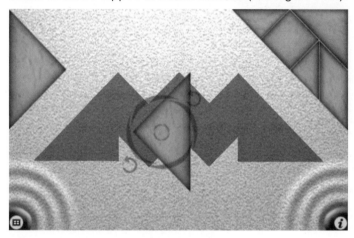

Figure 5-21. *Selection ring with rotation knobs*

That solution certainly worked but wasn't very elegant, and I didn't want TanZen to have a complicated heads up display. There had to be some way to solve the problem using the unique capabilities of the iPhone. That's when I brought multitouch into the equation.

What if I repurposed the rotation ring into a selection ring? Then movement and rotation modes would be determined by the number of fingers being used: select the piece you want to adjust, and use one finger for movement or two fingers for rotation. That sounded like an ideal iPhone solution to the problem!

After coding up this new idea, I had Lindi give it a try. She really liked that she could see the pieces now, yet still rotate them. Using two fingers to rotate was a bit harder than before, but if she used two hands, it was fairly easy to use a steering-wheel-style motion with her thumbs to turn a piece. Even my five-year-old daughter and seven-year-old son had no trouble doing it. This seemed like a workable solution! There was still something wrong, though.

Both my wife and my coworker found that they were trying to move nonselected pieces after they were finished with a selected piece. They'd start dragging a piece without tapping it first to select it, which moved the previously selected piece instead, since any movement was still mapped to it. Perhaps using the whole screen for manipulating a single piece wasn't the best solution. It would probably be better to limit the control scheme to just the immediate area of the selected piece. But how could the player be told where it's OK to move or rotate?

I went back to the trusty selection ring, and simply made it bigger (see Figure 5-22). I made it just large enough to allow Lindi to grab the ring, without covering up the piece. I then limited the movement and rotation finger motions to the ring area, instead of the entire screen. This allows selection and dragging of nonselected pieces outside the ring, yet still maintains the same movement and rotation logic for the selected piece. After much testing, Lindi and our kids gave TanZen their seal of approval. Whew!

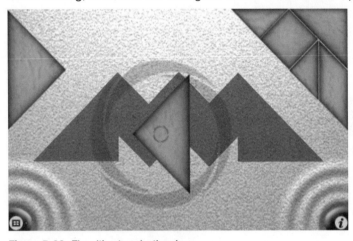

Figure 5-22. *The ultimate selection ring*

The Perils of Being 95 Percent Finished

Mere days before the opening of the App Store, most everyone was still on the waiting list, including me. TanZen was complete and included a fairly simple piece-manipulation scheme. But I was worried players were not going to understand it. With three possible things you could do to each piece, as well as the somewhat complicated nature of tangram puzzles themselves, I felt like I needed a way to show people how to solve a puzzle— I needed a tutorial.

I decided to spend a little time creating an animated tutorial, which would cover everything that could be done in the game, by walking players through completing one of the puzzles. I wanted to use minimal text, so it would be understood by anyone in the world. I figured I could code it up in an evening with no problems. Right as I was about to start, the App Store finally arrived.

The App Store Arrives!

On July 11, the App Store opened with about 500 applications, all from people involved in the beta program. My reaction to this event was mixed: I was very excited that the store was finally open but extremely annoyed that I was never allowed a chance to be a part of it. I had spent months of late nights getting TanZen ready in time for launch, and to see that goal unfulfilled through no fault of my own was, well, a bit of a downer. I moped through the rest of the day.

But at the end of the day, like a ray of sunshine, I got the magic e-mail from Apple saying, "Congratulations, you will now be allowed to pay your $99 to develop on a real device and submit applications to the App Store!" After over four months of waiting, the sheer joy I felt reading that email was beyond words. Then the real work began.

With the end in sight, I threw myself into my work. Not only did I have the tutorial to do, I still had a web site and an application icon to make. I knew I couldn't get everything done at the same time, so I enlisted the help of an artist friend, Jim MacQuarrie, who took some of the load off by creating the web site and helping to design the icon, shown in Figure 5-1. For the icon, I knew I wanted to use the actual pieces from the game to create the classic square tangram shape. However, all the versions I created looked dull and uninviting. After going through many iterations, I finally decided to combine my square-shaped art with my friend's idea of adding an orange border to bring a bit of brightness to the icon, which proved to be just the right balance of realism and eye-catching color.

While coordinating with Jim, I was also busily trying to finish that piece-of-cake tutorial. Boy, did I underestimate that task! The tutorial was probably one of the dullest, most annoying, and time-consuming things I'd had ever done as a developer. But after many days of coding carefully timed animations, dang if it didn't turn out to be one fantastic piece of work (see Figure 5-23). A few art tweaks to the *Info* screen (see Figure 5-24) to include the new tutorial, and my work was done, and my worries about people not understanding the game were over.

Figure 5-23. *The animated tutorial*

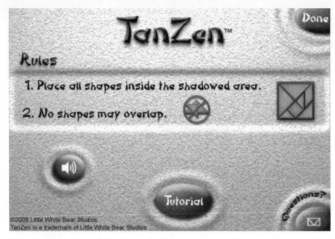

Figure 5-24. *The Info screen modified to include the new tutorial*

By the time the tutorial was finished, the App Store had been open for a week, and I was in a state of panic as I watched the list of games for the iPhone grow from a little over a hundred games to over two hundred. I felt like I was going to miss my opportunity to make some money off all my hard work. Everything was finished except for final testing. Rushing through the testing at this point could've been fatal, so despite my anxiety, I took a day or so to give the game a complete run-through. Good thing I did, as a couple new bugs were found!

Nearly a week and a half after the App Store opened, I finally submitted TanZen to Apple. The process went off without a hitch. I then waited and slept. The relief of finally being finished was replaced with nervousness. Would Apple reject the game? Was it good enough to be in the App Store? You have to remember that this was long before everyone realized that Apple lets nearly everything into the store. I was completely under the impression that Apple would judge the game based on some sort of quality standard.

Eight days later, I was sitting at work when the e-mail arrived to say that my application was ready for sale! I sprinted over to the office of the coworker who had helped me with TanZen before. Without comment, I revealed the e-mail to him. I think he might've been almost as excited as I was. I called Lindi, and she started screaming in excitement. It was a good day.

Recalling the First Days on the App Store

The first day that TanZen was available on the App Store, I saw only half a day's sales, since the game went up late in the day. But when the numbers came in, I was shocked. I had sold a whopping 66 copies! On day two, it sold twice that. I was amazed at how well it was selling, and I spent the next couple days obsessively watching the rankings change on iTunes as TanZen slowly moved up the list of puzzle games and into the Top 100 Games list. Reviews started coming in, and most of them were very positive. But there was a disturbing trend developing—some people were complaining about the two-finger rotation.

Responding to Rotation Issues

I was a little bewildered by the trouble two-finger rotation was causing people. I figured if all my kids could do it, so could everyone else. The tutorial emphasized using two thumbs to rotate, but a lot of people either didn't watch the tutorial and were trying to use a one-handed pinching maneuver or simply felt using two hands was too much work. So, to combat the problem of people skipping, or misunderstanding, the tutorial, I released a YouTube video detailing exactly how to rotate and included it on my support site.

After about a week, sales started to slump (I learned much later that this sales cycle was perfectly normal for any new application). I released a free Lite version of TanZen hoping that it would grab new buyers. It worked like a charm. Sales were better than ever!

And then the most wonderful thing happened. Apple decided to feature TanZen in the *New* listings, which is the best possible spot on the iPhone. Nobody really knew it at the time, but being featured was like winning the lottery. TanZen sales went through the roof, and within two days, the application was number 12 in the entire App Store! Lindi and I watched our credit card debt melt away as each day went by, and knowing that all the work we did was actually going to change our lives—wow.

I also felt a little nervous. I thought someone was going to figure out that I was just some guy with no gaming experience who bluffed his way to the top of the App Store.

Even though TanZen was highly ranked, the fact that the game's reviews were peppered with players complaining about the two-finger rotation was starting to bug me, so I decided to revisit the issue. I needed to design a single-finger rotation scheme that closely resembled the old scheme, so I could please old and new players.

Lindi and I really liked the move and rotate controls in TanZen. They were clean, fingernail-proof, and best of all, didn't involve a bunch of buttons and interface doodads. Plus, accidentally activating a move instead of a rotate was impossible. So, how could I take this nearly perfect solution and make it perfect for everyone?

The solution had to satisfy a set of conditions: Piece movement had to be fingernail friendly. Rotation feedback had to remain the same. And most importantly, Lindi had to like it.

Being the wise (lazy) programmer that I am, I decided to modify what I already had instead of creating something new. What would happen if I eliminated the second finger requirement, mapped movement to touches inside the selection ring, and mapped rotation to touches directly on the ring? I quickly coded up that idea and gave it to Lindi to try.

She hated it. She kept accidentally rotating a shape, when she meant to move it. The problem was that she had always moved pieces by dragging with the ring itself, never inside it. Now, I knew that not everyone was playing that way; instead, some were moving their fingers directly on top of the pieces. But I still had to satisfy the players my wife represented.

My next idea was to make the ring bigger, offering more room around the piece to activate a move without being on top of it. It was a little better, but Lindi was still making mistakes. So I made the ring even bigger. This process repeated a few times, until finally the ring was big enough to grab pieces the way she wanted to, yet still rotate without making mistakes.

Amazingly, with just a few simple tweaks, I managed to cover all the required conditions, keep the exact same interface look (see Figures 5-25 and 5-26), and still eliminate the evil second finger. Mission accomplished! But would current players accept it?

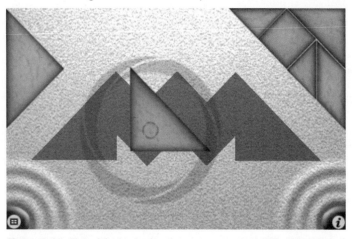

Figure 5-25. *The original selection ring was compact and allowed movement or rotation based on the number of fingers being used.*

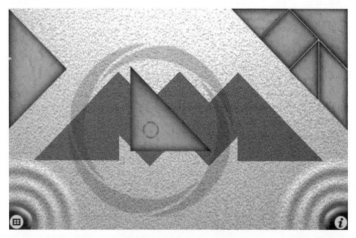

Figure 5-26. *The new and improved selection ring requires only one finger, with a move action mapped to the area inside the ring and rotation mapped along the edge.*

Users loved the new scheme. All hail single-finger rotation! Yes, a couple of people wanted the old method back, but not many did. Based on some of the video reviews and technical support e-mails I've read, many people didn't even realize the two-finger rotation was gone. They went along their merry way, placing that second finger, none the wiser that it didn't really do anything at all anymore. I'm going to call that a successful transition!

When to Say "Yes" and When to Say "Thanks, I'll think about it."

About a month after TanZen appeared on the App Store, I had gathered a ton of e-mail suggestions from players of the game. Many of the requests involved additions to the interface. I weighed each suggestion carefully, considering the possible added value to the game against how much it would compromise the interface. I also based some of my decisions on how long the feature would take to implement. If a feature is going to take a long time to complete, you need to decide if it will actually improve your sales, or if your time would be better spent doing something else.

The number one thing to remember about user requests is that you aren't required to implement any of them. You should give users what they need, not everything they want. If you add everything, your game will lose its focus and become a convoluted mess of features that only a few players will ever even look at.

You also need to be careful that your original intention isn't lost in user-induced feature creep. A lot of people wanted a little timer in the corner of the screen to add pressure to the game. And they wanted their best times displayed on the puzzle selection screen. While these features seem interesting, and potentially fun, they certainly didn't fit the Zen theme of this game.

Also, some players were disturbed by the lack of titles for the puzzles. They wanted to know which puzzle is a bunny and which is a bird. Usually, the puzzle forms were fairly obvious, and I considered the lack of text one of the defining aspects of the game, so I wasn't about to add titles.

Making the pieces go back to their default positions in the middle of a game was also highly requested. I should have listened to my daughter, as she had requested this feature months before. I had vetoed it back then, because I didn't want to add more buttons to the game. My opinion about extra buttons hadn't changed, but I did find a solution using the iPhone's accelerometer. Since I had been on the simulator for so long, I'd never even considered it. Within a couple hours, I added a fully functional feature that allowed users to shake the iPhone to reset a puzzle. The shake soon became one of the most talked about features: it's simple, handy, and completely invisible!

Players who were already familiar with tangrams wanted the game to be more like the classic version, where the puzzle is much smaller than the pieces, which makes the game much more challenging. I had considered this interesting idea as far back as my design document. I kept this suggestion in the back of my head and eventually added this advanced mode, called Masters Mode, to the game several months later (see Figure

5-27). And as you've probably guessed, Masters Mode integrated smoothly into the existing interface!

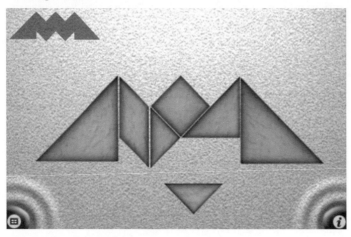

Figure 5-27. *An advanced puzzle mode for expert players*

A lot of players also asked for help in solving the puzzles. Some people pick up tangrams right away, and some really have to work at them. Because I received a lot of e-mail requesting hints and tips, I wanted to put them in the game somehow, but I didn't want to add any buttons. I examined all the touch interfaces I had already used in the game to see if there were any gaps that I could squeeze hints into. Fairly quickly, I figured out the answer: I had been using a double-tap for flipping pieces but not for anything else. Double-tapping anywhere other than on top of a piece did nothing.

I decided to assign hints to the double-tap, and I wanted the hints to be subtle, just like the rest of the game. Eventually, I decided to show a darkened shadow version of a random piece when a player double-tapped the game surface (see Figure 5-28). Yet again, a major feature was added to the game without cluttering up the interface.

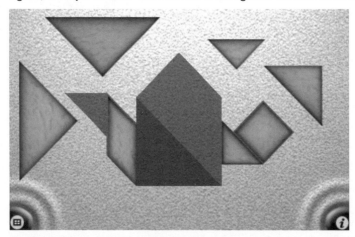

Figure 5-28. *A hidden hint system that only appears when users double-tap the playing area*

Surviving on the App Store

The first six months of the App Store were very much like the Wild West. Like a well-publicized gold rush, the App Store saw a lot of questionable developer activity, as Apple struggled to get hold of this wildly successful venture. The store was filled with fierce competition. Falsified reviews, both good and bad, were everywhere. Bogus updates clogged the submission process, as each update brought newly revived sales. Some developers made a ton of money, but most made little, if any at all. Application developers all lived and died by their rank on the store. As TanZen was featured right out of the gate, I was one of the lucky ones.

As the number of applications on the store increased so did the quality. Games from larger companies emerged at prices below $5. Suddenly, TanZen seemed vastly overpriced at $2.99, and its rank started to fall. I lowered the price to $0.99 in the hopes of becoming a low-priced hit. The gamble paid off, and TanZen made a second run at the top, and this time peaked at number 27 in the store, three months after it first came out.

There's a lot of discussion among developers about application pricing. Some people feel you should price your application at what you think it's worth. Some want to price based on a calculated return on investment. Others use rock bottom pricing to attract impulse buyers. Everyone has an opinion, but one thing is very clear. Given the current way the App Store rankings work, a lower price tends to sell more copies. In turn, selling more copies gets you higher on the rankings lists, as they are mostly based on the number of daily sales.

Visibility is everything on the iPhone. If you're not on a ranked list, you aren't making very much money at all. So in deciding your price, I would recommend examining the store, and pricing your app similarly to your competition. Yes, you put months of effort into your app, and pricing it low doesn't seem to make any sense. But, I've seen a lot of good apps fail, simply because the developer refused to lower their price.

An app is worth whatever people will pay for it. Originally, shoppers felt TanZen was easily worth $2.99. A year later, they feel $0.99 is the correct price. It's all about perception of value. If I tried to release TanZen today at the original price, it'd sell less than twenty copies per day, and drop down to zero sales very quickly.

Five months after TanZen's initial release, it finally fell out of the Top 100 Games list for the first time. Since then, it has become a permanent fixture in the Top 100 Puzzles list and has enjoyed a steady influx of new players every day. Even though U.S. sales account for most of TanZen's revenue, the game has enjoyed an incredible amount of sales in other countries as well—nearly 50 percent of all TanZen sales have come from outside the United States. I truly believe my decision to not include text in the main portions of the game and taking the time to create an animated tutorial are the prime reasons the game has been so well received worldwide. At the time of this writing, over one million people have tried TanZen, via the free or paid versions. Both Lindi and I are in awe when we think about it. All those late nights of coding, agonizing over every detail, and forcing ourselves to make the nicest looking game possible were worth it!

Creating a Second Game Without Starting Over

When TanZen was completed in late July of 2008, I was ready for a much-needed vacation. I had been working twenty-hour days for the final month or two of the project. During TanZen's first five months on the App Store, I continued at my day job, all the while enjoying all the extra income. I kept busy making updates to the game, but I wasn't finding time to create anything new. The App Store was not a steady source of income, as sales varied wildly from week to week. It was time to make a new game to bring in some more cash and spread out the risk.

When talking to people about the App Store, I liken the medium to the music industry. Applications generally become popular quickly or not at all. Most of the money is made in the first month an application is available on the store, and then the application falls into obscurity. The majority of the money is made by the top five percent of the applications. Sounds just like Top 40 radio, doesn't it? TanZen managed to buck that trend, through carefully timed updates and tremendous word of mouth support. I wanted our second effort to have the same amount of success.

If you follow the music industry analogy a bit more, you know that sophomore efforts by musicians are typically the make-or-break moment in their careers. If they make the same record twice, they risk being labeled as lazy. If they become too inventive, they risk alienating their original audience and could fail completely. I needed a game that would be similar enough to TanZen to please the existing players, yet different enough to make new people want to buy it.

I wanted to do another puzzle game, one that I could add to over time. I also knew I couldn't handle another several months of late-night coding. I searched the Web for popular puzzle games to get some ideas and came across the game of pentominoes, which had been around for at least a hundred years. Pentominoes is a puzzle game that uses twelve defined shapes (see Figure 5-29) that you must rotate and flip to create a larger shape. The game has been used for years in schools to teach spatial reasoning. Sounds a lot like tangrams!

Figure 5-29. *The twelve standard pentomino shapes*

To complement TanZen and appeal to its existing audience, I had to change the rules a bit. Instead of endlessly filling rectangles in different ways, as the traditional game has you do, I decided to create fun puzzle shapes that you'd only have to complete once. Additionally, since solving traditional pentomino puzzles is pretty difficult, I decided to include some puzzles that didn't require all twelve pieces, as a way to keep players from getting discouraged too quickly. These changes to the basic game concept would hopefully make the game more appealing to a broader spectrum of players.

Repurposing a Popular Interface

The similarities between pentominoes and tangrams are many, but there are a few key differences. Because pentomino games have twelve pieces as opposed to seven, I needed to modify the game to display a larger number of pieces. Since my code was modular, I simply created a modified version of the existing piece class and placed it in the game. Twelve subversions of that class later, I had all the shapes in the game (see Figure 5-30). I could move, rotate, and flip them. I placed a grid on the screen and had a working prototype of the new game based on the original one—all in about a day!

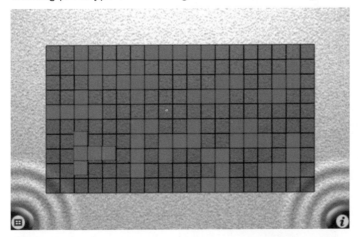

Figure 5-30. *A quick prototype to explore the game possibilities*

Making Interface Modifications to Fit the New Game Rules

With a working prototype, I could play the game and analyze what would and wouldn't work with the TanZen interface. For the new game, I needed pieces to interlock. Since pentomino pieces are based on squares, the puzzles are always grid based. Given these facts, a computer-assisted snapping feature would be a requirement.

After playing with the prototype, I decided that the large TanZen selection ring obviously wasn't the right interface for small, interlocking pieces. The pieces were all very close together, so too many pieces would be inside the ring, which would cause a lot of selection problems. So goodbye ring! Instead, I went back to the old standby of tapping to rotate. Pentominoes rotate at 90-degree angles, which meant users needed only four taps to make a complete rotation. Tapping actually worked well as an interface for this game, even though it failed for TanZen.

After a few days of trial and error, Lindi and I came up with piece sizes that were big enough to allow users to position them without fingers completely covering up the pieces. These larger sizes, along with the snapping feature, allowed them to accurately place pieces 100 percent of the time. We had a complete piece manipulation interface in no time at all!

Designing Around Limitations in Screen Size

Yet again, the limited screen size of the device would determine the UI. Given that a large portion of the screen would be taken up by the puzzle area, there wasn't a lot of space left to store the unused pieces. Simply tucking them away off screen was not an option. This type of game requires that you can see all the shapes at once, so you can form solutions in your mind. To fit all 12 pentomino pieces on the screen without encroaching on the puzzle area, I decided to put trays along both sides of the screen to hold miniature versions of the pieces (see Figure 5-31). This way, the player could grab one piece at any time and move it into the grid area, causing the piece to grow to full size. Even better, when a user didn't need a piece anymore, the piece could be moved off the grid, and it'd shrink back to the tray.

Figure 5-31. *Trays keep pieces out of the way, yet still in full view.*

Colors, Colors Everywhere

Game creation had been going exceptionally well so far. Reusing code and sticking with the TanZen art style saved months of development time. With the help of my wife, we had the entire game working, including a large list of puzzles, after only a month of late-night work. However, we had yet to design the exact look of the pieces. From experience with TanZen, I knew that the pieces' look was one of the most important decisions to be made.

Taking several cues from nature, I spent a few days creating sample piece textures in Photoshop. After nixing several wonderful samples, Lindi and I finally agreed on one of them: it had just the amount of randomness and imperfection that we were looking for. That left choosing the colors. Sounds easy right? Not so much.

I had found that using a single color for all the pieces was not an option, as all the pieces started to mix together, and confusion became a problem. We experimented with many looks—pastels, muted colors, earth tones, dark colors, light colors—but couldn't agree on the perfect look.

If you're ever looking for a way to send your marriage into divorce territory, try choosing a bunch of colors with your spouse. Imagine picking a color to paint your house. Now imagine picking the colors for all the houses on your street. And imagine that the choices you make will be judged by millions of people around the world. But in the end, we came up with a winning combination that we both loved (see Figure 5-32), and we didn't even have to involve any lawyers!

Figure 5-32. *Final piece colors*

Putting on the Finishing Touches

The game was now complete. Lindi and I came up with the name Zentomino, taking a cue from TanZen. I wanted the icon to have a similar look to TanZen's icon, so people browsing the App Store would immediately recognize it as a sister game. Using multicolor pieces in the icon looked a little busy, so I chose a single color instead; I created a square out of the shapes and slapped the TanZen icon's orange border around it. An icon family was born!

The game was now truly ready to be sold. In just a matter of weeks, we created an entirely new game, based on the code and general interface of our previous game. I quickly submitted the game to Apple, and it was approved in less than a week. After only a few months, Zentomino has sold nearly 30,000 copies. And the sales outside the United States have exceeded even TanZen's early days. By all accounts, the game has been a success!

Summary

It's been a year and a half since the iPhone SDK was first introduced, and boy, what a ride it's been! In that period, I went from a guy with an idea and a lot of credit card debt to a highly respected developer, with zero debt and a large fan base that is itching for even more games to play. None of this could have been possible if I hadn't taken the time to concentrate on interface design and all the fine little details that make up a great game. The games my wife and I create aren't fancy, nor are they complicated. But they're beautiful in their simplicity, and that's why people love them.

Hopefully, my story has given you some fresh ideas on interface design and maybe a little bit of inspiration. If you have a great idea for an iPhone application, by all means, create it! But don't forget: a great idea is only the beginning. A great iPhone application is 10 percent idea and 90 percent execution. The right user interface can make the difference between making $100 and $100,000. Take the time to make your application functional, beautiful, and memorable. Good luck!

Tim Novikoff

Company: Flash of Genius LLC

Location: Ithaca, NY

Life as an iPhone Developer: Flash of Genius: SAT Vocab

What's in This Chapter: This chapter describes my adventure developing an iPhone app while having no prior development experience. I focus mainly on the user interface design issues that came up along the way as I developed and tested Flash of Genius: SAT Vocab.

Key Technologies:

- *UIWebView*
- *UIButton*
- *UIAlertView*

Chapter 6

Flash of Genius: SAT Vocab

When I began developing Flash of Genius: SAT Vocab, I had virtually none of the technical skills that would eventually be required of me. I had never developed software for the iPhone, a Mac, or any device at all. I had never programmed in C, Objective-C, or any C language whatsoever. I was just a graduate student in applied math. My best markup language was LaTeX, a language for preparing mathematical documents, and my best scripting language was Matlab, a language for scientific computing. I had also never owned a business, been a member of a startup, or worked in any sort of entrepreneurial environment. Prior to becoming a graduate student, I had been a high school math teacher, and prior to that, I had worked as a voice-over actor and done various other odd jobs in show business.

This is all to serve as a warning: I'm not giving expert advice. More advanced programmers would surely have found more elegant solutions to the problems I've faced. Serial entrepreneurs would certainly not follow my way of going about starting a business. Experienced designers would find ample room for criticism in Flash of Genius: SAT Vocab.

Nevertheless, this chapter has a purpose. In fact, it has a few.

First, I want amateurs and first-time developers to come away from this chapter thinking, "Well if this guy can do it, I can too!" It's true. If you've got a general sense for programming, passion for what you're doing, and a modicum of grit, you can do it. You may not produce a number-one hit, but don't be surprised to see your application somewhere on a best-seller list. When I got my first e-mail from a customer, I asked him how he had heard of Flash of Genius. He said he noticed it at number 39 on the Top Paid Educational Apps list. I was stunned. Then, I watched it climb into the Top 20, which was a real thrill. Creating a successful application is not out of anyone's reach.

 I'll also write about some technical things pertaining to design and implementation. I eventually came to be relatively well-versed in the aspects of the API that were relevant to Flash of Genius. Because it's a flashcard application that displays each vocabulary word along with its definition, Latin roots, and a sample sentence, a lot of text markup is involved. I'll discuss some of the design limitations of the API, and the decision to use `UIWebView` in conjunction with `UIButton` to display flashcards as they had originally been imagined in the design phase when implementation was not being considered.

I'll also discuss some of the user interface issues that came up in the course of designing the application. I'd like to say that the decisions I eventually made were really no-brainers. For example, the decision to have the flashcard application be in landscape mode seems pretty obvious. After all, only in landscape mode does the iPhone feel like, um, a flashcard. Incredibly, though, many other flashcard applications botched even this simple UI decision, as well as others. So I'll fight the urge to skip the obvious and discuss simple decisions as well as more subtle ones.

Even though I think Flash of Genius: SAT Vocab eventually came out looking pretty good, I still urge you—no matter how inexperienced—to keep in mind that this isn't expert advice. It's just advice from a dude who managed to put out a successful iPhone application despite his own inexperience.

Checking Out the Competition

The basic idea behind a vocabulary flashcard application is to automate the usual process for studying vocabulary words. The usual process goes something like this: Take a stack of index cards, and on each one, write a vocabulary word on the front and its definition on the back. Then, study the words by looking at the cards one at a time, starting with the one on top. Try to recall the definition of the word on the front before looking at the back to check yourself, if necessary. After doing this for one card, put it back in the stack somewhere; put it far back if you don't want to see it again for a while, and not so far back if you're still shaky on the definition and want to test yourself again soon on that word. Then go on to the next card. Continue studying like this until you know all the definitions.

Most flashcard applications automate this process in roughly the same way. First, show the user the front of a virtual flashcard, like the one from Flash of Genius shown in Figure 7-1. Allow the user to indicate either that they know the word or that they want to see the definition. If they opt to see the definition, flip the flashcard over to reveal the definition and maybe some other useful information about the word (see Figure 7-2). Next, allow the user to indicate whether or not he or she had correctly recalled this definition before seeing it. Either way, continue by then showing the user another virtual flashcard. All of the user input is passed to an algorithm which dictates which flashcards get seen by the user and when.

circumspect

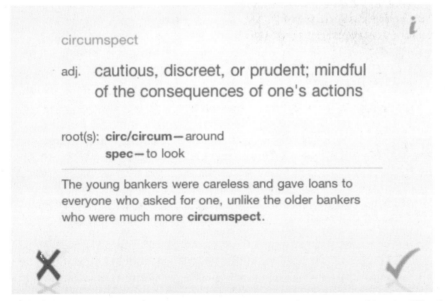

Figure 7-1. *This is the front of a flashcard in Flash of Genius. If the user taps the question mark, the card flips over to reveal the back of the flashcard, shown in Figure 7-2. If the user taps the check, the front of the next flashcard is revealed.*

circumspect

adj. cautious, discreet, or prudent; mindful of the consequences of one's actions

root(s): **circ/circum**—around
 spec—to look

The young bankers were careless and gave loans to everyone who asked for one, unlike the older bankers who were much more **circumspect**.

Figure 7-2. *This is the back of a flashcard in Flash of Genius. If the user taps either the "X" or the check, the front of the next flashcard is revealed.*

Literally hundreds of flashcard applications are available from the App Store, and many of them are quite slick. When I started, though, there were only a few, and most of them had clearly been developed in haste without much thought to UI. This gave me hope that maybe I wasn't too late; I could still make the first good SAT flashcard application. The following sections explain some of the more brutal UI flaws that I noticed in early flashcard applications before I began developing.

Mental Model Inconsistency

Most flashcard applications these days use a flip animation to go from the front of a flashcard to its back and use a different type of transition to go to the next flashcard (with a different front and back).

Some flashcard applications, though, used to make the mind-boggling decision to simply use a flip animation for every single transition. Thus the user could be looking at the front of one flashcard and then after two "flips" be looking at a different flashcard! That's not how real flashcards work. If you turn a real flashcard over and then back again, you end up looking at the same thing as when you started. That's how virtual flashcards should work too.

Applications that made this design error were messing with the mental model that the user has about how the application works under the hood. The idea of a mental model is to me the single most important notion when thinking about how people interact with technology. You could write a whole book about it. In fact, someone did write a whole book about it. The book is called *The Design of Everyday Things* (Basic Books, 2002). It's written by Donald Norman, a professor of cognitive science who's also a former Apple employee. It helped me think about UI design more than anything else I've ever read, and I recommend it very strongly.

Inappropriate Orientations

Another bizarre choice that many developers made was to have the entire application be in portrait mode. Making a watertight case against this decision is hard, but here are my thoughts. For one, portrait mode is not very reminiscent of flashcards. It also makes it difficult to display a bunch of information without making it look like a list, which is not an effective format for this type of material. Applications that chose to use only portrait mode would often also center all of the text, too. That layout looks fine for the vocabulary word itself, which occupies only one line of text, but the sample sentences generally look ridiculous. To me, center-aligned sentences remind me of sloppy fliers put up by high school kids running for senior class president.

There is also the question of hand placement. With a flashcards application, you basically need two buttons showing all the time: one to indicate that the user knows the definition, and another to flip the flashcard if the answer isn't known (see Figures 7-1 and 7-2). Every transition is prompted by one of these two buttons, so they should be very handy. Putting the application in landscape mode and then placing the buttons where I did presents the user with an intuitive way to hold the device and use the application—with two hands, using thumbs to control the application (like for a PSP or an Xbox controller).

It's a good idea to make the most common functionality of an application very suggestive of a particular way to hold the device. This way, you have a good idea of how the user is likely to hold the device when using your application, and you can plan your UI accordingly.

Small Buttons

Another all-too-common UI flaw among early flashcard applications, as well as applications in every category on the App Store, were unnecessarily small buttons. My feeling is that if an application has buttons that need to be pressed very often, these buttons should have a big fat target area so that the user never misses them. Figure 7-3 illustrates the size of the check button in Flash of Genius.

Figure 7-3. *A screen-capture from Interface Builder showing the target area of the check button. You can't miss it!*

This goes for the little *Info* button that comes with the iPhone API, too. The area of this button is just too small for many users by default. Luckily, there is a simple remedy for this: put a big clear UIButton on top of it in Interface Builder. I think this is widely done now.

Before making an iPhone application, it's obviously a good idea to check out what else is already in the App Store and make sure that you're making a new contribution. My own experience tells me that even if you see others going for the same functionality, if they don't get the UI right, the market is still there for the taking. Apple knows this quite well too, as it was not the first ones to make a phone with a built-in browser and music player, but it was the first to make a really slick one. (sorry Treo.)

Starting Development

Getting started was very hard. I wish I could say that I just buckled down and holed up until I learned everything I needed to know about iPhone development, but that's not how it happened. I was a full-time graduate student and could barely devote a few hours a week to the project. I actually paid someone to help me get started with Xcode and programming in C and Objective-C, and I paid a law school student to help me get the business started. All that went quite smoothly and was a great use of money saved up from my previous life as a high school math teacher. I'm very happy to have the knowledge and skills I picked up from these people, not to mention a couple more contacts for the future. Those contacts might come in handy if I ever decide to really make an effort at building a software company. Getting help with programming and starting a business was a success.

Getting help with designing the application and the icon was another story. I eventually found a great person to work with, but at first, I tried my luck with craigslist. Oops. I won't go into all the details, but I was severely disappointed when the first mock-up of the icon came back. We had agreed on an icon design over the phone that would involve little flashcards, but instead of index cards, the icon mock-up showed flash digital storage cards, like the MicroSD cards that used to come with digital cameras (see Figure 7-4). It turns out that the charming and well-spoken American guy I had talked to on the phone was just a front for an operation based in the Philippines, and something had gotten lost in translation on the way to the artist in Manila. After a similar incident with the phrase "idea light bulb," I realized it wasn't going to work. I had paid up front, and that was $100 down the drain.

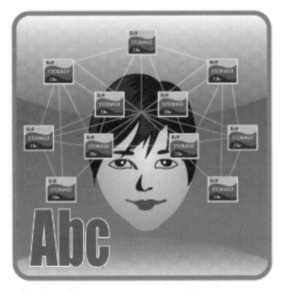

Figure 7-4. *The wrong type of "flashcard" is really only the beginning of what's wrong with this icon. It would never even scale down to the size of an icon on the iPhone. What a disaster!*

I eventually hired a professional named Jan Tedder to do the icon. She is a friend of a friend and very talented, and she did a great job.

I wanted a few things from the icon. First of all, I wanted anybody looking at the icon to be able to figure out that Flash of Genius was a flashcard application for studying SAT vocabulary words. Second, I wanted the icon to grab the attention of anyone with the SAT on their mind and certainly be attention-grabbing to anyone searching the App Store for "SAT" or "SAT flashcards." I also wanted the icon, and eventually the design of the entire application, to convey intelligence and professionalism. I wanted potential customers to see the icon and assume that this application was not just thrown together without thought, and that they could count on the definitions and sample sentences in the application to be top quality, which they were. I think that's what students look for in SAT study materials, so that's what I told Jan I was looking for in a design. You can see what she came up with in Figure 7-5.

Figure 7-5. *This is the first icon that Jan made for Flash of Genius: SAT Vocab.*

The College Board, the company that writes and administers the actual SAT, wasn't thrilled with the icon. Their lawyers are eternally concerned that people might think that any product with "SAT" in the name was made in conjunction with their enterprise, and they have trademarked the term "SAT". They asked me to have an icon made that included the full name of the application, Flash of Genius: SAT Vocab, and included an asterisk after "SAT" corresponding to a footnote on the iTunes product description page. So Jan made a new icon, shown in Figure 7-6. The College Board was happy with it, so was I, and that was that.

Figure 7-6. *This is the final icon that Jan made.*

One of the first things I turned my attention toward in this whole project was the icon, and it was one of the last things that finally fell into place. I'd say I spent a total of 40 hours thinking about the icon. This is absurdly long, and now that I've gone through the process once I think that next time it will go much quicker, but I do think it was worth every minute.

The fact is that without a decent icon, nobody will ever look at your application. The icon is to the application what a resume is to a job applicant; without a good one, you don't get noticed. It will also inform your users what to expect of the application, including how they expect to be able to interact with it. I think it's worth spending as much time on the icon as you need to get it right. For me it was a long time, but maybe for you it will be less.

For your entertainment, I've included some of the icon design ideas that didn't go anywhere (see Figure 7-7). In general, the stupider the icon here, the more I had a hand in its design. The biggest lesson I learned from the whole process was this: find a talented professional, tell them all about the application you're making, and then get out of their way!

Figure 7-7. *Here are some of the icons that didn't make the cut along with the final one (bottom-right).*

Designing the Flashcards

The main feature of Flash of Genius: SAT Vocab is the study mode, where users interact with flashcards. On the front of the flashcard (see Figure 7-1) is a vocabulary word. If a user knows the definition of the word, I want that user to tap the checkmark. Otherwise, the user should tap the question mark to see the back of the card.

On the back of the flashcard (see Figure 7-2) are the definition, the part of speech, the roots of the word if they are helpful, and a sample sentence. Users who flip over the card and discover that the definition they had in mind was correct should tap the checkmark. Users who didn't know the definition, or thought they did but in fact had it wrong, should tap the "X" button.

Almost all flashcard programs have roughly this functionality at their core, yet they are often implemented very differently. In my case, I used the UIWebView class to display all of the text and the UIButton class with a custom image for each button.

I didn't want to go with this implementation originally because there are a lot of downsides to it. For one, the resource files and code that govern the look and feel of the flashcards become highly nonlocalized: HTML and CSS files in one place, XIB files elsewhere, and Objective-C code scattered about as well. Another downside is that particular care needs to be taken to make sure that the resulting flashcard doesn't look like a messy mash-up of web design and iPhone API elements.

Despite this, the alternatives are worse. What was so bad about "going native" and forgoing the UIWebView class altogether? One word, really: typography.

The backs of the flashcards vary depending on their corresponding vocabulary words (Figure 7-2 shows one example). Some words have two roots, like "circumspect" (from "circum" meaning "around" and "spec" meaning "to look"), and some have one root, like "placid" (from "plac" meaning "to please"). Others have no root that would be of use to the average user, like "cloying" (whose tenuous relationship to the French word for "nail" just isn't useful to the average 15-year-old cramming for the SAT). The definitions of the words vary in length enough that some require one line of text, whereas others require three. And the sample sentences vary from two lines to four.

In addition to the varying lengths of things, the content of the flashcards also called for several different font styles. In the sample sentences, I wanted to emphasize the vocabulary word by putting it in boldface. I also wanted the ability to italicize foreign words in the sample sentences.

All these things meant that UITextView, UILabel, and other built-in objects were not really for me. The main problem with these classes was the lack of ability to vary font styles within a particular instance. That meant having to forgo any use of italics or boldface within sentences, which I wasn't keen to do.

Even if I could accept a uniform font style, the problem of varying sentence length would still have been an issue. Leaving room for three lines of text looks silly when only one is being used (see Figure 7-8). In theory, I could have varied the height of a `UITextView` according to the length of the text to go inside, and varied the placement based on the heights of the other `UITextViews` above it, but why bother if the font style was still going to be a problem?

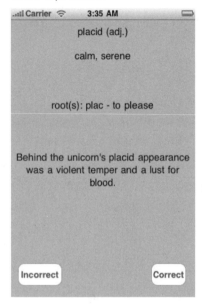

Figure 7-8. *This is how Flash of Genius may have looked had I gone with UITextViews instead of UIWebView and just generally not cared about user interface design at all.*

In the end, I decided to go with `UIWebView` for the markup of all the text. Besides giving me the ability to carefully manage the style and placement of the text on the flashcard, this approach had another benefit. By relegating the markup to a `UIWebView` instance, I would have the option of working with web design and HTML people to design and implement the flashcards. As it turned out, that's exactly what happened.

Designing the Buttons

In theory, I could have just used `UIWebView` and forgone the `UIButton` class altogether. If you hack hard enough, you can actually get the click of a hyperlink in a `UIWebView` to prompt a method call in the `UIViewController` class. Using such a technique, I could have had my buttons displayed as images embedded in the web view. But that comes with a downside too: lack of visual feedback.

Apple takes visual feedback very seriously when making their own software, and it shows in all the built-in applications for the iPhone. Consider the way the keys on the number pad turn bright blue as soon as they're touched (not to mention the tone they produce if the sound is on). Or consider the way any application icon darkens slightly when you tap it. These features all let the user know that the phone has registered the intended touch.

One of the great things about the `UIButton` class is the ability to supply different images for different states of the button. For example, if a button has a checkmark as its image for `UIControlStateNormal`, then image for `UIControlStateHighlighted` for that same button could be a slightly darker checkmark, or a checkmark with some shading around it, or whatever else I wanted. There would have been no comparable freedom had I used images within the `UIWebView` instead of instances of `UIButton`.

I went with shading around the checkmark, instead of just a darker checkmark, because thumbs are big. That is, the buttons were placed to coax the user to hold the device with two hands and use thumbs for pressing buttons. But when a thumb touches the checkmark button, it typically completely obscures the checkmark image. With shading for the highlighted state, a user can get the visual feedback that the button is being pressed from the area right around the thumb. I experimented with just making the checkmark bigger than the average thumb, and then using a darker checkmark for the highlighted state, but that just looked goofy, so I went with shading instead.

Figure 7-9. *These are the images for the default and highligted control states of the check button, respectively.*

As for the design of the actual checkmark and "X," here are Jan's thoughts in her own words: "I was going for buttons that were clean but still friendly and with a human, almost hand-written touch to them. The final product was sort of Web2.0y, which I think still resonates with the intended audience of high school kids, at least for now."

A couple of issues remained regarding the little omnipresent *Info* button on the top-right of the screen. First of all, I knew I wanted it to be a lowercase "i" because iPhone users already know that touching a lowercase "i" generally takes them to a settings page. But I also wanted it to look like it was part of the sleek flashcard design. The white glow that often accompanies the *Info* button when it is pressed (in the built-in Weather and Stocks applications, for example) is also really cool but only comes in white, which, of course, is no good on the white background of Flash of Genius. So I asked Jan to make an "i" specifically for Flash of Genius and to make another one with a dark glow of some sort for `UIControlStateHighlighted`. I liked how they came out, so I went with this instead of the dark version of the *Info* button that comes in the API.

i   *i*

Figure 7-10. *These are the images for the default and highlighted control states of the* Info *button, respectively.*

Testing the Application

With the buttons looking good and the markup looking the way it should on the back of the flashcard, I thought I had a complete application. I certainly felt like I had created a useful tool for learning vocabulary words. There was something I had been ignoring from the very beginning though: how does anybody figure out how the darn thing works?

No problem, I thought. I'll just write an FAQ and slap it onto my settings page! After I wrote a 2,000 word FAQ for my dinky little flashcard application, I realized this may not be the way to go. Besides, I was coming to realize, the truth is that if users need to go to a FAQ, I've already lost. Why should anybody ever have to go to one of those? This is the iPhone! Things should be totally intuitive!

Unfortunately, there are some unintuitive things about Flash of Genius. At the core of the application is an algorithm that determines which flashcards the user sees and when the user sees them. If the user gets a particular word wrong, that word will appear again in the near future, and so the user will get drilled on it until the definition sticks. If a user gets a word like "placid" right but then gets "placate" wrong, a lesson card pops up comparing the two words, emphasizing that they both come from the same root, "plac." There are some more sophisticated AI elements to the algorithm too, but I won't describe them here.

The whole idea behind Flash of Genius is that the users shouldn't have to worry about what cards they study, organizing them into virtual stacks, or any of that sort of thing. They just need to trust the algorithm that governs study mode. While that may make perfect sense to a programmer, it's pretty foreign to most nontechnical people. When I was showing early prototypes to people during development, I was surprised to see how few people even knew what "algorithm" meant.

My solution to this wasn't novel or subtle, but it did get the job done. I just showed a UIAlertView every time something potentially confusing happened for the first time. For example, the first time a checkmark or "X" button is tapped in study mode, a UIAlertView pops up to let the users know that Flash of Genius is going to take care of them (see Figure 7-11).

Figure 7-11. *I found one-time-use alert views like this one to be a decent way to get the user to understand how to use Flash of Genius.*

I watched a lot of people interact with my application without knowing what it was, and I found that this message was enough to get people to understand how the application works. I think something about the repeated use of the word "genius" calls to mind the Genius feature of iTunes. It signals to people that they're using some sort of "smart" technology. (Incidentally, iTunes's Genius feature came out before usability testing for the application, but well after I had named the application and formed Flash of Genius LLC. It was just a nice bit of good luck for me.)

It's important not to overdo it with these `UIAlertViews`, of course, but using just a few is OK in my opinion. I have four total.

I think one of the most important things when developing an application is to observe other people interacting with it, learning how it works in real time. When observing people, it's important to just watch quietly and resist the temptation to help them figure things out. After all, real users won't have you next to them when they start using your application.

A lot of changes were prompted by Flash of Genius's usability testing, and many were of the same character: making the application more resistant to bizarre user behavior. For example, after realizing that they could flip a flashcard by swiping the screen, many people decided to see if they could flip them very fast repeatedly. Why? I don't know. But that got me to disable user interaction during animations in a hurry! I would never have known that so many users would act this way with my application unless I had witnessed a lot of people doing so.

In addition to watching people use the application, I also periodically tried to get into the mindset of a first-time user and do usability testing myself. This process is useful too, but there's just no replacement for seeing a large sample of your audience interact with your application.

Launching the Application

Launching the application was very exciting. I wasn't expecting to get any feedback from users, but I did get some via e-mails, blogs that have mentioned Flash of Genius, and comments left on iTunes. Happily, almost all of it has been positive. Most comments just address the content itself— people like the quirky sample sentences, for example— but some users have complimented the application on the concept too, which of course feels great. I'm glad these could shine through. It's sad when users can't appreciate the content or concept of an application because of silly and avoidable UI issues. I'm happy to say that I haven't gotten a single comment critical of the design or usability of the application, and nothing along the lines of "I don't get how this works."

The only negative feedback so far, really, has been requests for more features. Some people asked for audio pronunciations, which I've now added. Others asked for more words, which I've added as well.

Unbelievably, Flash of Genius: SAT Vocab became the top-selling iPhone application devoted to SAT preparation after just a few months on sale. I still can't believe that!

I thought that once I launched the application it would be out of my mind, but it hasn't turned out that way at all. The application is my baby now, and I want to nurture it and help it grow up to be big and strong. My mind often races with ideas for new features, and I often look forward to finishing my graduate school work and spending more time on development. I thought the process ended with the launch, but it doesn't at all. When does it end? I don't know yet.

Summary

My biggest advice to first-time developers is this:

- Take user interface design issues seriously.

- Watch lots of different people interact with your application, and go back to the drawing board until you're happy with the learning experience that you're providing first-time users.

- Don't underestimate how good professional artists and designers are at what they do. You may not be able to imagine what they can do that you can't, but that will change after you work with a good one!

Developing Flash of Genius was an adventure for me, and I relished every minute of it. I went into the process as an entrepreneur but came out an iPhone application developer. I thought more than I ever imagined I would about UI issues. The iPhone's built-in functionality is very intuitive, so the bar is set high for developers. That said, you know as a developer that you're dealing with a savvy user base that will appreciate carefully crafted UI, cute design flourishes, and helpful visual feedback. You know that the time you spend on these things won't be wasted. For iPhone application developers more than others, spending time on user interface design is important, so don't ignore the details. Your users will thank you!

Chris Parrish and Brad Ellis

Company: *RogueSheep Incorporated*

Location: *Seattle, WA USA*

Former Life As a Developer:

Chris :

Formerly I was a developer at Adobe Systems working on print publishing applications such as PageMaker, InDesign and InCopy. I've been a long-time Macintosh programmer, reaching back to the early days when programming a Mac included pressing the magic programmer's switch on the side.

Over my career I've worked at the low-level coding with a variety of processor specific assembly language variants as well as the standard tour of the popular high-level languages such as Pascal, C, C++, Java and Action Script. I've toiled away in a variety of programming environments and IDEs including Think C, MPW, CodeWarrior, Visual Studio, Eclipse, Flex Builder and Xcode. I have been working with Cocoa and Objective-C since the introduction of Mac OS X and it is my platform and tool chain of choice.

I have a deep interest in graphics, imaging and audio and find the Mac and iPhone the premiere platforms to explore these technologies. I also have an academic background in signal processing and data compression where I spent some time doing research on audio waveform and satellite image coding techniques.

These days almost all of my programming is done using Xcode on a Mac. I also regularly rely on other Apple tools such as Interface Builder, Pixie, Shark and Instruments. I supplement Apple's tool chain with some great third party applications as well. TextMate and TextWrangler are frequently running in my dock as alternate text editors. We use Perforce almost exclusively for version control and I rely on simple GUI front-end RogueSheep created for it many years ago called P4Cocoa. I keep all my important notes and design work in Flying Meat's VoodooPad. I love prototyping and experimenting with graphics techniques in Quartz Composer and Core Image.

Brad :

Somehow I've crammed in over ten years of Adobe Photoshop and Illustrator experience into my short time on this earth. I was "that guy who knows Photoshop" most of the time, before I discovered interface design. My time spent in the Art department during college assisted me with learning how to manage time effectively while being simultaneously engaged in different projects.

I spend most of my time in Photoshop and have amassed a vast array of actions and shortcuts to enhance my productivity and final products. Occasionally I switch over to Adobe Illustrator for its vector tools. I also use Apple Motion explore movement and bring life to mockups.

When walking by my carefully-lit workstation you'll often find me using the Mac OSX zoom shortcut to analyze pixels, casually sipping a grande soy mocha, or tidying my pen cup.

Life as an iPhone Developer: Chris is the President, co-founder and one of several developers at RogueSheep. Brad works as RogueSheep's artist, designer and user interface expert. We regularly design and implement a variety of iPhone applications for clients as well craft our own creations for the iPhone and iPod touch.

Our most well-known application on the App Store is Postage, a digital postcard application in the Photography section. Postage won and Apple Design Award in the iPhone Showcase at the 2009 World Wide Developer's Conference.

In addition to a suite of postcard applications based on Postage we also have published a novel word game based on an award-winning toy called Word Spin. We also have a variety of applications developed on contract for our clients in the store or in progress.

What's in This Chapter: This chapter will guide you through what we think are the most important topics relevant to designing intuitive, natural and elegant iPhone applications. Along the way we'll tell you about the techniques we used to design Postage and give you examples of how we applied the theory presented to our application.

Topics include:

- Focus
- Flow
- Context
- Technique

Tools Discussed :

- Photoshop
- Motion
- Core Animation

Key Technologies:

- Tuning responsiveness and feedback
- Specifications and Mock-ups
- Preferences and configuration
- UIScrollView

Chapter 7

Postage

The idea for our application Postage was born at Apple's Worldwide Developer Conference in the early summer of 2008. The iPhone SDK had just become available, and our small crew of four longtime Mac developers was anxious to find an application with which to begin exploring this exciting new mobile platform. One colleague, Jeff, was using his iPhone to take pictures of San Francisco, where we had traveled for the conference, when he hit on the idea for a virtual postcard application. Jeff wanted to be able use the images he was capturing while on the road in a custom postcard that he could send digitally to his family back home. Ten months later, Postage for the iPhone (see Figure 7-1) finally saw its introduction on the App Store.

When we started to work on the design and features of Postage, we knew from the beginning that we would need to focus on several key areas. Being experienced Mac developers as well as users, we wanted to bring our expertise and knowledge from desktop development to create something for the phone that would rival what Apple itself would produce. First, we knew that the output would have to be top-notch and suitably high resolution. We had to wow our users and the recipients of their postcards with the capabilities of the iPhone. We also knew that we wanted our user interface to be ultra-intuitive and simple to use. Finally, we realized it was paramount to ensure that our application was focused and streamlined.

This last point, the focused nature of the application, became the central piece around which the rest of the design was anchored. Early on, we set a goal that a user would be able to launch the application and send a complete postcard as quickly as possible. If someone could spend one minute or less in our application and end up creating a beautiful and personal postcard, we would have succeeded.

To achieve that focus required designing a user interface that was not only intuitive and engaging, but one that also did not overwhelm the user. Following the lead that Apple has established for years with their own applications, we worked hard to make sure to present the user with just enough choices, at just the right times. We also found it important to conceive of a flow through the application that was natural for the task at hand. We did not want the user guessing at what to do next or how to achieve the desired result.

A critical component in our desire to create an intuitive user interface was to ensure that we chose and maintained a familiar mental context for the user. Our design for Postage demanded that the users feel as if they were working on a real postcard throughout. We made sure that the card was the focus from step to step and used animations and scripted motions to maintain that mental framework or context. In Postage, the interface animates around the card, which is always the central focus. To enhance the feeling of the context, we also made sure to provide user interface elements that supported the theme.

Finally, to turn our design into an experience that was visually engaging and seamless with the user's expectations for an iPhone application, we had to employ a variety of art, design, interface and programming techniques. Consistency in art design and lighting, reuse of familiar user interface elements in the proper locations, and leveraging the powerful frameworks provided by the iPhone OS were all instrumental in realizing the potential of the application we all had envisioned.

Figure 7-1. *Our application, Postage*

Keeping the Application Focused

Well-known blogger and Apple follower John Gruber said, on designing iPhone applications, "Figure out the absolute least you need to do to implement the idea, do just that, and then polish the hell out of the experience" (http://daringfireball.net/2008/11/iphone_likeness).

Designing for a mobile application is really quite a bit different than for desktop software. Limitations of the device itself, including screen real estate and user input methods, force us to make different choices. But beyond the specifics of the device interactions, it's important to consider when and how a mobile application is used.

A typical nongame iPhone application is going to be activated when the user is on the go and usually for only a few moments at a time. Because of this, it is critical to make sure that your application is responsive and allows the users to accomplish their goals with a minimum amount of fuss and time invested. The best way to achieve this is to make sure your application is well focused.

On the desktop, we are accustomed to applications that create new content being based around the idea of a document. Word processors, spreadsheets, image editors, and the like all typically operate with a motif of the user opening one or more documents and providing a variety of tools and menu commands with which to create and manipulate the content in those documents. Users can switch modes rapidly and jump between tasks easily. Often, interfaces on the desktop strive to present the user with many, many options for any choice to be made.

The open-ended nature of desktop applications does not translate well to the iPhone. In fact, it often opposes our goal to focus the application. One of the best ways to focus our application is to be thoughtful in the amount of choices offered to your user and how you present them.

Anyone who has spent much time building software applications knows that users frequently request to be presented with more choices and more features. It seems to be human nature to always conclude that more choice is always better. Although we all will say more choice is better when asked directly, the truth is that, for some tasks, more choice is really just a barrier to accomplishing the final goal. An application that overloads the interface with choices can easily overwhelm users and can even tempt them to give up before actually completing their tasks. Just remember this when designing an iPhone application: more is not always better.

> For some great thoughts on how too much choice leads to paralysis and unhappiness see the works of Swarthmore College professor, Barry Schwartz. His book, *The Paradox of Choice* (Ecco, ISBN-10: 0060005688) has some thought-provoking insights into the problems of overwhelming choices.

In many ways, our application is just like a content creation application where the user is working on a document; in our case, that document is a postcard. On the desktop, we might have chosen to allow the user freedom to work on any task in the steps required to create a postcard at any time. Following the typical desktop metaphor, we would likely offer the user a variety of tools with which to work on the different parts of the postcard in any random order. Photos would be added and edited with a photo tool anytime the user selected that tool. Text would follow in a similar fashion, with the user adding and editing text by selecting the text tool and applying it to the postcard. We would also likely have allowed the user to choose from a variety of fonts, colors, and positions for text and images, as well as effects and other design choices. Doing all of this on the phone would have lead to an application that was overwhelming with choice and difficult to approach. Most users would be stuck wondering how to even get started with such a variety of choices presented within the confines of an iPhone-sized screen and a touch-based interface.

Selecting Font Styles

When designing Postage, we instead decided to be very frugal in the choices and customizations offered to the user in many places. For instance, consider selecting the font for the message; we could have presented an interface that listed every combination of font and style available on the device. Instead, we carefully preselected a list of fonts that gave the user a variety of type styles that also matched our postcard designs well. Figure 7-2 shows how this careful preselection of fonts allowed us to present a variety of choices in a pleasant and compact interface in the application. We did the same for font color and image effects as well, which are covered in the next couple of sections.

Figure 7-2. *Frugal font controls in Postage*

Despite all this apparent limitation of functionality by limiting the choices available to the user, we have never had complaints about the lack customization in our application. In return, we have a streamlined and approachable interface that doesn't overwhelm the user yet still allows plenty of creative expression.

Selecting Font Colors

Selection of font color in Postage works in a similar manner to font selection. We could have crafted an intricate new color-picker control to allow the selection from the millions of possible colors the device is capable of displaying. Instead, we chose to present the user with a choice of around ten hand-selected colors. This design decision also had another beneficial consequence: by limiting the colors that can be used, we could now carefully select colors that we knew would look good for the particular postcard design the user was working with. Each postcard template in Postage comes with a specific list of colors matched to that design, and these are the only choices presented to the user. We made it intentionally difficult for the user to make a choice that resulted in a postcard that would look bad. By limiting the choices, we helped to ensure that the users' content looked great and therefore increased their satisfaction with the end result.

Using Image Effects

Image effects in Postage also work in a similar manner. Users can select from a variety of common image effects to enhance the photo placed on each of their postcards. Photos can be made grayscale or sepia, enhanced for contrast, or stylized with a glow or softening. In each of these cases, the underlying code has a variety of parameters that control the application of the effect to the users photo. It would have been possible to expose each of these parameters in the interface and allow the user complete creative control over the result. Image processing, though, was not the central activity of our application and therefore this level of exposure to controls was not within our stated mission to focus the application. Instead, for each effect, we carefully selected values that made a pleasing result on a variety of images. The user was presented with one choice for each effect. As Figure 7-3 shows, all a user has to do to apply a photo effect is to tap a single button. As before, this allowed the task to be efficient and approachable while still offering a variety of creative options.

Figure 7-3. *A single button press applies image effects and fonts.*

Setting Preferences and Configuring the Application

Preferences and configuration represent another important opportunity to focus your application. If you study Apple's applications on both the desktop and the iPhone, you will often find a relatively sparse selection of preferences exposed to the user. Conversely, on other mobile or desktop platforms that are not known for their ease of use and approachability, you will find applications full of preferences and configuration choices.

Presenting the user with many preferences and options for configuration makes your application seem unnecessarily complicated to the typical user. When presented with an interface that forces them to make many choices, most users will feel confused and decide that the application is too difficult to use. Often, poorly designed applications present an abundance of user interface elements for preferences and configuration or create flows through an application that force users to make frequent but relatively unimportant decisions.

Often, the problem is that many of these forced decisions are not what the user really cares about when using the application. These unnecessary decisions just get in the way of what the user really wants to accomplish with the software. While many hobbyists and computer professionals crave complete control over their software, most consumers would rather have an application that just works how they expect without the need to make changes to the application behavior. The iPhone OS even obfuscates preference setting by stashing user preferences for an application in a location that few people even realize exists (see Figure 7-4).

Figure 7-4. *The somewhat hidden application-level preferences on the iPhone OS*

The best application interfaces are those that keep preferences to a minimum and make sure that the choices exposed to the user are really those that matter to them. It was once said that every application preference represents a point where the development team could not make a tough choice. It's up to you to make those tough choices on behalf of your users. It's true that sometimes the choices you make will not please everyone. You will, however, make your users (outside that small minority) big fans of your application without them ever realizing why. When you design your application, make an effort to envision the average user in your market, and anytime you come across a fork in the flow of your application that might be solved by a preference, instead make the choice to have it work in the manner that will satisfy the majority of your users.

Sometimes, despite your best efforts, allowing users to set a preference is unavoidable. Originally, we shipped Postage with no application-level preferences at all, which was just what we had desired. Over time, though, Apple updated the iPhone OS and added a feature that many users wanted but fundamentally changed the output of our application. With the new iPhone OS, it is now possible to send an e-mail with an attachment using the owner's e-mail configured in the standard Mail application. Previous to this change, if a developer wanted to send an e-mail with an image attachment, it was necessary to use your own server or have the user reenter e-mail account information. We knew that entering all the details of an e-mail account would be a barrier for our users, so we choose to send our e-mails directly from Postage to our own servers. This allowed us to create and send a beautiful HTML e-mail with embedded image attachments.

With the new OS, it was now possible to send an e-mail with an attachment via the user's existing e-mail configuration. In addition, these e-mails could be sent as a background task, rather than forcing the user to wait for the e-mail to finish sending, as required when sending an e-mail with our own methods. Finally, this change meant that the users were sending the postcards directly from their own accounts rather than through our special account. A handful of vocal customers had been upset about privacy concerns and spam filtering caused by using a RogueSheep e-mail account rather than their own. Clearly, using this new operating system feature seemed like the perfect choice to satisfy our users and to enhance the experience of our application. Unfortunately, we soon discovered a consequence of this change; it was no longer possible compose an e-mail using HTML with an embedded image attachment if we used the iPhone SDK interfaces to send the e-mail. Suddenly, our beautiful postcard output that thousands of users had come to expect from our application was a little bit less cool than before. Making this change in functionality with its many benefits would be taking away a feature in the output that some unknown number of our customers may have come to expect. We were left pondering which path to take.

We eventually caved and enabled the choice of e-mail sending methods as an application preference. If that new functionality had existed before we shipped our application, we would have just used it and never created a situation that required a preference to satisfy new and existing users at the same time. Over time, we will slowly phase out the old way of sending the e-mail through our servers, starting with changing the default to new method. By giving our users a gradual change, we will bring them all over to the new method without any disappointment or shock.

Configuration can be thought of in a similar manner as preferences. Do everything you can to reduce or eliminate the configuration required by a user to start enjoying your application. The last thing you want is for someone to launch your application and give up before really experiencing the joy of it because of a barrier presented by configuration UI. This is especially true on the iPhone, where so many applications need to connect to some network-based service. Do everything you can to delay or prevent having the user enter account or similar credentials when using your application for the first time. We can't even count the number of times each of us has quit an application, never to return, when the first thing we are asked for on launch is to create or enter an account.

In our application, the primary form of sharing a postcard is by sending it as an attachment in an e-mail. As mentioned before, we built the application before Apple exposed the ability to send an e-mail with an attachment directly from your own application using the owner's already configured e-mail account. We knew that requiring the users to enter an e-mail account, one that they probably have already set up on the iPhone once before, would be seen as at best an inconvenience and at worst a reason to trash the application with a one-star review. Average users have no idea what information on the iPhone that developers are and are not allowed access to; they only know that they already send e-mail from the iPhone and can't understand why they would need to configure it again for your use.

For Postage, we chose to send the postcard through our own servers to eliminate the need for any configuration or account credentials. This created a slight burden for us in managing that service. It also costs us a few users who are concerned about an intermediate service involved in their communications. These concerns, though, are far outweighed by the benefit. Users are able to install our application, create a postcard, and send it just a few steps—with no configuration required.

Separating Tasks

Finally, focus can play an important role in the design of the individual screens of your application. All but the most simple of iPhone applications require several separate screens with distinct controls and data presented to the user. With the iPhone OS, Apple has provided us with a few standard controls to help us conceptually break up these separate screens (see Figure 7-5). The navigation bar provides a way for a user to step through a hierarchy of tasks or choices and is often coupled with one or more list views. A tab bar sits at the bottom of a screen and is appropriate for presenting separate subtasks or views on the data of an application. Finally, an application can present a modal view or alert that takes over interaction and demands immediate attention.

Figure 7-5. *Standard iPhone SDK controls for separating tasks or views of data*

You should use these standard controls to separate the presentation of your interface as appropriate for your application. When considering how to create these dividing lines among all the tasks that your application is capable of and what should be visible at any one time, you must be mindful of focus once again. Only display what is necessary for the task at hand on each screen associated with a navigation step or tab. Strive to have only a single item as the focus of the screen, and reduce the number of UI elements present to the minimum needed to manipulate that item. First, this strategy will help to ensure that the controls you present to the user are large enough to easily be targeted on the somewhat constrained real estate of the device. More importantly, it will help to keep your interface simple and welcoming. Consider that none of Apple's stock iPhone applications ship with anything resembling a menu bar or a menu full of actions that can be taken at a single time (pickers are always reserved for selecting from data to use, not actions to take).

Figure 7-6 shows two possible designs for a postcard application like Postage. On the left, the different aspects of the postcard are captured as items in a table view. The user could potentially work any the feature of the postcard by selecting that item from the table view and then drilling down to further details. While using a table view is a very familiar concept for anyone that has experience with the iPhone, there is one glaring problem with this design. There is no way for the user to see how all the different choices for the style and customization of the postcard are affecting the final product. There is no preview of the fruits of the user's labor. In addition, there is no suggestion of what to do next to complete the task.

On the right is another approach where the user can do a whole slew of tasks from this one screen. Using the tools from the toolbar, new photos and text can be added at any time. The user can tap an item on the postcard to select it as the item that has focus and is manipulated by changing any of the style controls. Other controls are available to send the postcard by e-mail and to a social networking site. Finally, a menu gives the user access to a variety of additional tasks.

Figure 7-6. *The wrong way to present a variety tasks in an iPhone application*

So what's wrong with Figure 7-6? To begin with, there are simply too many controls on each of these screens. How does the user even know where to start? The always-present *Share* button is just begging the user to accidentally send off an incomplete postcard. The idea of the selection itself is potentially poor as well. While common on the desktop, the iPhone OS rarely introduces the notion of a selected item outside of a picker. Finally, all these controls are scrunched on one 320 × 480 screen, making each control hard to see and almost impossible to target with a fingertip. While this application design might imply a lot power, it likely to scare off most casual users before they get too far.

While both of these examples are somewhat contrived, its not too uncommon to see applications in the App Store that make many of these same sort of mistakes. These examples work to demonstrate the sort of thinking you must apply to create a streamlined user experience on the iPhone.

In the final design for our application, we decided to divide the subtasks of creating a postcard into separate steps and to use a navigation bar as the method for moving between these steps, as shown in Figure 7-7. Using the navigation bar allowed us to focus the controls present on each screen to just those relevant for the current task: pick a postcard, pick the photo, enter the message, style the message, and share the card.

Figure 7-7. *Navigation of postcard creation steps in Postage*

When necessary, we further segregated the visible controls using a control that toggles the choices present in custom horizontal button bar. For example, when on the *Pick Photo* task, we divided the controls present between choosing a photo and applying effects to the photo, as shown in Figure 7-8. When the user is choosing a photo, the horizontal button bar displays buttons for sources that the photo can come from. When the user applies effects to a photo, the horizontal button bar changes to display buttons that apply effects to the current photo.

Figure 7-8. *Dividing the photo picking task into subscreens with a custom tab bar*

In the Postage design that we shipped, each navigation step in the creation of a postcard is somewhat modal, allowing only the manipulation of one aspect of the postcard at a time. Each of these steps is scripted in a specific sequence as well. For instance, choosing a postcard design is the first step, followed by placing a photo, and finally, choosing and styling the message. At each step, the user is focused on that single task—whether that is picking a photo, styling the message, or sharing the postcard—and is not permitted to jump to any arbitrary step in the process, though movement between the previous and next step is allowed at will.

In our some of our early mock-ups, like the one show in Figure 7-9, we had attempted more of a modeless approach with each subtask as a tab in a tab bar. We soon felt that this approach would work against our goal of a user creating a postcard in just a few minutes. It created too many choices and too many opportunities to generate an incomplete postcard. For instance, what would happen if the user tapped the *Mail* button before any of the others? Should that be an error or warning, or should the application send a blank postcard?

With Figure 7-9's design, we also felt like we were forcing the user into a more complicated discovery process in learning the application. By instead choosing to step the user intentionally through each task, we could ensure they didn't miss a step and only had to focus on a small amount of user interface detail at a single time.

Figure 7-9. *Rejected navigation and flow for postcard creation in Postage*

MODAL VS. MODELESS

User interface experts long ago identified two different styles of interaction with a user. In a `modal` interaction, the user is not permitted to do any other action or task until the current interaction has been completed. In a `modeless` interaction, the user is permitted to continue other tasks or interactions and to deal with the modeless interaction at their leisure.

The classic example of this distinction is dialogs. A modal dialog will stop the user from any further interactions until the dialog is dismissed. This is typically reserved for an alert or similar dialog that is an indication that the user must make a choice before continuing because of current conditions. A modeless dialog, however, will float around without demanding that it be handled. Floating tool palettes and many spell-checking dialogs are common examples of modeless windows that do not demand the focus of the user's interactions while present.

When we had finished our preliminary specification, we felt that our design for Postage did well in focusing the interface for a killer mobile application experience. We acknowledged that the central task for this application was creating a digital postcard and thoughtfully separated those tasks into discrete steps that allowed that allowed us to create carefully crafted interface elements for each specific task.

Because each task was so focused, we had room in the visual design of those separate views to make sure the interface was uncluttered and easy to understand. We had space to create clear interface elements, while still showing off much of the users content and the postcard that was being created.

We still had an important element left to address before our design work was done. We had not yet completed the flow and description of interface behaviors between each task. Where should the user start in the process of creating a postcard? How would we transition between each step in the process? The answers to these questions about sequence and flow came from measured analysis of the mental map, or context, we wanted to create for the user in our application.

Analyzing the Context

Context is extremely important when designing any application interface. So what is context? When we talk about **context**, we mean the setting or mental model of the application or portions of the application. Context has been used throughout the modern exploration of graphical user interfaces to help guide users into the use of software applications.

The classic example of an application context is the desktop metaphor ubiquitous on personal computing platforms. Most operating systems provide the user with a desktop that serves as a mental model for the content of their computer. The desktop contains folders and files that represent the data and the hierarchal organization of that data. Often, the desktop contains a trash can, or similar object, used to dispose of files. Hard disks, CDs, or DVDs also appear on the desktop to allow the user access to these storage media. Frequently, the context is enhanced by representing physical objects the user may be familiar with separate from their computer. Files look like paper documents, and folders look like common filing folders.

Context has been used to great effect on the desktop for many years. iTunes, DVD Player, and other media-playing applications style their interfaces to similar to real-world music and video players. The Mac desktop application Delicious Library allows users to catalog all of their physical media such as books, CDs, DVDs, and games. Delicious

Library uses the metaphor of a bookshelf as the interface motif, which is immediately recognizable.

This same notion of context is applied in a variety of applications on the iPhone as well. Consider the Messages application that presents text messages as word bubbles or the Maps application that uses pushpins to represent points of interest on the current map view. Eucalyptus is an excellent iPhone OS book-reading application that uses a bookshelf metaphor for browsing books and a graphically rich representation of turning a real page when flipping between pages of a digital book. All of these uses of context help a user quickly understand how to interact with your application and aid in setting the proper expectations for how your interface behaves.

All developers should consider the mental model their users will develop when using their application. It's important to maintain this context with consistency throughout your application. This mental model that you build for your users will allow them to quickly become comfortable and fluent in your application. When you meet the users' expectations for that mental model, they will perceive your application as natural, intuitive, and a pleasure to use.

When possible, presenting and maintaining this context visually within your application can be of great benefit. Several of Apple's applications have an immediately visible presentation of the context. The Camera, Compass, and Voice Memos applications that ship with the iPhone all provide elements of real and familiar physical objects to set the stage in the user's mind. The Notes application looks like a familiar pad of legal paper. When you launch Notes, your mental model of the application begins to instantly develop around your notions of a pad of paper. Many times, the small visual details make a big difference in maintaining your context. In Delicious Library, deleting a book results in an animation that burns the book up into smoke, but deleting a DVD shatters it into pieces. These little details help reinforce the model of books and DVDs in the application.

Be careful not to break the context you have developed for your user. Few things are more jarring when using an application than sudden, unexpected behavior. If you set up a mental model of a real-world object in your application, you must strive to maintain the behaviors of that object, or you risk disappointing your user.

Considering Context in Postage

Early on in the design of Postage, we knew that we wanted to present a mental model of a physical card. Throughout the application, we designed the user interface so that the postcard was always the central focus, and the interface animated in, out, and around it. From the moment after you pick up the postcard design until you send the card to its recipient, each intermediate step always has the postcard you are creating as the thing focused in the view. The key to maintaining this context through each step is animating the view of the postcard to zoom in and out of the area that is the focus. Picking the photo zooms in on the area of the postcard where the photo is placed. Styling the message zooms the view of the card to the text area. Preparing to send the card zooms to a full preview. In each individual step, the interface elements animate away and build up around the card by sliding up and down (see Figure 7-10). In this way, the interface feels secondary to or separate from the postcard. The card becomes the permanent context, and the controls present at any point are just the tools used to manipulate the card for the current task.

Figure 7-10. *The user interface animating around the postcard*

The context of working on a postcard that feels separate from the user interface is one of most unique aspects of our user experience and, we think, one of the most critical components to its success. Apple provides us, as developers, with an incredibly powerful tool in Core Animation. While it may be easy to dismiss Core Animation as a means to provide eye candy, we feel that Postage demonstrates an example of how an animating user interface actually enhances the usability and pleasure of using an application.

We also employed the use of themed elements in the design of our application to continue to support the context. When sharing a postcard, we present an animated envelope that the card slides into. The card sliding into the envelope helps to maintain the illusion of the card as a separate physical object while also supporting the motif of postal mail associated with postcards. Sending success and failure messages are presented as stamps on the envelope mimicking postal practices in the physical world. All of these simple embellishments add to the context and delight the users.

Facing Potential Problems with Context

Not all applications lend themselves to an emulated physical model to build a mental image around. Sometimes even when they do, the models are contrived or overused, or perhaps the disparity between the physical and virtual objects is too great to be effective in placing the user in a familiar context. These limitations don't mean, though, that your application doesn't have context and would not benefit from consistency. Sometimes, the context simply is the consistency you develop in the way you present your data, controls, and application behaviors.

Make sure to use familiar controls and gestures for user interaction in your application. iPhone users are already trained in many interactions and user models by the consistency deployed in the built-in and most third-party applications. Most importantly, do not change the behavior of a familiar button, control, or gesture. For instance, you may be tempted to use the default search button icon (a magnifying glass, tilted to the left) to change the zoom or magnification of the current view. The problem is that even though the magnifying glass maps well to the action of changing the scale of what is viewed, it has already been established in many places on the iPhone to mean "search." You risk confusing the user when you reuse this standard button for a different, even if logical, action in your application. If you develop your own controls be sure to apply them with consistency throughout your interface as well.

Don't suddenly change the meaning of a button without changing its visual appearance significantly to match. Similarly, be careful not to overload the meaning of a button that users already have expectations for. A button with a triangle pointing to the right might be a tempting proposition to use for advancing through a list of items. However, a triangle pointing to the right inside a round button is universally accepted to be a control that starts media playing. If you use this button in an application to step through a list of songs (see Figure 7-11), you run a high risk of confusing your users, who might mistakenly assume the button means that the current song should start playing.

Figure 7-11. *Trying to assign a new meaning to a familiar button causes confusion.*

Broken metaphors can be worse than using no metaphor at all. For instance, imagine an audio application that had a vertical slider and a small knob that turns left to right. Both of these controls are metaphors for physical input devices found on many audio devices. Because of previous experience with these sorts of real world controls, most users are going to expect that turning the knob in your interface to the right will increase the value associated with the control. Similarly, they will assume that raising the slider to a higher position will increase its value. If your application reversed either of these expectations, users will consistently find themselves manipulating the control to get an unexpected result.

These same concepts apply to gestures on touch devices like the iPhone. The touch interface of the iPhone OS lends itself to manipulation of photos by grabbing, pinching, sliding, and rotating. In Postage, we wanted to allow the users to rotate their photos to fit perfectly on their postcards. Apple doesn't provide a standard way to rotate with a gesture, so this is a behavior we needed to implement ourselves. When you create your own behavior, you potentially have a lot of freedom in how you map the user's finger movements to the rotation of the photo. The natural gesture for most users is to place two fingers on the photo and twist them to rotate. We found it was very important to make sure that points where the user touched the photo originally remained exactly under the fingertips as the user moved around. If you think about it, this is exactly how rotating a real photo on your desktop by twisting your fingers would behave. This attempt to emulate the laws of physics makes the mental model of how your interface works immediately meet your users expectations. Every attempt we made in Postage to map the finger-twisting to rotation in a manner inconsistent with the metaphor of spinning a real photo with your fingers always felt wrong.

Using Familiar Controls in Postage

In Postage, we employed many standard Apple controls and gestures:

- Selecting a postcard design operates with a standard scroll view that pages with the familiar swiping gesture.

- A standard page control conveys how many postcard templates are in a category just like Safari or the Stocks application.

- We used a standard navigation bar to implement the means to step through each task in creating a postcard.

Our navigation was somewhat unique in that we allowed movement forward through the steps in the navigation bar. Most applications use the navigation bar item on the left to step back to the previous navigation step but drill down further into the hierarchy using a list of table in the main view. We wanted to advance forward using the navigation bar, so we developed the custom button shown in Figure 7-12 that carries the user forward in the same style as the right side navigation buttons (this same technique is used by the iPod application for navigation back to the *Now Playing* track). We made sure to maintain this navigation bar behavior throughout the application. Once you discover that you tap the right navigation button to move forward in the application, the behavior is consistent throughout.

Figure 7-12. *The Postage navigation bar with forward and backward navigation steps*

The sending screen of Postage also employs familiar controls for sharing a postcard with e-mail, as shown in Figure 7-13. Our e-mail–sending screen uses a layout of fields very similar to the standard Apple Mail application. We also developed custom controls to tokenize the recipients in the *To* field and to add contacts from the address book just like the standard Mail application. It took a lot of work to add all these behaviors to our e-mail–sending screen, but the result is that users are instantly familiar with how to use this part of our application if they have used e-mail on the iPhone already. Fortunately with iPhone OS 3.0 and later, you can now do almost all e-mail–sending tasks, including attaching files to an e-mail using Apple's standard controls, without having to leave your application. The sort of custom controls we had to employ in Postage are likely no longer necessary for e-mail, but the lesson still applies if you find yourself needing to emulate an existing action common to other applications on the iPhone within you own code.

Figure 7-13. *Recreating a familiar set of controls to send email*

As noted before, we designed and developed a custom tab bar and horizontal button bar controls for many of the task-specific screens in Postage. We took great care to make sure to reuse this paradigm throughout the application. The horizontal button bar may be an unfamiliar control when you first encounter it. Once you learn what to expect from it and how it interacts with the main view and the tab bar controls though, it is consistent throughout the entire application. This reduces the learning curve of our application greatly.

After you arrive at the mental model you want your users to have when using your application, you will be able to choose your user interface controls and their visual styles to help support that context. In Postage, we used animation, familiar controls, and a consistency from screen to screen to develop and maintain the postcard as the focused element of each screen. Our animations helped to establish which visual elements are user interface controls and which elements are the content the user is working on. By animating the interface control elements around the postcard, we established its permanency and gave the postcard some substance in the Postage application model. We now had a great postcard model visually represented in the interface, but we still needed to consider how we would place controls on the screen and in which order and what physical locality. These decisions would create the flow of our application as the user moved from starting a postcard to completing it.

Creating the Application Flow

Every application has a natural flow of the user interface. Often, the flow is concerned with locality of controls and groups of controls and the order of operations or tasks. On the desktop, many applications are designed so that controls that are less specific in their effect are grouped together and placed in an area that is the first place a user will naturally look. Controls with effects that are more detailed or reduced in scope are then also grouped together and placed at a natural spot for the user to move to after using the first group. Popular Mac OS X programs, such as iTunes and iPhoto, employ a source list on the left that lets the user select from groups of music or photos. After selecting from this source list, the controls to the right reflect the selection on the left and allow more detailed manipulation, viewing, or listening. On the iPhone, we often see a similar flow with table views and navigation bars. Selecting from a table view often narrows the data the user is working on from a large choice in a list. Each selection burrows further into more specific selections of the data, moving from left to right in the interface. All well-designed applications are careful to make this flow as natural and consistent as possible.

One of the most natural flows (at least for Western societies!) is a left-to-right flow that follows the reading order. In Postage, we used a left-to-right flow to naturally progress from one step to the next. We also employed a control hierarchy that flows from top to bottom. Controls at the top of the screen in the navigation bar make big changes and switch tasks: moving between steps, sending a finished postcard, and starting a new postcard. Controls at the bottom have effects local to the current screen or task: changing the font, applying a color, or choosing an effect to apply to a photo.

Sometimes, you may find you need to guide the user in the flow of your application. You may want to employ some form of hint to give your user an idea of what they can do next. This is a special concern on the iPhone where the number of pixels available on the screen, while fantastic for a mobile device, is far less than what we have grown accustomed to on the desktop. We just don't always have room for labels, titles, and other descriptive instructions.

Giving Hints About Flow

While testing Postage, we found that new users sometimes double-tapped a postcard design on our first screen to select it. Our design actually called for using the navigation bar to move to the next step. We contemplated having both a double-tap of the postcard as well as tapping the right navigation button carry the user on to the next step. In the end, we decided against dual controls for two reasons:

- First, we would have a hard time supporting the same double-tap in later stages of the interface. We felt this would have broken our context or expectations of our users when the same behavior would vary in result from screen to screen.

- Second, we knew that most all steps after the first one would require tapping the right navigation button to move to the next step. We felt that, at some point, the user would have to learn that the right navigation button is how to move on.

In the end, we decided to have double-tapping that first screen present a small pop-up hint that momentarily indicated that the right navigation button would advance to the next step. At that point, we felt we had trained the users who did not naturally see the right navigation button to begin to look there to advance through the application.

Figure 7-14. *Giving the users a hint*

We also deployed similar hints in other locations in the interface. The photo-picking screen allows the user to scale, position, and rotate the image. While the scale and position actions might be familiar to the user from the built-in Photos application, rotation was potentially a new concept. We also felt it was possible that the user might not think to touch the photo to manipulate it. To resolve this problem without permanently sacrificing valuable pixels, we choose to once again momentary display a textual hint when a photo has been picked.

Postage also uses another important form of hinting. Our horizontal button bar was a fairly novel control that many users might not be familiar with. We needed to give the users some indication that the control would scroll with more choices if swiped left or right. To solve this dilemma, we borrowed a technique that is employed throughout the iPhone user interface whenever a vertical list or table is displayed. All of Apple's applications, and most third-party ones, are careful to make sure that at least one partially obscured cell or item is visible in any list or table view. In other words, the height of the entire table is never a whole multiple of the height of the table cells. When users see this partially hidden item, they are naturally compelled to swipe to make the cell visible.

We used the same technique for our horizontal button bars. We took great care to size our buttons so that half of a button is always shown when the bar is scrolled completely left or right. This gives the user an immediate hint that more exciting buttons are just waiting to be scrolled into view! We also added a small technique to further guide the user into exploring the choices available by scrolling the button bars. When an obscured button is tapped, the whole button bar automatically is scrolled so that more of the hidden controls are made visible. This quickly shows the user that more awaits them with a simple swipe.

Unfortunately, even Apple doesn't always follow it's own lead in UI design. The Stocks application that comes with the iPhone is a perfect example of how *not* to implement a scrolling list (see Figure 7-15). The table view that lists each security you are tracking is sized so that it is exactly an even multiple of the height of the cells in the table. When there are more rows in the table than can be shown at once, there is no indication that any content is being clipped by the view. On the desktop, this design would not be a problem, because a scroll bar would be used to indicate the content was bigger than the view. On the phone, scroll bars are only visible when scrolling, so there is no indication that anything is missing. How will you know it's time to cash in on that APPL you bought four years ago for a vacation home in Hawaii if the tricky Stocks application hides that data from you?

Figure 7-15. *Which one is a scrollable list?*

Showing Instead of Telling

You can improve the flow of your application by helping your user more quickly ascertain the meaning of your controls. An effective technique in for this is the "show; don't tell" principle. The old cliché that a picture can tell a thousand words may be overused, but it still holds true. We are all used to the fact that a well-conceived and familiar icon can more succinctly convey the meaning of a button than a simple label.

Sometimes, you can carry the notion of showing instead of telling one step further than a good icon and graphically depict a sample of a button or control's action directly on the control. Our design for Postage used this technique repeatedly when presenting the user with a stylistic or creative choice. Figure 7-16 shows the buttons that apply image effects to a postcard's photo. Each button uses the same icon image on the button to give a sample of the exact effect that the button will apply. Even though each button is labeled with text, we could not really rely on that description to convey the nature of each expressive effect. By showing a sample of the effect on each button it was possible for us to convey much more meaning in the same amount of screen real estate as an effective finger-sized target.

It's important to note that the effectiveness was increased by using the same source image (in this case, a beachside palm tree) for each button. In this way, the user can quickly see the original image on the *Normal* effect button while each successive effect button such as *Sepia* or *Contrast* is applied to the same reference image for comparison. A further refinement of this idea would have been to use the user's actual photo as the image on each button. In this case, the users would be seeing an even clearer representation of the effect on their own photos. While this choice might have been even better, we decided not to do so because of the performance implications. A few of the image effects in Postage require a decent amount of pixel processing. On first-generation iPhone and iPod Touch hardware, the creation of the button images could have delayed the responsiveness of the interface, so we choose to work with a static prerendered image instead.

Figure 7-16. *Buttons that show their actions*

We repeated this same technique for the font and color buttons that apply text styling in our application. We crafted our font buttons such that each shows a sample of the letter "A" with the font and style associated with the button applied. This is similar to the technique of showing a font's name in the same font in a menu item but more compressed for the constrained space available on the mobile device screen. Our color buttons follow the same pattern by simply showing the exact color each button will apply. In both of these cases, we were able to forgo placing a label on the buttons and thus reclaim valuable screen space.

Avoiding Icon Overload

Having made the case for more pictures and fewer words, let's take just a moment to swing the other direction and caution you from going icon crazy. Designing an effective icon, especially for a small control, can be a real challenge. When we have a chance to use a preestablished icon, we do. For instance, the play button represented by a triangle pointing right is nearly universal and a great choice when you have a button that starts something playing. Many of the icons Apple provides in the iPhone SDK are also very familiar to your users.

When you find you need a custom icon, consider if you might be better served with a text label on your button instead. In Postage, we used button with no icon and just text labels in several places. In many of the screens, there were two or three sets of horizontal button bars we wanted to have available to the user on a single screen. We added label-only buttons next to the button bar to switch the content of the bar (see Figure 7-8). Effective icons for these conceptual actions would have been nearly impossible to convey without the assistance of a text label or repeated exploration by the user. Knowing we needed the label either way, we opted to increase the size of the label for clarity and drop the icon entirely. We also made use of labels in the navigation buttons that move the user back and forth between steps. The shape of the button tells the users the direction they are stepping, forward or back, and the text is related to the title of the previous or next navigation step helping to maintain context between tasks.

Be careful when using Apple's provided icons. If you use one of these icons, or even one you create yourself that is close in appearance to a stock SDK icon, to mean something different from the way Apple uses the icon, you risk having your application rejected when you submit it to the App Store for review. Make sure you only use these stock icons to mean the exact same action that Apple uses in its applications. Using the icons as they're intended is a good idea anyway, because it helps maintain the context, or mental map, that makes our user's feel so happy

Tuning Responsiveness and Feedback

One last area you can tune the flow of your application is in the responsiveness and feedback of your interface. Whenever possible, you should make sure that a user's action is greeted with some visible reaction. A user will quickly become confused or frustrated when an application fails to visually or audibly respond swiftly to a gesture. This can quickly lead to the user accidentally repeating actions or prematurely quitting a task or your application altogether.

Despite their tiny size, the iPhone and the iPod Touch are fairly powerful devices. The iPhone OS and the CocoaTouch frameworks provide the means to easily thread actions for concurrent execution. Although the constraints of memory size and bandwidth, as well as processor throughput, prevent massive concurrency, its more than reasonable to be able to update your user interface to indicate progress or even allow a user to carry on with other actions while engaged in a lengthy computing task. Depending on your application and the tasks you are engaging in, you will have to be cautious of memory limitations and judge the proper course for each case in your own application.

Many iPhone applications fail this issue of responsiveness when working with the photo picker control that allows users to take a new photo. It's very easy to code your application so that you begin to perform a potentially slow operation with the user's new photo image before the photo picker view is dismissed. When this happens, your application will appear to have frozen almost immediately after the user has taken the new photo. An impatient user may quit in this circumstance before realizing that your application is working hard on the next step, not locked in an unresponsive state.

In Postage, we defer use of the newly acquired image until the photo picker view has been completely dismissed. Because our processing of the image can take a second or two after choosing a new high-resolution snapshot fresh from the camera, we also make sure to display a standard indeterminate activity indicator (the spinning wheel) where the newly processed photo will appear in the postcard design.

> Pace your progress or activity indicators at the location on the screen that your users are most likely focusing their attention. It is very tempting to place a progress indicator in an out-of-the-way location, but for many situations, this placement will make it easy for the users to overlook the indicator entirely.

We also had to take on some extra programming work in Postage to make sure that we used threaded background tasks when appropriate. Applying an effect, especially blur-like effects, to a full-resolution photo from the camera can take several seconds. In order to keep our application responsive during this processing, it was necessary to process the image using a background thread and to indicate the progress with an activity indicator on the main thread in the user interface. Similar situations arise frequently when accessing network resources as well.

Make sure you test your application on a device, and on something besides the top-of-the-line device, to understand the responsiveness of your interface. Although extremely useful, the iPhone simulator included with Xcode will fool you into thinking that your iPhone is as fast as the 8-core Mac Pro you do your development on. At the time of this writing, the top-end iPhone is the 3GS, which is significantly faster and has much more memory than the previous-generations of iPhone and iPod Touch. The 3GS effectively runs circles around its siblings, and if it's your only development device, you run the risk of creating an application that has serious problems with responsiveness for owners of older hardware.

By applying all of the concepts we have discussed here related to flow, we managed to create an application interface that users have almost universally found intuitive. Our attempts to give the users hints and provide them with controls and metaphors make Postage feel very natural to use. By carefully devising the flow through the application and guiding the user through the major tasks of creating a postcard, we made sure that a user didn't have to wonder what to do next. As often as possible, we tried to visually show the user what to do or what would happen rather than explaining with instructive text. We were careful to be consistent with how the user navigates through each step of the application and created a top to bottom flow with navigation steps at the top and controls that manipulate the user's content at the bottom. The result was an application that doesn't require prior instruction or explanation for use and a very happy population of customers that rarely ask for support or have difficulties achieving their tasks.

Exploring the Postage Development Technique

We used a variety of techniques during the design and implementation phases when building Postage; these allowed us to leverage the design concepts we have discussed so far to create the final polished application. Some of the same tools and methods we applied will undoubtedly help you create an outstanding application of your own.

Creating Prototypes and Mock-ups

One of the most important techniques you can employ when designing the next killer iPhone application is to make judicious use of prototypes. It is often impossible, or very nearly so, to determine the effectiveness of a particular design decision, interface control or application layout without some hands-on experience, even if it is simulated.

Create wireframes or mock-ups of your user interface before you start coding. Try your ideas and early designs in a medium that provides some level of interaction. Many application designers and developers prefer to construct a paper or cardboard simulation of the interface. Sometimes, coding a simple prototype of a particular control in isolation in a separate application serves as the mock-up. There are also a variety of software tools that can assist in designing your mockups.

Photoshop is the go-to tool for any designer working on interface designs. Judicious use of layers in Photoshop documents will allow you adjust your designs and try different approaches by placing controls on separate layers that can be disabled and enabled as needed. Another interesting tool for creating wireframes for application design is Balsamiq Mockups (http://www.balsamiq.com/). Balsamiq has a variety of iPhone controls and icons built in.

Modeling interaction with mock-ups and prototypes is also an important technique. Doing these before you lay down a bunch of code can increase your efficiency and result in less code you have to throw away. Apple's graphics tool, Motion is a great way to try out animations, timing curves, and pacing. Briefs (http://giveabrief.com/) is a great new tool that lets you create interactive prototypes that run on your iPhone with no programming required. Finally, if you have more of a development background, Interface Builder (part of the Xcode's suite of tools) is a great way to try out designs using Apple's standard controls. You can easily drop in buttons, images, table views, and the like and even try them out with some limited capability directly in Interface Builder without writing any code.

We often employed real-world objects to stage animations and transitions in Postage. For instance, we used real envelopes and slips of paper to prototype the animation when sending a postcard in the application. We also leaned heavily on Photoshop and Motion to do many rounds of initial mock-ups before the first line of code hit the compiler. Figure 7-17 shows an example of how we used Motion to try on of a variety of possible transition animations in Postage. Motion allowed us to try several ideas quickly, which encouraged experimentation. If we had tried to do this in code first, we would have been far less likely to explore new options and push our creativity because of the overhead in making the required changes.

Figure 7-17 *Using Motion to prototype animations*

Photoshop was an essential tool in the creation of the array of mock-ups for our interface design. Leveraging layers and embracing the spirit of experimentation, our designer was able to explore many different layouts and styles before we settled on our final design. Figure 7-18 shows a variety control styles we considered for the buttons that switch the category of postcard designs. In the end, we settled on using icons rather than words, but this early prototyping helped us find our visual style in addition to leading us to the more friendly design we finally used.

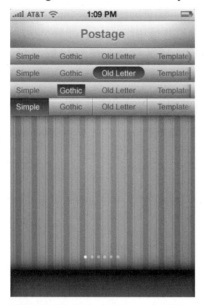

Figure 7-18. *Trying buttons styles in Photoshop*

Everyone prefers a different set of tools and techniques for prototypes, so experiment to find what works best for you.

Writing Specifications

Many application developers tend to leap directly to writing code without any sort of specification of how the application will look or behave. We would argue that even a lone developer can benefit from creating a specification before getting too deep into the actual nuts and bolts of crafting a new application. When working on a team, some specification, even a simple one, is almost a necessity to coordinate and communicate among the designers and engineers.

There are many benefits to generating a specification early in your project. Describing the exact behaviors of your application in a specification before beginning implementation helps by forcing you to think about the complicated interactions and issues before running down a rabbit hole that is hard to dig out of when you have thousands of lines of code and pixels committed down the wrong path.

A specification is also a good medium to communicate animations, specific visual effects, and complicated behaviors and interactions between designers and engineers. Although our specification for Postage was not necessarily exhaustive, its existence before we started slinging code allowed a number of developers to quickly jump into the project on an ongoing basis with a common direction and consistent theme to work from. Our specification called out specific pixel distances, exact colors, and desired transitions and animations. It allowed our engineers to quickly capture the vision of the application crafted by our designer and bring the application he had in his head to life with fewer iterations and false starts than if we had not started with the specification.

Another interesting benefit of creating a specification is that it can give your design some time to bake. Several months passed between the first iteration of our application design and the final specification we used to build what we delivered to the App Store. This long, if not necessarily planned, baking time allowed for thoughtful consideration of many of the critical design choices we had made. Sometimes, the perfect solution looks a lot less appealing after a few days pass or new information is obtained. We had plenty of time to iterate through different designs without committing engineering effort that would have been wasted on code that ultimately went unused. Figure 7-19 contains a sampling of the variety of designs we looked at over the course of the design phase for the template-browsing screen in Postage. What we ended up with in the end is drastically different than these mock-ups. The value of exploring the designs cheaply before we started implementation was a key component in creating an application that was as easy to use and visually compelling as Postage became.

Figure 7-19. *Early design iterations for browsing postcards in Postage*

It's hard not to push the edges of the hardware capabilities of the device when designing sophisticated user interfaces for iPhone OS applications. Our early specification for Postage called for a visual effect of overlapping turn edges for the backgrounds of each postcard design. As the user browsed through the available designs, left-to-right swipes of the horizontally scrolling to view a new postcard design would show the turned vertical edge of the current postcard overlapping the background of the next card that was coming into view. Figure 7-20 shows the detail of how we wanted this to look in the application.

Our initial implementation of this on the iPhone worked easily and looked amazing. The problem was that, at the early stages, we only had a handful of Postcard design templates to choose from. Once we started adding more and more design templates (we eventually shipped with over 50 designs), we discovered that we frequently slammed up against the limit of available memory on the device, and our application was forcibly terminated. To combat this problem, we had to start loading the foreground and background image elements of our postcard designs in a more lazy manner, making sure to purge art assets we didn't immediately need based on the design that was currently visible.

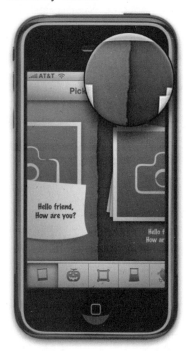

Figure 20. *Overlapping background images in our first implementation*

While this looked so simple on the whiteboard, the actual realization of this turned out to be a protracted development nightmare. We found that, despite our best efforts, we could not create a browsing experience that loaded the art assets we needed on demand for browsing without causing one of two ugly problems. Either the application would become unresponsive for moments at a time while scrolling through designs, or we would be forced to display a low-resolution proxy or placeholder of a postcard design before it was completely loaded from storage to display. Both experiences left the act of browsing our beautiful postcard designs feeling somewhat second-rate.

In the end, we found our solution, though it came with a price. Our postcard art assets started life in the PNG file format. PNG is the preferred native format for iPhone UI resources, and it supports the transparency we needed to make our cool overlapped edges. What we discovered, though, was that loading our PNG files specifically was what caused our momentary hiccup, which resulted in our unresponsivenes or the need to display a low-resolution proxy while waiting for the image to finish loading. If we switched to using a JPEG file format, the load of the art assets for each newly visible postcard template was no longer causing interruptions in our applications. Sadly, the change to JPEG meant that we had to sacrifice transparency in our background images, thereby eliminating our ability to have overlapping edges.

What is the lesson you can take from this? Specifications are a great way to plan out your application, but you have to allow for knowledge that you gain when turning that specification into real-running code that will inevitably lead to unanticipated changes. If you go wild with your design ideas, there will be places where the limitations of the real world will force you to rein in your interface ambitions some. Spend some time exploring the more complicated aspects of your intended design, and see if the device and SDK are capable of your intent.

> Postage contains over 40,000 lines of code! We spent approximately 35 person-weeks of development with as many as 5 engineers and 1 designer building the application over a 2-month period before shipping the first version.

Considering Art

Many art techniques can be used to support our design goals of focus and flow in an iPhone application. For instance, it is important to focus the user's attention to the proper portions of your interface. Postage is a creative application where the primary focus of the interface should be the user's content. To support this, application interface elements such as the navigation bar and tab bar controls are intentionally colored with gray tones in order to be neutral against the color and vibrant postcard designs (see Figure 7-21). Subtle gradient drop shadows are used at the boundaries between the interface elements and the postcard to enhance the separation between interface and content.

Figure 7-21. *Using neutral interface colors and shadows to highlight the content*

Consistency in art is also effective in maintaining context and enhancing the cohesive feel of an application. Users may not be able to point out exactly why, but subconsciously, they will sense this consistency and perceive the higher quality of design. An application with art that is consistent with itself and the iPhone OS will simply feel more correct or Apple-like.

Note that all lighting on the iPhone is from the top of the screen down. Make sure all your gradients, highlights, and drop shadows maintain this lighting for normal user interface elements. Strive to use consistent button styles as well. Pay careful attention to the pressed and highlighted states of your buttons. If you are creating custom buttons, you will likely want to include your own highlighted and selected states as well.

Tuning the Touch

One of the most unique and prominent properties of the iPhone is its touch screen interface. Using the iPhone OS is an inherently tactile experience, and touch-based gestures require thoughtful tuning so that an application feels right. In many cases, your application will rely on standard SDK controls, such as the UIScrollView, that have been well tuned by Apple for its complicated interactions. For this reason alone, you should try to base your interface on Apple's control classes when possible. If you hunt around, you will find there are a variety of applications in the App Store that have decided to implement their own scrolling. While many of these attempt to mimic the feel and response of the regular SDK control, few get it correct. Its truly a difficult problem and requires more work than you want to spend when you can almost always get the behavior you want from the SDK control. The difference in responsiveness to the touch is noticeable and makes these applications feel wrong to users accustomed to the scrolling behavior in most other applications.

In some cases, though, you may find yourself with a legitimate need to implement a new control with sophisticated reactions to gestures from the user. In Postage, the user is allowed to scale, position, and rotate a photo image placed into a postcard design. The rotation behavior by twisting two fingers on the screen is a custom behavior and not present in any of the standard Apple controls or supported gestures. Early implementations of our rotation felt squirrelly or imprecise. We went through many different iterations of how this rotation gesture was implemented before we found the final behavior that felt natural and gave the expected results.

Animations will require fine-tuning when used in your application's interface. For many simple transitions between sets of controls the default parameters controlling an animation are usually sufficient. In Postage, we used Core Animation to provide several custom animation sequences in our user interface. One of the more interesting animations is the effect that is applied when a new category of postcard is selected in the design browser. The new postcard design that appears when selecting a new category animates onto the screen by dropping in from the top. The animation ends with the postcard bouncing as it comes to rest from its drop. This bounce helps to make the postcards feel more like real objects in the application. Getting the bounce to behave realistically and at a speed that kept the application from feeling unresponsive required many iterations. To help the process, we even used a motion graphics application (Motion from Apple's Final Cut Studio suite) to model the animation timing. Apple's visual graphics programming tool Quartz Composer, which comes with Mac OS X, is another great way to tryout animations.

Our animated transition between steps that changes the focus of the visible area of the postcard the user is creating also required fine-tuning. Each of these transitions is a fairly complicated animation that swaps out user interface elements and moves the view and scale of the current postcard to highlight the area of the design being manipulated at the new step. We went through several iterations of the timing of these animations before the pace felt correct for the balance between responsiveness of the application and providing our goal of providing visual cues that established the postcard as something more tangible in the user interface.

THE TOOLS

We used a fairly large list of developer, media, and graphics applications to design and build Postage, including these:

- Photoshop
- Illustrator
- LiveView for iPhone
- Final Cut
- Motion
- Perforce
- SimFinger
- Xcode
- iPhone Simulator
- iPhoto
- Mail
- Snapz Pro
- Digital Color Meter

Summary

Pulling all of these ideas together to create and implement your iPhone application is a lot of hard work. You have to care about each and every pixel on our screen, the timing of each animation, and the exact characters in the label on each button. You have to think hard about your users' expectations and their preconceived notions. Sometimes, you have to push the boundaries of the technology you are developing with. You have to be willing to throw away what you created and start over and even lop off your personal favorite idea or feature. In the end though, you'll be proud of your work, and your users will appreciate all the blood, sweat, and tears.

For my team and I, the hours of agonizing over all the small details resulted in much critical acclaim from the community and media that culminated in a coveted Apple Design Award in 2009. We hope the tips and guidelines presented here will help you create the next award-winning user experience on the iPhone. We can't wait to see what you come up with.

Keith Peters

Company: Infrared5

Location: Wellseley, MA

Former Life As a Developer: Flash Developer for several years, developing games and rich Internet applications. For the last couple of years working at Infrared5 in Boston.

Life as an iPhone Developer: Currently working on several high profile iPhone apps with Infrared5, and have pushed out a bunch of apps and games on my own. Most notable is Falling Balls, which rose to number on on the free applications list.

■ *Falling Balls*

■ *Vector Blocks*

■ *Bug Out!*

■ **Wire Draw**

■ **Dust**

■ **iAttractor**

What's in This Chapter: Deconstructions of two games: Falling Balls, and Gravity Pods, both of which started out as Flash games, some of the UI challenges encountered in porting them to the iPhone, and how those were overcome.

Key Technologies:

■ *Touches vs. Accelerometer for UI control*

■ *Creating an onscreen keyboard replacement for fine control*

■ *Drag and drop onscreen UI elements*

Chapter 8

Falling Balls and Gravity Pods

I'm a Flash developer from way back and a somewhat recent convert to the religion of Cocoa and iPhone programming. In Flash, I've always gravitated toward game programming or applications with creative user interfaces and interaction. I was never a huge fan of laying out rows and columns of generic user interface controls and wiring them together to move data around. That's just boring to me.

Naturally, when I started on iPhone development, my first few projects were attempts to re-create the kinds of things that I'd done in Flash. Now, most of the tutorials you find out there on iPhone development show you how to use Interface Builder to lay out various UI components and how hook them up to display some data, so I figured I'd use this chapter to talk about the more unique interfaces that I've always found much more interesting. In particular, I'm going to use examples from two games that I originally created in Flash and later ported over to the iPhone.

If you're not coming from the Flash world, don't worry; this chapter is not about porting Flash games to the iPhone. It is about the challenges involved in creating nonstandard user interfaces on the iPhone, some of the problems you might run into, and some ideas on how you might go about solving them.

These challenges can be seen as falling into three broad areas:

- The first challenge area has to do with the hardware that the iPhone lacks, notably the keyboard and mouse. Yes, you can call up a software keyboard, but that is strictly for entering characters into a text field. You are not going to use the W, A, S, and D keys on that keyboard to move a character around the screen, as you would in many desktop and web games. And yes, taps and touch screen gestures can fill in for a lot of mouse functionality, but as you will see, there are some big differences there too.

■ The second challenge is keeping in mind the capabilities the iPhone does have that your usual desktop computer doesn't. This includes the multitouch screen and accelerometer, as well as things like touch gestures—swipes, pinches, and so on. While gestures with the mouse have been attempted now and then over the years, they've never really caught on. Perhaps it's the coordination required to move, press, make a gesture, and release. A finger swipe on the iPhone's touch screen, however, is the most natural thing in the world. It's important to keep all these new features in mind when building your user interface.

■ The third, and perhaps most challenging, area is in not *misusing* what you do have to make up for what you lack. You need to avoid things like the overused shaking gesture when the gesture makes no sense for the function it is performing or using actions the user would never dream of doing, like a three-finger double-tap (yes, I've seen it done).

The whole idea behind these new, more physical and tangible input methods is to use them to make a user interface that works in the same way that real-world objects work. You might need to explain how to do a particular action one time, but this should result in an exclamation of "Ah! Of course!" and never "Hmm . . . OK, I better write that down."

In this chapter, we'll look at how some of these challenges presented themselves while developing my Falling Balls and Gravity Pods games and look at some of the solutions I attempted and finally settled on.

Creating Falling Balls

The first iPhone game I created was called Falling Balls. It was based on an unnamed game I did in Flash back in 2001. The premise of the game was utterly simple. As you pressed the left or right cursor keys, a little stick-figure man ran back and forth at the bottom of the screen. From the top-left corner of the screen, round spiky objects fell down and bounced their way left to right. For each spiky ball that made it to the right side of the screen without hitting the stick man, you got one point. If any did hit him, he died, and the game was over. You can see the original game in Figure 8-1.

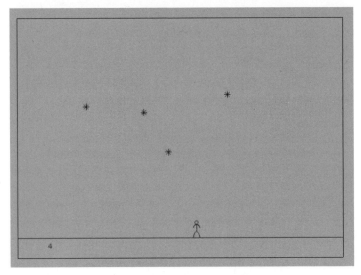

Figure 8-1. *The original Falling Balls game from 2001*

This was more a quick proof of concept than a very polished game. I put it up on my site, `www.bit-101.com` along with the FLA file, the Flash source file that contains both the code and graphics for anyone to play around with.

A couple of years later, someone grabbed the source code and graphics for this game and created a Facebook game called Tangerine Panic. They changed the spiky balls into orange circles, added some music, and gave the stick figure some commentary. They also have the stick man following the mouse rather than being controlled by the cursor keys. Figure 8-2 shows a shot of Tangerine Panic.

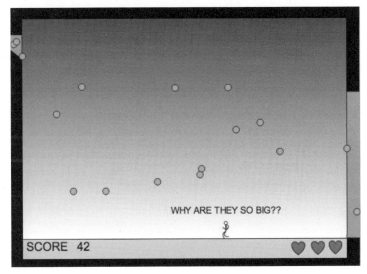

Figure 8-2. *The Tangerine Panic game*

When I started delving into iPhone development, one of the first things I did was to get a circle to move around the screen and bounce off the sides. When I had that working, I tried to think of some compelling game that could be built on top of that. I remembered my old Flash game, and Falling Balls was born. A few weeks later, inexplicably, it was the number one free game in the App Store!

Building the Game

The graphics and audio for the game are extremely simple. Graphically, the game contains a stick figure that runs back and forth and balls that fall down and bounce. I also added a blood spatter that displays when the stick man is hit and some sound effects that consisted of a funny boing sound and the Wilhelm scream (check http://en.wikipedia.org/wiki/Wilhelm_Scream).

In this chapter, however, we'll just be rebuilding one piece of the Falling Balls game, the stick figure that runs back and forth, as this mechanism is the key to the whole game and is what took the most amount of time to sort out.

To start with, create a new application in Xcode, choose View Based Application, and name it FallingBallsRemake, or just download the files from this book's Source Code/Downloads page at www.apress.com. To get the running stick figure, I went right back to the original Flash file, copied each frame of the running sequence I had made back in 2001, and saved each of these as an individual PNG file. These images are very simple, and there are only six of them. I've supplied these for you as files named run1.png through run6.png.

In your project, right-click the resources folder, and choose to *Add Existing Items*. Select all six images at once, and click OK. You'll then want to make sure you copy these images into the chosen folder and add them to your project's target, as shown in Figure 8-3.

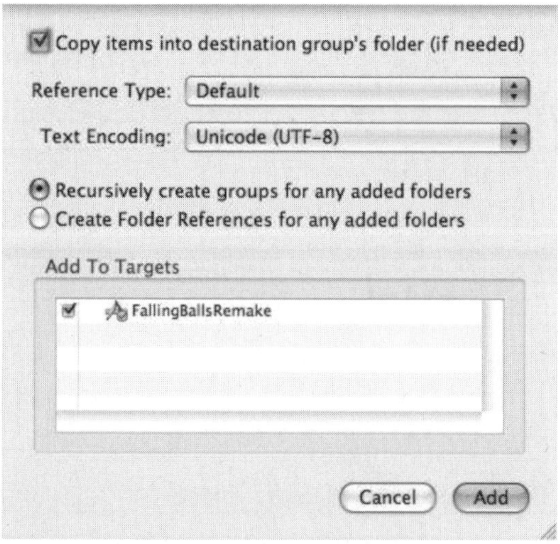

Figure 8-3. *Adding resources to your project*

These six images form one half of the run cycle, so after displaying all six, you have to display the fifth image again and then move back down to the second one to make a smooth loop. You can do all this in the view controller. The interface code will look like this:

```
#import <UIKit/UIKit.h>

@interface FallingBallsRemakeViewController : UIViewController {
    UIImageView *stickman;
}
@end
```

And the implementation looks like this:

```
#import "FallingBallsRemakeViewController.h"

@implementation FallingBallsRemakeViewController
- (void)viewDidLoad {
    [super viewDidLoad];
    stickman = [[UIImageView alloc]
                initWithFrame:CGRectMake(225, 270, 30, 30)];
    stickman.animationImages = [NSArray arrayWithObjects:
                                [UIImage imageNamed:@"run1.png"],
                                [UIImage imageNamed:@"run2.png"],
                                [UIImage imageNamed:@"run3.png"],
                                [UIImage imageNamed:@"run4.png"],
                                [UIImage imageNamed:@"run5.png"],
                                [UIImage imageNamed:@"run6.png"],
                                [UIImage imageNamed:@"run5.png"],
                                [UIImage imageNamed:@"run4.png"],
                                [UIImage imageNamed:@"run3.png"],
                                [UIImage imageNamed:@"run2.png"],
                                nil];
    stickman.animationDuration = 0.7;
    [stickman startAnimating];
    [self.view addSubview:stickman];
}

- (BOOL)shouldAutorotateToInterfaceOrientation:
        (UIInterfaceOrientation)interfaceOrientation {
    // Return YES for supported orientations
    return (interfaceOrientation ==
            UIInterfaceOrientationLandscapeRight);
}

 - (void)dealloc {
    [stickman release];
    [super dealloc];
}

@end
```

The variable, stickman, is declared in the interface as a pointer to a UIImageView. In the viewDidLoad method in the implementation, we allocate the UIImageView and call initWithFrame, passing in a CGRect of its initial location. Then, we assign its animationImages property an array of UIImages. These are created using the static imageNamed method of UIImage. Make sure that you have added these images to your project first. Also make sure to set the last element to `nil`, which signals the end of the array.

The final steps are telling the `UIImageView` how fast to play the animation, telling it to start animating, and adding it to the view. The speed of the animation is controlled with the `animationDuration` property. This value represents the time it takes to play a single cycle of the animation. With some experimentation, I found that 0.7 seconds seemed to look about right.

Next, we call `startAnimating` and pass `stickman` as a parameter to `addSubview` for the view controller's view. This will make the stick man visible as a part of that view. Also note that we implemented the `shouldAutoRotateToInterfaceOrientation` method to force the game into landscape mode. You should wind up with something that looks like Figure 8-4 when you run it in the simulator.

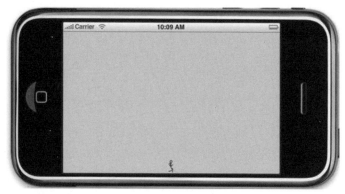

Figure 8-4. *The game in the iPhone simulator*

Adding the Game Controls

In the original Flash-based game, the stick man was controlled with the left and right cursor keys. Since we don't have a hardware keyboard on the iPhone, this wasn't an option. I considered following the cue of Tangerine Panic and having the character just track the x position of the user's finger. This task is really easy; just add this method to your view controller:

```
- (void)touchesMoved:(NSSet *)touches withEvent:(UIEvent *)event
{
    UITouch *touch = [touches anyObject];
    CGPoint point = [touch locationInView:self.view];
    if(point.x < stickman.center.x)
    {
        stickman.transform = CGAffineTransformMakeScale(-1.0, 1.0);
    }
    else
    {
        stickman.transform = CGAffineTransformMakeScale(1.0, 1.0);
    }
    stickman.center = CGPointMake(point.x, 285);
}
```

This code is assuming a single touch and grabbing a pointer to that UITouch object through [touches anyObject]. It then converts this UITouch into a CGPoint by calling locationInView, passing in the view. The conditional statement checks to see if the touch is to the left or the right of the stick man. If it's to the left, you want to flip the stick man on the x axis, so he appears to be running to the left. Otherwise, keep him facing to the right. Finally, we make a new CGPoint with a fixed y position and set the stick man's center to that new point.

This actually seems to work pretty well on the simulator, but if you try it out on a real iPhone or iPod Touch, you'll find it pretty unusable for one important reason: a finger is *many* times larger than a mouse cursor. In other words, the stick man will almost always be completely hidden behind your finger.

I knew simply following the user's finger was over before I even started. My next thought was to use touches in a more general sense: If the user touched the left side of the screen, the man would run to the left. If the right side of the screen was touched, he would run that way. This proved to be a bit more complex than I thought it would be due to the way touches work. You only get notified when you touch down, move, or touch up. There is no built-in concept of holding a touch on a particular point. Again, this solution worked fine in the simulator where you have to release the mouse before touching another location. But things were not so clean on a device with real multitouch capabilities.

Then, it dawned on me that I could simply use two large, hidden buttons—one covering the right side of the screen and one covering the left. When the left button is pressed, the man runs left; the right button makes him run to the right. This proved to be a whole lot simpler than trying to track touches, and it worked perfectly the first time around. The moral of that story is to avoid getting fancy when you have a ready-made solution.

At this point, all the elements of the game were in place, but it still lacked something. Touching the screen to move this way or that left me feeling kind of flat. I was just about to release it anyway when I had a startling realization (or at least a startling recollection) that the iPhone has an accelerometer. It was exactly what the game needed. Tilting the device to the left or the right to make the stick man run that way gave the game a physical reality; you felt like there really was a little guy in there that you were influencing. Using the accelerometer draws you into the game in a way that simply touching the screen does not. Remember that the *user interface* is how the user interacts with your application—it's not just screen layout of controls. Thus your control scheme, even if it is not visible, is a huge part of the UI.

Accessing the accelerometer is pretty easy but requires a few specific steps. First, we need to tell the compiler that the view controller wants to implement the UIAccelerometerDelegate protocol. This is done in the header file, by adding the name of the protocol in angle brackets:

```
#import <UIKit/UIKit.h>
@interface FallingBallsRemakeViewController : UIViewController
            <UIAccelerometerDelegate> {
    UIImageView *stickman;
}
@end
```

Next, in the implementation file, we need to set the view controller as a delegate to the accelerometer, which tells the accelerometer to call a specific method in the view controller when accelerometer events occur. We can do this in the top of the viewDidLoad method. I won't show the rest of the method, which includes setting up the images and does not change:

```
- (void)viewDidLoad {
    [super viewDidLoad];
    [[UIAccelerometer sharedAccelerometer] setDelegate:self];
    …
```

After that, we need to create the method that the accelerometer will call:

```
- (void)accelerometer:(UIAccelerometer *)accelerometer
        didAccelerate:(UIAcceleration *)acceleration
{
    NSLog(@"x:%f, y:%f, z:%f", acceleration.x,
                              acceleration.y,
                              acceleration.z);
}
```

This method gets passed two pointers. The first is a pointer to the accelerometer object itself, and the next is to a UIAcceleration object that contains information about how the device is oriented in 3-D space. For now, we're just logging the x, y, and z properties of that acceleration object. Note that, from this point on, you'll actually need to run the game on a real iPhone or iPod Touch, because at the time of this writing, the simulator does not simulate the accelerometer. When you get it up and running on your device, you should see a long list of output statements like this (they're all on a single line if there is space in the console):

```
2009-04-05 17:28:06.883 FallingBallsRemake[1123:20b] x:0.145349,
y:-0.036337, z:-0.981105
```

I usually start by throwing in a log statement in my accelerometer functions and make sure it's working before I go writing my actual accelerometer code, as it's really easy to make a small error and that causes the code to fail silently. Once you've got those log statements firing off like they should be, you'll be ready for the real code.

You'll notice, as you tilt the device back and forth, that the acceleration.y value will range from 1.0 when the device is tilted 90 degrees to the left (from the default landscape orientation) to –1.0 when the device is tilted 90 degrees to the right. We can use that value to control the direction and speed that the stick man will run in. The accelerometer:didAccelerate method becomes the following:

```
- (void)accelerometer:(UIAccelerometer *)accelerometer
        didAccelerate:(UIAcceleration *)acceleration
{
    if(acceleration.y > 0)
```

```
    {
        stickman.transform = CGAffineTransformMakeScale(-1.0, 1.0);
    }
    else
    {
        stickman.transform = CGAffineTransformMakeScale(1.0, 1.0);
    }
    float newX = stickman.center.x - acceleration.y * 30.0;
    if(newX < 10)
    {
        newX = 10;
    else if(newX > 470)
    {
        newX = 470;
    }
    stickman.center = CGPointMake(newX, stickman.center.y);
}
```

First of all, don't forget to remove or comment out the touchesBegan method if you created it. We're not using that anymore. Here, in this accelerometer method, we're going to do something similar in terms of flipping the stick man so that he faces the direction he's running in. If the device is tilted to the left, we make him face left and run left, and the opposite occurs if the device is tilted to the right.

After that, we can just subtract the acceleration.y value from the current center to establish a value for the new x position. Actually, the values from 1.0 to –1.0 will make the stick man move pretty slowly, so we first multiply it by a figure like 30.0 to get him to run a bit faster. You can play with this value to get a motion you like. Before applying this value to the stick man's center x position, we clamp it to a minimum of 10 and maximum of 470, to keep him from running totally off the screen.

If you've followed along, you should be able to tilt your device one way or the other and have the stick man run the way you are tilting. While relatively simple, this is the exact type of code that can be used as the start of any number of games. Change the stick man graphics into a rolling ball and implement some vertical motion as well as horizontal, and you're well on your way to creating the next rolling-ball-in-a-maze game!

Creating Gravity Pods

The second major game I worked on for the iPhone is called Gravity Pods. In truth, at the time of this writing, I am still putting the finishing touches on the iPhone version. The original Gravity Pods was created in 2007 and was quite successful. I followed it up with Gravity Pods 2 in late 2008. While creating that sequel, I realized it would make a great iPhone game, and in fact, this realization that drove me to learn Objective-C and iPhone programming.

The basic premise of the game is to aim a gun, shoot a projectile, and hit a target. However, various fixed, moving, and even rotating walls block the way. Also, there are the gravity pods for which the game is named. These warp the path of the projectile, allowing it to go around corners, and so forth. Judicious placement of these pods by the player, as well as placing additional items such as repellers, bouncers, and black holes, help meet the goal on each level. Figure 8-5 shows the original Flash-based Gravity Pods game.

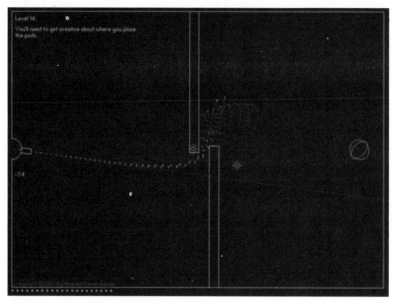

Figure 8-5. *The original Gravity Pods game*

The first version of the game was almost completely mouse driven. This caused a bit of frustration in some cases, as the difference of just a pixel or two in the location of a gravity pod could result in a major difference in the overall path of a projectile. So in version 2, I added more keyboard support, allowing the user to finely position the location of a pod using the cursor keys, as well as dragging and dropping with the mouse.

I knew that dragging and dropping with any degree of accuracy on the iPhone would be even tougher than with a mouse, so a similar kind of supplemental, fine-tuning control was going to be a necessity. But how could I do this without cursor keys?

It didn't take long to realize that the accelerometer was out. No way could it be used for pixel-precise control. I thought about gestures like sliding up, down, or sideways to move a pixel in any direction. The problem, though, was that I still needed drag-and-drop functionality to move the pods large distances, and it was difficult to disambiguate a drag-and-drop gesture from a slide indicating pixel-precise adjustment.

I finally came up with the concept of on-screen buttons to move the pods one pixel in each direction. In other words, making my own custom on-screen keyboard. You can see a current development screenshot of this in Figure 8-6.

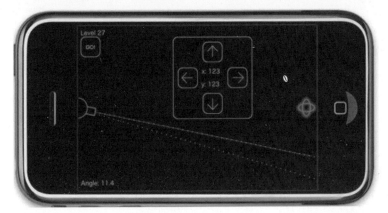

Figure 8-6. *Gravity Pods on the iPhone*

Now, keep in mind that on-screen navigation keys are probably not the kind of thing you want to use all the time. For instance, moving a character around in real time would not be very workable with virtual buttons like this. Because the buttons are images only, with no tactile feedback, it's all too easy to let your fingers stray slightly in the heat of game play, and the results would be quite frustrating. But for a situation where you require minute control of the position an object, this solution works out pretty well.

The next challenge was to decide where to put these buttons. Another challenge of developing for the iPhone is the limited screen real estate available. If you start filling it up with on-screen controls, you have no room left for the game itself. Yet the buttons have to be big enough that the user can hit them without trying too hard. I tried putting them across the bottom and along the sides, but I felt they just took up too much space. Additionally, I wanted these buttons to be laid out in kind of a cross pattern as shown in Figure 8-6. Laying out buttons in a horizontal or vertical strip saves more screen space but is less intuitive to the user.

What I finally came up with is a kind of heads-up display (HUD) that is only on-screen when you need it. Essentially, when you select one of the positionable items the HUD pops up, allowing you to use the buttons to position the item. When the item no longer has focus, the controls go away.

While the HUD solved most of the problem, I was still stuck with the decision of where to place this panel so that it wouldn't be in the way of the draggable pods. I went through various iterations, trying to dynamically and intelligently place the control panel in a part of the screen away from the currently selected pod. For example, if the pod was near the bottom of the screen, the HUD should be near the top. If the pod was near the left edge of the screen, the HUD was on the right side. Coding that behavior took a lot of logic and wound up not working too well. Even if the HUD was not covering the selected pod, it might be covering some part of the screen the user was interested in, and there was no way to tell what part of the screen that might be. In the end, I just decided to make the panel draggable too, letting the user place it in the best place at any given time. Again, simplicity was the best answer.

Building the HUD

The example for this section is in the project named HUD. To make it as simple as possible, I did as much as I could in Interface Builder. Figure 8-7 shows the layout of the view in HUDViewController.xib.

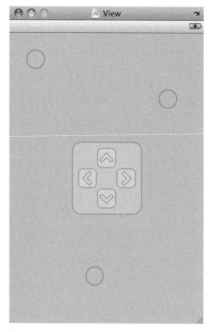

Figure 8-7. *The layout of the main view*

Three UIImageViews are set to display an image called pod.png, which is just a red circle. These are all set to have their alpha values at 50 percent, and you'll see why shortly. They also have a tag of 1. This is set in the View Attributes panel in Interface Builder. In the center is the HUD, which is a UIView. It has a UIImageView with hud.png for the background (the rounded rectangle) and four custom UIButtons with images showing left, right, up, and down arrows. These four buttons will be connected to four IBAction methods in the view controller, and the HUD will be connected to an IBOutlet in the same class. The HUD's alpha value is set to 0.0, causing it to be invisible when the program first launches.

All of our custom code for this example will be in the HUDViewController class. Here is the interface for that class:

```
#import <UIKit/UIKit.h>

@interface HUDViewController : UIViewController {
    UIImageView *selectedPod;
    UIView *hud;
    CGPoint dragOffset;
    BOOL hudIsDragging;
}
```

```
@property (nonatomic, retain) IBOutlet UIView *hud;

- (IBAction)moveLeft;
- (IBAction)moveRight;
- (IBAction)moveUp;
- (IBAction)moveDown;

@end
```

Here, we have a variable for the selected pod, which can be any one of those three
UIImageViews. Then come the HUD itself, a UIView, and a couple of variables that we'll
use for dragging the HUD. The hud variable also has a property declaration. Finally, you
can see the IBAction methods I just mentioned. Don't forget to go into Interface Builder
and connect the buttons to the IBActions and the HUD itself to the hud IBOutlet.

The implementation follows. I'll give it to you all at once, and then we will go through it in
more detail.

```
#import "HUDViewController.h"

@implementation HUDViewController
@synthesize hud;

- (void)viewDidLoad {
    [super viewDidLoad];
}

- (void)touchesBegan:(NSSet *)touches withEvent:(UIEvent *)event
{
    hudIsDragging = NO;
    UITouch *touch = [touches anyObject];
    UIView *touchView = [touch view];
    if([touchView tag] == 1)
    {
        [UIView beginAnimations:nil context:nil];
        [hud setAlpha:1.0];
        [UIView commitAnimations];
        [selectedPod setAlpha:0.5];
        selectedPod = (UIImageView *)[touch view];
        [selectedPod setAlpha:1.0];
    }
    else if(touchView == hud)
    {
        hudIsDragging = YES;
        CGPoint touchPoint = [touch locationInView:self.view];
        dragOffset = CGPointMake(hud.center.x - touchPoint.x,
                                 hud.center.y - touchPoint.y);

    }
    else
    {
        [UIView beginAnimations:nil context:nil];
        [hud setAlpha:0.0];
        [UIView commitAnimations];
        [selectedPod setAlpha:0.5];
        selectedPod = nil;
```

```
        }
    }

    - (void)touchesMoved:(NSSet *)touches withEvent:(UIEvent *)event
    {
        UITouch *touch = [touches anyObject];
        CGPoint touchPoint = [touch locationInView:self.view];
        if(hudIsDragging)
        {
            [hud setCenter:CGPointMake(touchPoint.x + dragOffset.x,
                                       touchPoint.y + dragOffset.y)];
        }
        else
        {
            [selectedPod setCenter:touchPoint];
        }
    }

    - (void)moveLeft
    {
        [selectedPod setCenter:CGPointMake(selectedPod.center.x - 1,
                                           selectedPod.center.y)];
    }

    - (void)moveRight
    {
        [selectedPod setCenter:CGPointMake(selectedPod.center.x + 1,
                                           selectedPod.center.y)];
    }

    - (void)moveUp
    {
        [selectedPod setCenter:CGPointMake(selectedPod.center.x,
                                           selectedPod.center.y - 1)];
    }

    - (void)moveDown
    {
        [selectedPod setCenter:CGPointMake(selectedPod.center.x,
                                           selectedPod.center.y + 1)];
    }

    - (void)dealloc {
        [hud release];
        [super dealloc];
    }

@end
```

Let's begin with the first part of the touchesBegan method. This method is called when the user touches the screen. We initially want to know if the user has touched one of the pods. If so, we want to set that pod as the selected pod and indicate visually its selected state. Earlier, I mentioned that all the pods had an alpha of 50 percent. We'll indicate a selected pod by increasing its alpha to 100 percent. You might want to add a glow or drop shadow or swap the graphic with something that makes it look more selected.

```
- (void)touchesBegan:(NSSet *)touches withEvent:(UIEvent *)event
{
    hudIsDragging = NO;
    UITouch *touch = [touches anyObject];
    UIView *touchView = [touch view];
    if([touchView tag] == 1)
    {
        [UIView beginAnimations:nil context:nil];
        [hud setAlpha:1.0];
        [UIView commitAnimations];
        [selectedPod setAlpha:0.5];
        selectedPod = (UIImageView *)[touch view];
        [selectedPod setAlpha:1.0];
    }
    else if(touchView == hud)
    {
        hudIsDragging = YES;
        CGPoint touchPoint = [touch locationInView:self.view];
        dragOffset = CGPointMake(hud.center.x - touchPoint.x,
                                 hud.center.y - touchPoint.y);

    }
    else
    {
        [UIView beginAnimations:nil context:nil];
        [hud setAlpha:0.0];
        [UIView commitAnimations];
        [selectedPod setAlpha:0.5];
        selectedPod = nil;
    }
}
```

We get the single touch from the NSSet, touches, and find out what view that touch originated in. Remember we tagged all the pods with a tag of 1. By default, objects have a tag of 0, so we know if the tag is 1, the object's a pod and we need to do a few things.

First, we want to show the HUD. We do that by setting its alpha to 1.0. Wrapping that line inside the pair of beginAnimations and commitAnimations calls causes the HUD to fade into view, rather than instantaneously appearing.

Next, we set the currently selected pod's alpha to 50 percent. Then we set the selectedPod variable to the pod that was just touched and set its alpha to 1.0 (100 percent).

If it wasn't a pod that was touched, we check to see if it was the HUD. We'll cover that chunk of code shortly. Finally, neither a pod nor the HUD was touched, the user just touched an empty area of the screen. In this case, we again set the selected pod's alpha back to 0.5 and set selectedPod to nil, meaning no pods are selected.

Before we move on to the HUD itself, let's finish up with the pods:

```
- (void)touchesMoved:(NSSet *)touches withEvent:(UIEvent *)event
{
    UITouch *touch = [touches anyObject];
    CGPoint touchPoint = [touch locationInView:self.view];
    if(hudIsDragging)
```

```
    {
        [hud setCenter:CGPointMake(touchPoint.x + dragOffset.x,
                                    touchPoint.y + dragOffset.y)];
    }
    else
    {
        [selectedPod setCenter:touchPoint];
    }
}
```

Here, we get the location of the single touch in the view. If the HUD is not being
dragged, the pod moves to the point being touched. This code assumes a pod is
selected of course. But it doesn't really matter. If no pod is selected then selectedPod
will be nil. Sending methods to nil is no problem in Objective-C and is more efficient
than an unnecessary check to see whether or not it is nil. There you go—drag-and-
drop pods!

Now, let's move on to look at the HUD. In touchesBegan, if the view that was touched
was not a UIImageView, we check to see if it was the HUD itself that was touched. If so,
we run the following code:

```
hudIsDragging = YES;
CGPoint touchPoint = [touch locationInView:self.view];
dragOffset = CGPointMake(hud.center.x - touchPoint.x,
                         hud.center.y - touchPoint.y);
```

This sets the hudIsDragging Boolean variable to true. You saw where we used that in
touchesMoved. Then it gets the (x, y) point that was touched and creates a new CGPoint
that is the difference between that and the center of the HUD. In the case of dragging a
pod, we simply snapped the pod's centers to the point that was being touched.
Because the HUD is much larger, that behavior wouldn't look natural at all. So we save
this offset point and use it in the touchesMoved method when the HUD is being dragged:

```
if(hudIsDragging)
{
    hud.center = CGPointMake(touchPoint.x + dragOffset.x,
                             touchPoint.y + dragOffset.y);
}
```

The final bit of code is just the four move methods. As you recall, these were connected
to the four buttons and simply move the selected pod a single pixel in the specified
direction.

Now, you can select or deselect any pod by tapping on it and draging it around
manually. When a pod is selected, the HUD will appear, enabling you to position the
selected pod in any direction, pixel by pixel. When no pods are selected, the HUD
disappears, freeing up the screen real estate. Furthermore, the HUD is draggable,
allowing the user to position it wherever is convenient.

Summary

The goal of this chapter was to show you some nonstandard user interfaces, some of the challenges associated with creating them, and a couple of examples of how these challenges can be overcome, for example, trying out different input methods likes touches and the accelerometer and exploring the idea of an onscreen keyboard for fine control of game objects. I hope this chapter has, at least, sparked some ideas of things you can try on your own.

Jürgen Siebert

Company: **FontShop AG**

Location: **Berlin, Germany**

Former Life As a Developer: **Jürgen Siebert (54) studied physics and became a scientific journalist and book author in 1984. Two years later he founded Germany's leading design magazine PAGE in Hamburg and was editor in chief since 1991. After that he joined FontShop in Berlin to develop typographical projects like FUSE, FontBook, the design conference TYPO Berlin and the FontFont typeface library. Since 2001 he is CMO of FontShop AG and responsible for market communication (Fontblog) and new business tools like FontShuffle.**

Life as an iPhone Developer: **FontShuffle was the first app that opens the world of typefaces on a mobile device. It is a reference tool, developed by Jürgen Siebered and programmed by software architect Jonas Witt (Metaquark, Berlin)**

What's in This Chapter:

- **Understanding the world of typefaces**
- **The anatomy of letters**
- **Fonts for screen design**
- **Identifying typefaces**
- **Typographical classifications**
- **Font inspirations via FontShuffle**

Key Technologies:

- *User interface*
- *Font rendering*
- *Customized font samples*
- *Classifying references*

Chapter 9

FontShuffle

In this chapter, you'll see how FontShop released FontShuffle and put the world of type under a simple user interface so that you can browse through 500 years of type design with a fingertip. During the discussion, you will also learn how to differentiate and describe typefaces. Finally, you'll gain the knowledge to choose the right fonts for your publishing or programming projects and how to get maximum readability on screen or paper.

FontShuffle is a typeface reference tool for print and media designers, but it's also handy for typography novices. Compared to printed catalogs, it delivers search results faster and generates custom text samples of every typeface it offers. While most professional references require previous knowledge of the history of type design or typeface anatomy, FontShuffle uses an intuitive visual interface. Hundreds of font families are sorted by formal similarity, so anyone can browse and compare related typefaces.

Introducing FontShuffle

Since its start in 1989, FontShop produced printed typeface catalogs. After some years, formerly slim catalogs have grown into the well-respected *FontBook*, which is still the only independent typeface catalog showing the most popular fonts of more than 90 type foundries.

The latest issue of *FontBook* weights 6.6 pounds and contains 1,760 pages. It is heavy, hard to handle, and expensive. Only professionals can afford the "yellow bible," as they like to call it. The editorial team is very conscious of the fact that *FontBook* is reaching its limits. For example, binding 1,760 pages is a real challenge. The alternative would be a two-volume issue that might be even more difficult to handle.

Creating a PDF for reference purposes is fine. But, we all know that browsing a book on the monitor of a desktop computer is unedifying. Additionally, comparing items on distant pages is nearly impossible. The mobile momentum of printed books is inestimably valuable. That's the reason why a complete industry believes in the success of e-book–reading devices.

When the iPhone came out and we saw the first applications, it was suddenly clear that FontShop has to join that new mobile platform. One of the reasons was, of course, that selling special fonts for the iPhone might be a future business. The iPhone operating system in its current version doesn't allow the installation of third-party fonts. Nobody knows at the moment when and how that will happen.

By accident, FontShop Germany was working on its new web site at that time. One of the brand new features for it was a visual search function with the working title FontShuffle. The concept and the technical structure of that application were finished. And as an isolated application with a playful approach, it seemed to be ideal for an iPhone transfer—and so it came to be.

Although we are all confronted with printed text every day, and a lot of readers have sympathy for well-designed pages, not everybody is aware of what is happening behind the scenes of typeset words. Therefore, in this chapter, I will first dip into the terminology of typography and the art and techniques of arranging type. This will help understanding the functionality of and the skills required to develop (and use) FontShuffle.

Entering the World of Typefaces

The terms "typeface" and "font" had more clearly differentiated meanings before the advent of desktop publishing. A **typeface** usually comprises an alphabet of letters, numerals, and punctuation marks—all designed in a matching appearance by a type designer. Usually, typefaces build a family with members such as Roman, Bold, Italic, or Small Caps. Like every family, type families have names. An example of a very popular type family name is Helvetica. Helvetica is used for the iPhone operating system. Helvetica Book and Helvetica Bold are two members of that family (see Figure 9-1).

Helvetica Regular ABCdefg123
Helvetica Italic ABCdefg123&$
Helvetica Bold ABCdefg123&
Helvetica Bold Italic ABCdefg

Figure 9-1. *Four members of the typeface family Helvetica: Regular, Italic, Bold, and Bold Italic*

Understanding Fonts

To understand why a font is not a typeface, it's useful to know where the term came from. "Font" (or previously, "fount") is derived from the Middle French word *fonte*, meaning something that has been melted. In type founding, metal was melted then poured into a hand mould with a matrix to cast each individual piece of movable type.

"Font" is a word that describes a (technical) variant of a typeface: every time a specific variant of a typeface was cast at a specific size, a font was created. Therefore, a **font** is a particular casting of a typeface belonging to that type family.

In electronic publishing nothing is cast, but fonts are digitized from the design created by a type designer. Size doesn't matter anymore because digital (vectorized) fonts are scalable. For example, digital fonts are files named `helvetica_book.ttf` or `helvetica_bold.ttf` where `helvetica` indicates the name of the represented typeface family; `bold` describes the weight (i.e., member) of that family, and `.ttf` tags the digital format, in the case of Helvetica, TrueType.

Figure 9-2 shows the depictive representation (icons) of such font files and their nomenclature. The `.otf` tag stands for OpenType font.

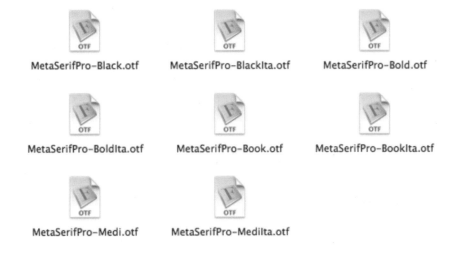

MetaSerifPro–Black.otf   MetaSerifPro–BlackIta.otf   MetaSerifPro–Bold.otf

MetaSerifPro–BoldIta.otf   MetaSerifPro–Book.otf   MetaSerifPro–BookIta.otf

MetaSerifPro–Medi.otf   MetaSerifPro–MediIta.otf

Figure 9-02. *Digital fonts on computers are managed by their operating systems (e.g., Windows Vista or Mac OS X) and contain the glyphs and the metrics of a typeface.*

Why is this stuff important? Well, compared to world peace, it's not. However, nomenclature is important because being understood is important. The term "font" is omnipresent in print and media design but often used in an inexplicit way.

NOTE: Everybody who understands the definitions of "typeface" and "font" will come to the conclusion that the name FontShuffle is not properly chosen, because the application is a typeface reference. Exactly. The reason for using this name is the name of its publisher (FontShop, which is a correct name because we are selling fonts) and the underlying technology that is provided by fonts on our servers.

Characters and Glyphs

A font stores the image (**glyph**) of each character of a typeface. This could either happen as a bitmap in a bitmap font or by mathematical description of lines and curves in an outline font, also called a vector font. Bitmap fonts are found in the operating systems of many mobile devices and in computer games. In print and publishing, vector fonts are *the* standard.

Computer systems and many applications use outline fonts too. The system's rasterizer renders the character outline to decide which pixels should be black and which ones white. Rasterization is straightforward at high resolutions, such as those used by desktop printers and in prepress publishing systems. For computer screens, where each individual pixel can mean the difference between legible and illegible characters, some digital fonts use hinting algorithms to make readable bitmaps at small sizes. Font sizes are measured either by pixel or the traditional point units.

Let's have a look into the glyph set (see Figure 9-3), which is the inventory of letters and symbols that defines a font. Besides the uppercase and lowercase characters (2×26), the figures (10), and the punctuation marks, a digital font carries at least 100 more glyphs, like accented letters, ligatures, and letter-like symbols (e.g., currency symbols).

abcdefghijklmonpqrstuvwxyz

ABCDEFGHIJKLMNOPQRSTUVWXYZ

01234567890 .,;:!?¿¡»«[(\|/)]--

ÂÁÀÃÄÅÇÉÊËÈÍÎÏÌÓÔÒÖÕØÚÛÙÜŸ

áàâäãåçéèêëíìîïñóòôöõúùûüÿ

&ßæÆœŒ$¥£ƒ€µ∂π∆∫∏∑fifl‰%

¢§•¶ªº®©™...÷±≤≥∞≠¨∆1‡★#

Figure 9-3. *Fonts contain many more characters than 26 letters. A minimum glyph set is the ACSII standard, which has 256 characters.*

Digital fonts may also contain data representing the metrics used for composition, including kerning pairs, component creation data for accented characters, and glyph substitution rules for Arabic typography and connecting script faces and for simple everyday ligatures like "fl".

Common font formats include Metafont, PostScript Type 1, TrueType, and OpenType (here, these are sorted in chronological order with OpenType being the latest and most advanced format). Applications using these font formats, including the rasterizers, appear in Windows and Macintosh operating systems, Adobe Systems products and those of several other companies. Digital fonts are created with font editors such as Fontographer, FontLab, TypeTool, or DTL FontMaster.

The Anatomy of Letters

It's not necessary for most font users to know the precise difference between a counter and an eye or a tail and a shoulder, but knowing is fun and can make you feel smart. Instead of resorting to a term such as "that curvy connector bit in the middle of the funny-looking g," you can use a real term like "the link in a double-story g." It is important to speak precisely if you have to defend a font decision you made for print or GUIs.

There is a standard set of terms to describe the geometry around letters and the parts of a letter. These metrics and parts are often referred to as **letter anatomy** or **typeface anatomy**. By breaking down letters into parts, a designer can better understand how type is created and altered and how to compare typefaces effectively.

In Figure 9-4, the most important parts of the character being discussed are labeled or circled. A few extra terms, such as baseline and x-height, are included to help understand and describe the geometry around the letterforms.

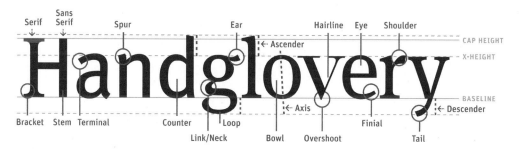

Figure 9-4. *The design components of Serif and Sans Serif letters*

The **baseline** is the invisible line on which characters sit. Every font has a baseline. Interestingly enough, it's the only property of a digital typeface that is interpreted in a common way (e. g., if you type a ten-letter word and set every letter in a different typeface, all the letters will sit on the same baseline).

All other metrics, like the x-height or the cap height, may differ from typeface to typeface. What might be hard to understand, even for people who are mathematically talented, is that there is no fixed start (zero point) in the world of typefaces; on the contrary, every typeface comes with its own coordinate system.

Luckily, the metrics are consistent within a typeface. Rounded letters, such as "e," and acute-angled letters, like "v," may extend slightly below the baseline. That is purely for optical reasons to tell our eyes that curves and pikes are sitting on the same base level as "m," "x," and "l." Without such an overshoot, they would appear to hover above the baseline.

You will find the same phenomenon at the x-height, which is the line that falls at the top of many lowercase letters and also at the curve of letters like "h" and "d." That line, which some call the meanline, is referred to as the **x-height**, because it is the height of a lowercase "x." This height can vary greatly between typefaces and is responsible for the optical size of an alphabet. The formula goes like this: the larger the x-height, the bigger the writing. For better understanding, compare it with an all capitals setting, and imagine lowercase letters as high as uppercase (i.e., maximum x-height).

The **cap height** (see Figure 9-5) is the distance from the baseline to the top of uppercase letters like "H" and "J". The cap height is a fixed distance within one font, but it might be different among the members of one type family (e.g., Regular, Bold, or Black), and it is certainly different between two typefaces because it cannot be standardized.

Helvetica FF Quadraat Futura Bauer Bodoni Franklin Gothic Gill Sans Stempel Garamond Letter Gothic FF Meta Bell Gothic

Figure 9-5. *The height of a capital letter (cap height) in digital typography is not an absolute value, meaning that the uppercase "H" of miscellaneous typecaces has differing heights.*

The reason for this deviation is that there is always an imaginary space around letters that is needed for accents, ascenders, and descenders. The amount of space that has to be reserved for that purposes depends on the design of a typeface. The total (square) area for any letter of a typeface, including the nonprinting space around it has been called em-squad since hot metal times. In metal type, the em was the height of the metal body from which the letter rises. It is comparable to the bounding box from digital type design.

The part of a lowercase letter that extends above the main body of the letter is called the **ascender**. Letters with ascenders are "b," "d," "f," "h," "k," "l," and "t." Some fonts have very long ascenders and descenders in comparison with the letter bodies, giving them an airy, elegant feel but cutting back readability. Fonts with short ascenders and descenders look more compact and sturdier. Note that the ascender might end beyond the cap height. This is very common in classical sans serif text typefaces.

A **descender** is the part of a lowercase letter that extends below the baseline. Letters with descenders are "g," "j," "p," "q," and "y." Note that this is similar as extending above the x-height.

OPTICAL SIZE AND READABILITY

Font users often wonder why some typefaces look larger than others at the same point size on their computers. Two variables are responsible for that effect:

- *The real cap height*: Although two fonts are set with the same point size, their cap heights might be different. The reason for that difference is that type designers have some degree of freedom to decide how large they define an uppercase letter within a fixed letter design area, which is called the **bounding box**.

- *The x-height*: Although some fonts have the same cap height (like in the following illustration) one might appear larger (and thus better readable) than another. The simple reason for that is the bigger x-height that results in larger lowercase letters. The illustration includes two extreme examples for the optical size of a typeface. Verdana on the one hand, made for maximum readability on computer screens, and on the other hand, the geometric Futura made in the 1930s for elegant hot metal printing. You can also see that Apple's decision in choosing Helvetica as the iPhone's system fonts was, from the point of readability, not so bad, although Helvetica is not an ideal screen font (like Lucida Grande, Verdana, or Georgia) due to its geometrical design (see also Figure 9-6).

Verdana:

Ramburgef

Ramburgef quick brown fox jumps over the lazy Duis autem vel eum iriure dolor in hendrerit in vulputate velit esse molestie consequat, vel illum dolore eu

Helvetica:

Ramburgefe

Ramburgef quick brown fox jumps over the lazy Duis autem vel eum iriure dolor in hendrerit in vulputate velit esse molestie consequat, vel illum dolore eu feugiat nulla facilisis at

Gill Sans:

Ramburgefei

Ramburgef quick brown fox jumps over the lazy Duis autem vel eum iriure dolor in hendrerit in vulputate velit esse molestie consequat, vel illum dolore eu feugiat nulla facilisis at vero

Futura:

Ramburgeferi

Ramburgef quick brown fox jumps over the lazy Duis autem vel eum iriure dolor in hendrerit in vulputate velit esse molestie consequat, vel illum dolore eu feugiat nulla facilisis at vero eros et accumsan et

Choosing the Right Typeface for Screens

Since you've already learned a lot in this chapter about the properties of typefaces and the consequences of readability, you are well prepared for a delicate question: what is the right typeface for a graphical user interface?

I'd like to answer with a fictional scenario on the iPhone. Let's assume the iPhone operating system offers a free-type world. It doesn't, and both the application UI elements and your data are rendered in Helvetica. I do not criticize Apple's decision to use Helvetica as the overall system font family, but it is less unique and harder to read than Lucida Grande on Mac, as explained in the sidebar on distinctive glyph features.

I respect Apple's decision to jump on the current type fashion trend of a neutral, static typeface. However, I would appreciate the choice of some alternative fonts in some applications like Notes or Contacts. Why Notes? Marker Felt is a nuisance—ugly, hard to read, and space wasting. I often import magazine articles that I like to carry with me into Notes. Such text is unreadable in Marker Felt. Fortunately, I found a way to display them in Helvetica.

The problem with Helvetica in Contacts is the similar letterforms. In text where we read complete words, it doesn't matter if uppercase "I" and lowercase "l" and "i" look nearly the same. But if you are browsing through international names, alphanumeric postal codes, or weird Skype and Buddy names, Helvetica is not an ideal typeface for such a purpose (see Figure 9-6).

I did some experiments in Adobe Photoshop to test alternative screen fonts for the Contacts application. After a series of alternatives, I ended up with a typeface called FF Unit that was designed by Erik Spiekermann and Christian Schwartz in 2004. FF Unit has two merits compared with Helvetica: it runs narrower (without losing legibility), which is good for long family and company names, and it has more distinguishable glyphs (see Figure 9-6).

Figure 9-6. *Compare the original Contacts typography, Helvetica (on the left) with an alternate typography with increased readability, FF Unit (on the right): FF Unit was developed with distinguishable and space-saving letter forms in mind. Note the dancing pleasent-reading semi-old-style figures.*

DISTINCTIVE GLYPH FEATURES

What makes a typeface good to read on screens? Two conditions are responsible for comfortable on-screen reading:

- *Hinting:* Although screen resolution has increased over the years, it's still a low-resolution output device, where each individual pixel can mean the difference between a proper (legible) or a destroyed (illegible) text-sized character. Because of that risk, digital fonts for screens use hinting algorithms to make readable bitmaps at small sizes.

- *Glyph design*: Typefaces that are meant for screens should be checked against the following properties:

  - Simple letter forms (e.g., Sans Serif)

  - Large counters and eyes (e.g., "d," "b," "o," and "e,")

  - Open counters (e.g., "c," "e," "C," and "G")

  - Distinctive features in homologous forms (e.g., "i," "l," and "I")

  - Tabular figures (e.g., |1|2|3|4|)

  - At least two weights with marked contrast (e.g., Regular and Bold)

The following figure shows three typefaces with increasing legibility (from left to right):

- *Helvetica*: Geometric with poor readability

- *Lucida Grande*: Open design and good readability
- *FF Unit*: Distinctive characters and perfect readability

Ilia Richter Ceocilstr. 1 123456789	Ilia Richter Ceocilstr. 1 123456789	Ilia Richter Ceocilstr. 1 123456789
Helvetica	Lucida Grande	FF Unit

Identifying Typefaces

This is not the appropriate book to dive deeply into the history of type. Much has been written about the evolution of letters: how their forms took shape, from the Roman capitals to the Carolingian minuscules, and how the Latin alphabet was used by the first printing presses of the Renaissance age.

Looking back from where we stand now, we could say that the original forms of our uppercase letters are around 2,000 years old, while those of the lowercase letters would be over 1,000 years old. In the last 500 years, neither case has changed in its basic forms. What has constantly changed are the outlines of the letters, influenced by new inventions in reproduction and by the unique spirit of each epoch. Since the invention of sans serif typefaces over a century ago, many new stylistic forms have already emerged.

Serif vs. Sans Serif

Although the classification of typefaces is a tool for experts, the digitization of visual communication has brought more people in contact with typefaces than ever before. Nearly every computer user knows some fonts of his or her operation system and likely used fonts like Helvetica, Times, Verdana, Georgia, or Comic Sans.

The most familiar classification of typefaces for text setting is dividing them into the two groups of sans serifs and serifs. **Serifs** are semistructural details on the ends of some of the strokes that make up a letter. A typeface without serifs is called **sans serif**, from the French *sans*, meaning "without." Some typography sources refer to sans-serif typefaces as Grotesque (in German *Grotesk*) or Gothic, and serif types as Roman.

Serifs are thought to have originated in the Roman alphabet with inscriptional lettering, words carved into stone in Roman antiquity. The Roman letter outlines were first brushed onto stone, after that the carvers followed the brush marks which flared at stroke ends and corners, creating serifs. Because serifs originated in inscription, they are generally not used in handwriting.

The first sans serif font appeared in 1816 in a type sample book by William Caslon. Actually, it is amazing that the simple idea of dropping the serifs at the ends of strokes didn't occur earlier. But the biggest part of the serif persistence was, of course, due to plain habit. When more examples of sans serif fonts appeared, they seemed so controversial that the first name given to them was "grotesque," and they were very rarely used except in advertising.

Some years later, bold and slender weights of this type could be found everywhere in newspaper headlines, on posters, and in brochures. The new typeface style caught on quickly and began to appear all over Europe and the United States.

The use of sans serif typefaces was limited almost exclusively to typesetting for titles and headlines. The body text remained intact, true to the classic form of roman type. This situation would endure for nearly 100 years. Not until after World War II did sans serif fonts truly revolutionize the world of text publishing.

Explosion of Type Styles

During the golden age of advertising in the second half of the 20th century, with the advent of mass magazines, TV, and photo typesetting, the variety of type styles exploded. This wave was surpassed in the 1990s when type design programs like Ikarus M, Fontstudio, and Fontographer became designers' favorite toys.

After 500 years, the expert chain of type design, type cutting, type casting, type-setting, and preparing to print was unified in one person on one single machine that fits on everybody's desktop. As a consequence, the variety of type designs for digital applications increased tremendously. Most of the new type designs are based on exiting forms or derived from geometrical constructions. Some foundries (like FontShop's FontFont label) develop contemporary designs; others (like The Font Bureau, Inc.) do beautiful revivals of former hot metal typeface families.

To most typeface users, the huge variety of typefaces is confusing. Sometimes, the question arises, "How many typefaces do we need?" The great type designer Adrian Frutiger used to answer, "How many sorts of wine do we need?" And the answer is, "There is no limit!"

Other people might ask, "Will there be an end to type design?" No, there will never be an end, like there is no end in literature and pop music. The limited number of items from which all these arts and crafts are made allow unlimited variations that always seem new to our ears and eyes.

Classification, though, provides the solution for getting rid of chaotic opulence caused by a base stock plus continuously new publications. Let's again compare type design with popular music. The annual Grammy award trophies are given in 110 categories. These categories are similar to music styles. If a music fan has a favorite style, let's say jazz, the options to shop in music stores or to select a radio station decrease dramatically. Suddenly, a confusingly vast medium gets simple for everyone. The same is true with typefaces.

Classification of Typefaces

Several classification systems may give us support in grouping the large number of typefaces available. Obviously, each of them will not be discussed within this book. Rather, we will look at a system that includes the groups most commonly mentioned in classification systems.

In the recent years, design universities and typographers have followed two approaches in type classification:

- Historical developments
- Formal principles

The first approach is comparable to art history and worked fine for centuries, when type design developed continuously and was the job of specialized experts.

A first historical type classification scheme suggested in 1954 by the French typographer Maximilien Vox offers 11 categories:

- Humanist
- Garald
- Transitional
- Didone
- Mechanistic
- Lineal
    - Grotesque
    - Neogrotesque
    - Geometric
    - Humanist
- Glyphic
- Script
- Graphic
- Black letter
- Non-Latin

The "Vox-System" was adopted in 1962 by the Association Typographique Internationale (ATypI) and in 1967 as British Standards Classification of Typefaces. Three years before, the German Standard Association DIN (*Deutsches Institut für Normung*) developed a similar system called DIN 16518.

The disadvantage of all these models is that they work fine for scientists but are laborious in everyday use. With the advent of desktop publishing, a lot of type users joined the revolution from adjacent disciplines like architecture, marketing, and journalism. Suddenly, a new generation of students had to deal with a lot of fresh software and hardware challenges that moved the focus of interests from history to the present.

Around 2001, the German design teacher and typographer Hans Peter Willberg published a small booklet called "Type Signpost" (*Wegweiser Schrift*) in which he suggested a new visual way to sort typefaces without any historic reference. His two basic elements are form and style.

Forms are as follows:

- Serif
- Sans serif
- Slab serif
- Script
- Black letter

Every form is supported by the following styles:

- Dynamic
- Static
- Geometric
- Decorative

This simple matrix is an easy-to-use method not only for understanding the world of type but also for finding and mixing appropriate type styles for a project.

FontShuffle uses a mixture of both classification systems.

Exploring FontBook and FontShuffle

The subject of type classification is not new to FontShop, the publisher of FontShuffle. Since its start as an independent font mail order house in 1989, the FontShop network has had to deal with a large number of multifaceted fonts from various type libraries. In the beginning of our business, these fonts were simply ordered alphabetically in catalogs, according to their family name. Such a system of sorting was sufficient for experienced professionals.

During the first half of the 1990s, when thousands of career changers entered desktop publishing, an alphabetical reference book spaced out long-time type lovers and new talent, who did not know hundreds of typeface by their names. For that reason, we started *FontBook* (see Figure 9-7), not to be confused with the font management component called Font Book that came out with Mac OS X 10.3.

Figure 9-7. *In 1993, the first edition of FontBook profiled 8,000 typefaces in alphabetical order, each marked with a classification number from 1 through 9.*

The first *FontBook* was published in 1993, had 600 pages, and was accompanied with a separate 60-page "StyleFinder" brochure. It referenced over 8,000 fonts (including Eastern European and non-Roman letterforms) and 15,000 symbols and ornaments from 30 international type developers.

All Latin fonts were sorted in alphabetical order, making 26 chapters from "A" to "Z." Alphabet displays and text patches for all weights and families, together with comprehensive historical and technical data, made the *FontBook* indispensable for anyone working with type. Each typeface family was marked with a classification number between 1 and 9, representing the styles sans serif, serif, slab serif, script, graphic, display, black letter, symbol, and ornaments and non-Latin or special accents. If any user wanted to search by style, the separate "StyleFinder" was the perfect tool, delivering all fonts sorted with the nine classifications.

Two years later, the amount of new fonts had increased greatly, so that FontShop decided to publish a second volume of *FontBook* in spring 1995. It was also delivered with a separate "StyleFinder" brochure that showed all of the typefaces (over 10,000) of both volumes alphabetically in one-line listings according to seven different style categories, plus pi and symbol. Because the "StyleFinder" showed in which of the two books a particular font could be found, it served as the central search engine.

The "StyleFinder" from 1995 (see Figure 9-8) shows on its cover exactly the same basic type style categories of today's "StyleFinder." In the following years, that rough classification has continued unchanged through the recent fourth edition of *FontBook*, published in August 2006.

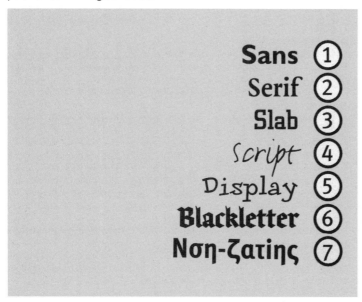

Figure 9-8. *This clipping of the "StyleFinder" cover from 1995 shows the first appearance of the FontShuffle categories.*

FontShop's Typeface Categorization

During its 20 years of existence, FontShop never thought about a second level of classification for its customers, (i.e., subdividing the sans serif section into Humanist, Static, Geometric, Gothic, and so on). In print, such a detailed offer might cause problems. For example, not every type friend knows that the serif-family Jenson is Venetian styled and not French or baroque, so readers might require three or more searches before finding this typeface specimen.

Browsing through categories on a digital platform is far faster. Plus, if you don't have any clue what a typeface named Ergo looks like, you can start a text search.

When FontShop Germany developed the concept for its new web site, one of its programmers, Rainer Pleyer, had the idea to offer a visual search for fonts in addition to the font name search. He scribbled a basic structure and named it FontShuffle, because it was constructed like a game. Then, it was my turn to realize that feature.

Naturally, my starting point was *FontBook's* structure, or rather the original "StyleFinder" structure just slightly modified: sans serif, serif, slab serif, script, black letter, and display.

At that point, I thought about the correct naming for the categories and the subcategories since using just "category" is too general: "category" is the generic term for words like species, order, class, or kingdom. Because the term "family" is well established in the world of typefaces, I just took a closer look into biology and borrowed its nomenclature. For example, Helvetica Italic's classification follows:

- *Class*: Sans Serif
- *Order*: Static
- *Family*: Helvetica
- *Genus*: Italics

After the nomenclature was settled, I concentrated on the orders, since the classes are well defined. I'll cover orders in the next section.

Although I am not interested in doing so, the biological model is expandable upward and downward. The species might be the weight of some Helvetica Italic (e.g., Helvetica Italic Bold), and the phylum of a Helvetica might be the Roman letter space, belonging to the kingdom of phonographic scripts, and so on.

Maybe it is because I'm a physicist that I decided to give each of the six FontShuffle classes exactly six orders: I love simple and symmetrical models. I did tried using nine orders, but that was far too fine.

Classes and Orders of Typefaces

The FontShuffle orders are a mixture between the historical model and Willberg's form-style matrix, in which form equals class and style equals order. For the huge class of Serif typefaces, I decided to stay primarily with the historical classification, partly because of the roots of these typefaces' designs and partly because of their stable design principles that outlast decades or centuries.

For the younger classes, like sans or slab serif, I've chosen mainly the style order. The script class carries attributes, like handwritten or simple, that only work in that class. Black letter is a special case with less elbow room not only in usage but also in classification: I left it with the traditional naming.

The display section is a very special thing: it's a catalog of its own, with some order names that are actually used for classes (sans, serif, slab, and script) as well as two style orders (decorative and experimental). What is a display typeface? It is more or less a lettering design, made for advertisements, posters, headlines, initials, catch lines, and so on. One half of the display typefaces are single weights, and the other half is organized as families, like text typefaces usually are.

The treatment of the display typefaces is the result of 15 years of FontBook experience, seeing the display section increasing from edition to edition. That area is growing disproportionally, because a lot of young type designers are producing typefaces entirely using the display approach.

The FontShuffle classes and orders since version 1.1 are shown in Figure 9-9.

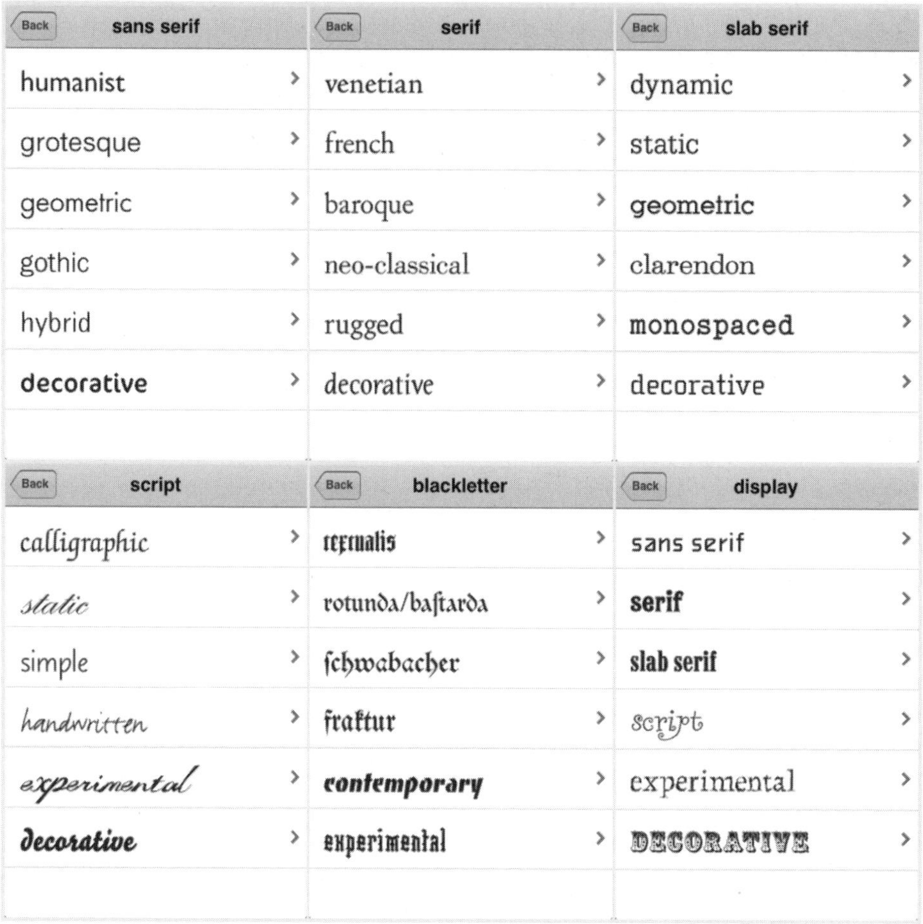

Back sans serif		Back serif		Back slab serif	
humanist	>	venetian	>	dynamic	>
grotesque	>	french	>	static	>
geometric	>	baroque	>	geometric	>
gothic	>	neo-classical	>	clarendon	>
hybrid	>	rugged	>	monospaced	>
decorative	>	decorative	>	decorative	>

Back script		Back blackletter		Back display	
calligraphic	>	textualis	>	sans serif	>
static	>	rotunda/baſtarda	>	serif	>
simple	>	ſchwabacher	>	slab serif	>
handwritten	>	fraktur	>	script	>
experimental	>	contemporary	>	experimental	>
decorative	>	experimental	>	DECORATIVE	>

Figure 9-9. *FontShuffle structures the world of type into six classes, each with six orders*

FontShuffle Step by Step

FontShuffle is an intuitive travel guide through the world of typefaces, developed for iPhone and iPod Touch. Although the application is aimed at beginners, professional users will also love its simplicity. The program opens the empire of type via a hierarchical system, arranging typefaces by similarity.

With just two fingertips, any user is able to head for a type design visually, without any previous knowledge: you don't need to know the name or style of any desired font, but you will learn names and styles as you use FontShuffle.

Getting Started: Search Level 1

The starting screen of FontShuffle serves as search level 1 (see Figure 9-10). It offers the following six common typographic classes: sans serif, serif, slab serif, script, blackletter, and display. The name of each class is set in an appropriate typeface to give visual support.

Figure 9-10. *Direct doorway to the world of typefaces: FontShuffle's start screen*

Choosing the right typeface for this display is typographically delicate. At one extreme, the terms should speak for themselves, meaning they should appear equally balanced. Presenting them in different typefaces causes noise—in positive words, typographic staging will give these equal weighted search terms different impressions in the users' eyes. The solution for this problem is finding a typeface superfamily that covers almost all type design styles. Surprisingly, only one typeface that complies with that condition: Lucida.

Lucida is an extended set of related typefaces designed by Charles Bigelow and Kris Holmes (B&H) between 1983 and 1994, and it includes a variety of styles: serif and sans serif, Roman and italic, normal and bold weights, scripts, black letter, icons, and symbols. This extra-large family of type styles is often called a superfamily, or clan, because it extends beyond the usual font family that contains just Roman, italic, normal and bold. Because of the richness and variety of its different styles, Lucida allows new forms of typography for electronic communication, printing, and publishing.

Between all the different Lucida styles, the capital heights, x-heights, and main stem weights are coordinated. Lucida makes it easy for users to achieve variety and harmony by mixing and matching different fonts in the same text and page. The designed coordination of so many different styles means that, when different Lucida fonts are used together, the effect is lively and interesting but without the confusion of randomly mingled and uncoordinated fonts.

> **NOTE:** Lucida Sans Demibold (which has identical outlines to Lucida Grande Bold but with tighter kerning on numerals) is used in Apple's Mac OS X operating system, as well as many programs, including Front Row. A fact not widely recognized is that the icons, symbols, arrows, asterisks, and geometric glyphs in Microsoft's Wingdings fonts were originally designed as Lucida icons, arrows, and stars, so the characters harmonize with Lucida Sans and Lucida Bright designs. Those three Lucida symbol fonts were purchased by Microsoft, who remapped the keyboard layouts and changed the names to Wingdings, but the symbols still harmonize with Lucida fonts.

Finally, the directory of FontShuffle is set in Lucida Sans, Lucida Serif, Lucida Typewriter, Lucida Handwriting, and Lucida Blackletter. Only the last category, Display, could not be served by Lucida, because no typical display version is available (i.e., a version with shadows, flourishes, or other decoration). We've chosen FF Bokka Shadow instead. It embodies perfectly the sixth class representing decorative headline fonts.

Searching by Typeface Name: Search Level 1, version 1.1

When FontShuffle 1.0 came out in December 2008, it was loved from the first minute by professional typographers. However, what they missed became request number one in our update feature list: a typeface name search. We've included that in version 1.1 directly at the top of the opening screen. The search is equipped with an automatic suggestion feature. So if you are not sure where to find Oranda, Letter Gothic, or Serifa, just type the first letters, and FontShuffle will present possible search results you can jump to directly (see Figure 9-11).

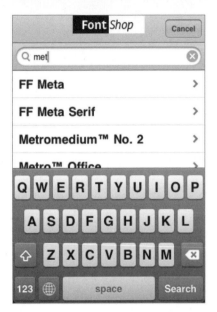

Figure 9-11. *Additional automatic suggestion font name search added in FontShuffle version 1.1*

Displaying Classes: Search Level 2

The second level of FontShuffle is six rooms (i.e., classes) each filled with six orders; that means 36 (6 × 6) stylistic pigeonholes, as discussed earlier. Thus, the application offers a finer classification than any known type specimen books or catalogs, including FontBook, which offers alphabetical sorting within its six classes.

FontShuffle, therefore, combines the historical classification with the much simpler formal Willberg classification. Some classes offer a mixture of both (e.g., serif), and others deal with pure formal features (e.g., sans serif).

As in search level 1, each of the six orders is set in an adequate typeface (see Figure 9-12). But while the classes-entry screen endeavors to keep the typographic exuberance modest, the orders screens strive for maximum differentiation. As a matter of fact, the typography dominates the wording all over level 2—that's the basic principle of a visual typographic search.

Figure 9-12. *The typeface orders (e. g., sans serif) are set in their adequate typeface styles.*

Displaying Families: Search Level 3

When you arrive at level 3, after two taps, you're at the final straight: the font family plane. And you're close to a desired type design. Six closely related typefaces are presented with the same sample word: Hamburgefontis (see Figure 9-13).

What is the significance of that term? First, it's an isogram, a word without a repeating letter. Second, this test word contains most of the various shapes and strokes found in a typeface (e.g., cap height, ascender, and descender). When designing your own fonts, it is often recommended that you begin your work by creating the characters that spell out Hamburgefontis. By concentrating on designing and fine-tuning these characters first, the bits and pieces can then be applied to most of the other characters in the font. When submitting new designs or design ideas to a type foundry for consideration, designers often submit (or are asked to submit) the test word Hamburgefontis set in both mixed case and all caps as a printout or PDF or as a digital font. If you try to protect your type design, some patent offices request that sample in Word too.

Figure 9-13. *The font family plane uses the common typeface sample word "Hamburgefont."*

It is essential for level 3 to deal with a uniform sample word for all typefaces. An alternative would be to present each typeface with its name. In that case, fonts with short names (e.g., Meta) won't have much chance to express their characteristics. Then too, the differences between the remaining fonts are very small after two filtering processes. Dealing with a uniform specimen word helps the user's eye to focus completely on the design attributes of each typeface. The name of each typeface (family) stands below the sample word in a decent gray for reference.

If none of the presented six fonts meet the user's needs, it is time to shuffle by pushing the red Shuffle button or just shaking the iPhone or iPod Touch. Both operations have the same result: fonts that haven't been shown until now will be thrown among a new search result sextet. Now, the user can compare and judge from a new mixture of similar typefaces.

FontShuffle 1.0 offered a selection of exactly 12 different variants for every class in level 3. This selection could be extended without distributing a new version of FontShuffle. That happened for the first time in January 2009, when FontShop added another 200 fonts to the basic 432 ($6 \times 6 \times 12$).

The basis for such remote controlled additions is FontShuffle's clever organization.

The "Hamburgefontis" sample words are generated on a FontShop server as PNG images and delivered into FontShuffle's cache when it starts the first time and connects with the server via Wi-Fi or G3. No fonts will be transferred to or installed on the iPhone or iPod Touch, just images. After that initial query, the application works up to level 3 without being connected to the Internet.

This infrastructure allows secret updates (e.g., expanding the typeface catalog). Adding new fonts to the FontShuffle directory is simple. We put them onto the FontShop server and add the corresponding "Hamburgefontis" to the inventory. When FontShuffle queries the server the next time it asks for updates, any new font sample words will be downloaded.

Shuffle or List View: Search Level 3, version 1.1

Soon after the premiere of FontShuffle, some users expressed the request for an alternative to the display that gave the application its name: the shuffle mode. Type friends do not want to play around but want to get the full view, especially when they are experienced or under time pressure. For that reason, FontShuffle 1.1 offers a more professional list mode in parallel to the playful shuffle mode. Users decide, via a toggle button, which mode they prefer (see Figure 9-14).

Additionally, the list mode allows users to mark up to five favorite fonts. After switching back to the shuffle mode, these marked typefaces will be fixed. That way, it is possible to research other alternatives without losing sight of two or three bookmarked favorites.

Also new in version 1.1: "Hamburgefontis" changed to "Ramburgefonstiv" (see Figure 9-14). Why? Well, let's analyze the changes step by step. First, the new test word has one more glyph; 15 glyphs instead of 14 means (at least mathematically) 7 percent more information.

The "H" is very important for type designers, because it is always the exact caps height of a font, and caps height is a basic metric—often not just for a single font but for a complete family. The "R" does not deliver a 100 percent exact cap height, because for optical reasons, its upper loop has an overshoot beyond the caps height. But for the evaluation of a type design, it is more valuable because it carries more design information than the "H or "E," (e.g., curves, a counter, contrast, an angle, and a connection).

The additional letter "v" contains hints on the treatment of acute angles like in "w," "x," "z," and "V." Finally, the letter quartet "stiv" is composed of the two pairs "st" and "iv," which are very common in the everyday writing in English and many additional languages.

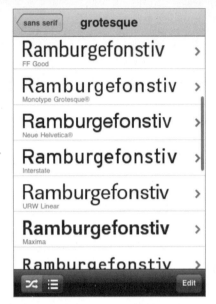 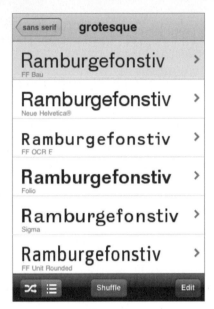

Figure 9-14. *New since FontShuffle 1.1: toggle between list and shuffle mode*

Displaying the Font: Search Level 4

With level 4, we've reached the terminus. It opens after your third tap, or maybe after a session of passionate shuffling or back and forth browsing. Now, it's time to choose a typeface. As a default, the well-known sample sentence "The quick brown fox jumps over the lazy dog" appears. That text is editable or expandable up to 100 glyphs. After a tap, the standard keyboard appears for typing, or deleting, sample text.

> **NOTE**: While levels 1 through 3 are available without any Internet connection, level 4 definitely needs a Wi-Fi or 3G connection for the dialog with FontShop's font server. The customized specimens are generated in real time on FontShop's server after the *Done* button has been tapped, and an image is sent to the iPhone—not font data. That image could be then stored in the camera roll or sent via e-mail.

Any customized sample text will be stored in FontShuffle until you next change the text. If you want to go back to the default text, just click the Reset button on the keyboard interface, which is shown in Figure 9-15, left.

Figure 9-15. *Individual font samples can be mailed or "printed" (that is, stored in the camera roll)*

You can type sample text with a maximum of 100 letters. Tap *Done* to request the font sample from the FontShop servers. If a type specimen becomes important to a user or project, you might want to keep it. That's no problem: just tap the camera icon at the bottom of the sample page (see Figure 9-15, right) to send the current type sample as an image into the iPhone's camera roll, and it will be stored to your desktop computer with your next synchronization. Or sent it immediately via e-mail to your computer or a friend.

A somewhat hidden feature appears when the iPhone or iPod Touch is turned to landscape position: the character set of the currently selected typeface appears on four lines (see Figure 9-16).

Figure 9-16. *A wide-screen character set appears when you topple the iPhone*

Summary

FontShuffle is a multipurpose tool for type enthusiasts. First, it unfolds the world of typefaces across a hierarchical simple-to-understand classification system. Alternatively, it offers a font name search. Also, it allows exploring a desired font with individual sample texts up to 100 characters. Such a typeface sample could be stored into the iPhone's camera roll or mailed to friends and clients.

Eddie Wilson

Company: *Eddit Incorporated*

Location: *Midlothian, Virginia*

Former Life As a Developer: *I provide UI design for web, desktop and mobile applications. I also teach web design at Virginia Commonwealth University. Top 5 pieces of software: Photoshop, Illustrator, LiveView, Textmate, and Safari.*

Life as an iPhone Developer:

Snow Reports

- *Category: Sports*
- *Provided: Design, development*
- *URL: http://bit.ly/snow_reports*

Streaks

- *Category: Productivity*
- *Provided: Design*
- *URL: http://bit.ly/streaksmi*

What's in This Chapter:

Snow Reports for the iPhone

- *Why Design for the iPhone?*
- *Programming? That's for Programmers*
- *My Process*
- *Details of the UI*

- *Coming from a Web Design Background*
- *Icon Design*

Key Technologies:

- *Standard and Custom UI objects*
- *Project Planning*
- *Moving from web to mobile design*

Chapter 10

Snow Reports for the iPhone

Surfing has been a passion of mine since my first successful ride. It's one of the rare things in life where I can forget everything else and just enjoy the moment. I skipped my ten-year high school reunion because it landed on the weekend of a surf trip. I spend almost half the year going on four-day surf trips every other week. My accomplice on these trips is a longtime friend who got me into the sport. Since we go so often, we like to keep it simple, and cheap. It's a three-hour drive to the coast, at which point we set up at a state-run campground for $20 a night. We each have a tent, small bag for clothes, our boards, and a cooler. These may sound like the bare essentials, but it's still a lot to put into the back of an SUV, so we're always looking for ways to lighten the load.

We have our favorite breaks, but we're usually chasing the waves wherever they are that day. The only problem is that it's tough to drive around looking for the perfect conditions; before you know it, lunchtime rolls around, and you haven't even touched the water. We would start the morning out by calling the local surf report to see where the waves were hiding. As the day went on, more calls were made to local surf shops, friends, and so forth. Everyone always had a hunch that waves were better down the road. The pursuit of the perfect day ensued.

Fast-forward a few years; true mobile access to the Internet became a reality. I picked up an iPhone and *voilà*! I was able to see all the surf report data I wanted via Surfline.com. It was great, but it still took a little longer than I thought it should to click, load, click, load, check this spot; and click, load, click, load, check that spot. If only I had an application on the iPhone, like the Weather application; I could have a list of tracked spots and just pick the best one—problem solved. And the application would be on my phone, which went great with the whole living-out-of-a-truck-for-four-days thing.

Three months later, I released my first iPhone application, Snow Reports, which allows you to create a personalized report from all of your favorite ski resorts, worldwide—wait a second. I don't ski or snowboard. How did that happen?

So You Like to Design, Huh?

Did I mention that I am a designer? It's my other passion, and sometimes, the two collide ("The deadline is Monday? Ugh. I'll be out of town on 'business' for a few days, so . . ."). Add on top of that the fact that I am now happily married and the father of two wonderful daughters, and you can see exactly how much spare time I have to develop iPhone applications.

Anyway, I am what many would call a graphic designer. To be more specific, I'm an interactive designer, which means I focus my talents in the realm of web and desktop application UI design. I have the good fortune of being able to work out of my home, under my company eddit, inc. It's just me, my home-office, and my clients. I love what I do, but there's just one tiny catch; I've always been a service provider for others. A client comes a knocking; we form a working relationship, and many projects ensue. It's wonderful to help someone else in leveraging design for their organization, but the work I do is always for others. I needed to develop a product—something that was 100 percent my own creation.

Why Design for the iPhone?

I knew I wanted to design for the iPhone the second Steve Jobs held it up at Macworld in 2007. I didn't even know if you could develop applications, but the rumor mills were buzzing with the potential. As you well know, the iPhone is a revolutionary device, driven by a revolutionary platform. Regardless of all the upcoming devices that claim to have nicer features, they all must pay homage to the iPhone for inventing the market and the concepts that these upcoming devices are based on. So far, none of them do it better, as a total package, than the iPhone, if you ask me.

Before the iPhone, I didn't think much of mobile design or devices. I've had clients that needed portions of their websites to be mobile-friendly, but I always considered it an extension or port of their standard web site. I didn't know anything about applications for the Blackberry and was altogether turned off by the design of most smart phones previous to recent models. My own phone was a candy bar Sony Ericsson that I was not willing to give up. For me, a cell phone was a phone, and that was that. I didn't want it pretending to be an e-mail client, trying to connect to a useless WAP weather service, or taking pictures that I will never use because they are all 320×240.

So what exactly was it that sold me on the iPhone? It all comes down to the fact that it's a device that runs a mobile platform allowing it to make phone calls, check e-mail, browse the Web, and more. It is not a cell phone with these features implemented on top. This shift in model allows the iPhone to integrate almost perfectly with its desktop equivalent and become a true mobile platform for development. And if you're going to have developers, you will definitely need designers!

The iPhone was also a completely new medium, and at the time, I was itching for something to explore. The following summer, I stumbled on my first idea, so all I needed to do was knock it out, right?

NOTE: In any situation like mine, there are always small, random circumstances that propel things along. When the iPhone was announced, I could not conceive of paying $500 for it, and the drop to $400 a few months later didn't make me any more comfortable. A week after Macworld 08, the day that I was purchasing an updated Macbook Pro, a good friend happened to spot a post about AT&T selling refurbished iPhones for $250. Since I was already spending a few grand, I felt like it should just be an Apple day and picked up one.

Isn't Programming for Programmers?

I am not a programmer. Please read that sentence again, and hopefully, you will find some comfort in it. I enjoy programming but would never give myself that title, as my mind is just not able to grasp concepts at the level that a professional programmer must. I'd like to think I'm a smart person, and I understand the basics, but when a discussion about programming starts up (yes, I hang out with programmers), I quickly become an observer and not a participant. Still, over the course of my career as a freelancer, I have had to wear many hats, and the programmer hat is one of them.

For my web projects, I've become very fluent in standards-based markup (that is, learning XHMTL and CSS and leveraging JavaScript libraries). In addition to this, when needed, I've built low-level CMS features into client projects (by learning PHP and MySQL and working in the server environment—yuck). For my clients that have promotional-oriented projects, I use Flash to provide a robust interactive experience (which means learning Flash ActionScript). All in all, it has made me a well rounded contractor and brings me to one of my key principles:

All professional designers must know a bit about programming for the environments that they design for.

In my opinion, this is a requirement if you want to design for the Web, desktop, or mobile devices. Knowing the capabilities and limitations of the environment I am working in enhances my design work. I can foresee, to some extent, how a programmer will work with my designs to implement them effectively. During the implementation process, I am able to talk to the programmers and understand and diagnose issues they run into. Much of what we consider "design" lies in programming the flow and interactions of a web site or application. As an interactive designer, my job truly begins when I finish a Photoshop document. This is never truer than when designing for the iPhone.

Exactly how comfortable am I with the concepts of programming? Before I developed Snow Reports, I knew a lot about variables, loops, functions, and `if` statements. I knew nothing about objects, classes, controllers, views, threads, or anything else in between. Memory management? You might have well just asked me how to walk to the moon, as all of this was well above my head, and it looked like I needed to know a lot about all of it to make this application a reality. So why even bother?

Why Snow Reports?

As I mentioned before, my initial idea was to develop a surf-reporting application. I wanted to launch it quickly, as I figure it was only a matter of time before another group developed one. As Harry Callahan said, "A man's got to know his limitations." So I decided to present the idea to a good friend and associate of mine who was a talented programmer. He loved it, was quick to start picking up the environment, and had a great idea: I love to surf, and he loves to go snowboarding, so let's make two applications, hence the birth of Surf Reports and Snow Reports.

That day, we documented both applications—what we wanted to achieve, ideas for future updates—and split up responsibilities between the two of us. While my partner was getting himself familiar with Xcode and Objective-C, I started looking into potential data providers. For Surf Reports, I wanted data from Surfline.com, and after some research, we decided to go with OnTheSnow.com (see Figure 10-1) for Snow Reports.

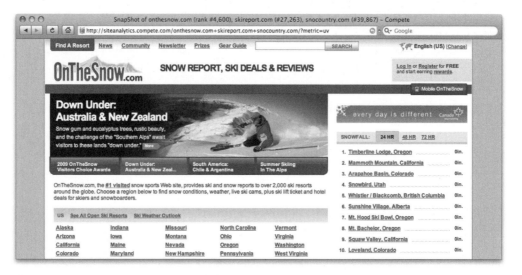

Figure 10-1. *OnTheSnow.com, the data provider for Snow Reports*

We didn't want to invest any money, so we agreed to offer complete branding of each application under the name of the data provider in return for access to their data and 100 percent of the sales revenue. We needed an angle that made this look like a win-win for both sides.

Our pitch to the data providers was that sales profits would never amount to much more than the costs for these companies to develop the applications themselves (in most cases, costs far exceed potential profits). They would have to hire designers, programmers, and assign project managers, in addition to promoting and supporting the final application. If they worked with us, they would enter the iPhone market with zero costs. We could just hear their responses, "You want to develop an iPhone application that uses our data, put our logo on it, and as far as the public knows it's ours? For free? Where do I sign?"

Sounds like a win-win, doesn't it? I proceeded to e-mail, call, e-mail, and call until I got the address or number of a decision maker for each of these companies. Shortly thereafter, three events changed the course of my initial application idea:

- OnTheSnow.com was very interested in our proposal and wanted to get started right away.

- Surfline.com was not interested. I discovered why a few months later when they released Surf Report in partnership with Oakley—talk about brand recognition.

- My programming partner had a day job, and right about the time we were getting started, he landed a nice promotion. While I was happy for him, it meant that he would have to pull out of our side project.

Why Learn iPhone Programming?

I was sitting in my office, a little on edge, looking at the situation:

In my favor, I had these things:

- What I thought was a pretty good application idea

- A signed usage agreement from OnTheSnow.com for their data and brand

- Complete flowcharts, architecture, and UI designs for the application

- Total personal investment to see this through to the end

But theses were the problems:

- No programmer

- Complete panic

Still, I wanted to design for this platform, so I needed to roll up my sleeves and learn Objective-C. It was definitely the steepest slope I have ever tried to climb. I enjoy a challenge, but most challenges push your talents and skills to their limits and beyond. This one required learning a whole new set of skills just to get in the door.

Altogether, version 1.0 took me a month to get out the door. That may sound quick, but during that time, there was an abundant amount of frustration, endless Googling, extreme lack of sleep, a growing pile of delayed client work, and a wonderful wife who was growing more and more curious and irritated about what her husband seemed so intent on learning to do. A little later in the chapter, I'll point out some great techniques I learned to climb the steep learning curve, but first I'd like to walk through my process from initial idea to submission to the App Store. Without a solid submission process, that month could have turned into three months, and Snow Reports might not have made it out the door.

My Design Process

As you may or may not already know, designing an interactive project (like an iPhone application) is much more about what your application achieves and how it behaves than how it looks. To manage these layers of complexity, a solid design process is necessary to carry you through all of the steps. The process I work with not only keeps me organized and on track, it protects me from making mistakes that won't get noticed until further down the line, resulting it a lot of wasted work.

> **TIP**: Looks are not what matters, as much as I hate to admit that sometimes. Have you ever thought to yourself, "Man this web site is impossible to use but it looks so sweet, so I'll keep using it"? I didn't think so, but you may have found yourself thinking, "This web site is really great to use; I just wish they would make it a look a little better." Spend your time worrying about how your application behaves rather than the way it looks. Ease-of-use is paramount over visual appeal. It may not win you a design award, but it will result in happy users, and you can always hire a designer to skin your application later.

The basic steps in my iPhone development process are to define the project (goals, requirements, budget, timeline), acquire third-party resources, create a flowchart for the applications's main functionality, wireframe each view, skin the design, develop and program the application, and finally, test, test, test and deploy.

Defining the Project

I always start a project, whether for a client or myself, in a text document: Pages, Word, TextEdit whatever you like. Even projects I do internally are treated as professional projects. I call the document the Project Planner, and it contains the following:

Project name: Write down the name of the application. If I don't have a name yet, I'll write some keywords here and later on maybe they will inspire me.

- Snow Reports

Project definition: Write one sentence that explains exactly what the application does. Why only one sentence? If someone walked up to me on the street and asked, "I heard you have an iPhone application for sale, what is it?" this would be my answer.

- Snow Reports gives you the ability to create a personalized report of all your favorite ski resorts worldwide.

Project goals and features: Forgive me for being bossy but set goals, goals, goals. You must define your goals. Goals give you a foundation for the structure and features of your application. Without a good list of goals, you can end up with an application that has no clear purpose and no defining qualities. A list of goals also gives you boundaries that put a stop to feature creep, the natural ability for any project to grow out of control with new features and changes that prevent it from ever seeing the light of day.

- Provide users with snow report data from OnTheSnow.com.

- Allow users to create a list of ski resorts they wish to track.

- Each report will provide resort and conditions data

- Each report will allow the user to further access information about the weather for that resort and any available resort images and cameras.

- Each report will also allow the user to call the resort and visit the resort's web site.

I know telling you to choose application features seems obvious, just like saying that every business needs a business plan is obvious. So make sure you do it! Making the plan ahead of time doesn't mean you can't change it later on, but at least it's all in a document that can be easily referenced. Keeping something in your head is the same thing as keeping it in flux. If you write it down, it's out of your head, and you can move onto the next step (basic premise of the GTD philosophy). Once these goals are achieved in your application, you're done (at least with a beta version)! Sorry about the rant; I'm done now.

The goals I had for Snow Reports are pretty simple. You might find yourself going to a second next page in your document with all the goals and features you want to cram into your application. If this is the case, you need to put them in order of importance. Once you have them all down and sorted, *cut the list in half*. Save any features that are not 100 percent necessary to achieving your application's key goals for a list for version 1.1. All of your thoughts up to this point are just guesses at what potential users might want, so your 1.0 release should be as skinny as possible without being limited. As people use your application, you will start to get e-mails that start with "Love your application, but would be better if I could…" or "would be a five-star app if it had an XYZ feature." Once you've gotten plenty of feedback, you can compare user requests with those features you put off and see what is worth implementing. This process of delaying some implementation details does a few things: version 1.0 of your application will be easier to develop and launch, you're able to make decisions based on user feedback not guesswork, and you'll have plenty of updates to push out in the future. Updates let users know that the lights are on and someone is home and working to make the application better, which is always a good thing.

Third-party resources: I list out all the third-party resources I'll need to complete the application. These are skills or assets that I cannot create or provide myself but that I need to beg, bribe, or (god forbid) pay to acquire:

- Draft a data usage agreement, and have OnTheSnow.com sign it.

- Acquire a vector version of the OnTheSnow.com logo and brand guidelines.

- Get documentation on working with their API.

Acquiring Third-Party Resources

Once everything was documented for Snow Reports, I needed to make sure that I had a signed data usage agreement from OnTheSnow.com. I can only imagine the state of insanity that would occur if I were halfway through development only to find that the folks at OnTheSnow.com had changed their minds before signing. Likewise, I recommend that you identify and acquire your third-party resources up front.

Do you need data for your application? You will need to find a data provider, contact that company, and negotiate to gain access to its data. Do you need to purchase or have sound effects created? Do you need to purchase any stock icons or graphics? List all of these requirements, *especially* if they have costs attached to them. Three sound effects might be cheap, but if you need fifty of them for a game, the costs can quickly add up. It's no use worrying over the development of an application if you can't get the data or the media it needs to function.

Finding a Good Data Provider

While I can't speak much about sound effects, I do know a little about finding a good data provider. In choosing a provider, you can look at statistics, or you can put your ear to the ground by talking to people who actually use the data providers. For statistics, I prefer to use `http://compete.com/` (a close second is `http://trends.google.com`). Compete.com's data may not be detailed (see Figure 10-2), but it's free, and when comparing one site to the other, it's perfect for gauging general popularity.

Still, numbers of visits don't tell the whole tale, so it's important to get on some forums or chat rooms and get the feel from the community. A popular site may have all the traffic today, but the community might be onto a new and better data provider that just recently launched. After talking to friends who ski and snowboard, checking forums and looking at statistics, I found that OnTheSnow.com was the most popular site for ski reports.

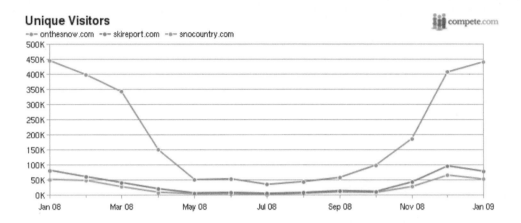

Figure 10-2. *OnTheSnow.com is the clear winner when it comes to monthly traffic, according to Compete.com.*

As I mentioned before, I proceeded to e-mail and call nonstop until I found a contact at the parent company of OnTheSnow.com, Mountain News. After I explained the concept to him, he was very interested in it, so I drafted up a quick data usage agreement. He ran it by his team, and I had a signed agreement a few days later. Now, it was time for the real fun to begin!

> Tip Remember that companies are run by people, and people always want to be part of a win-win situation. I was able to launch a great application, and OnTheSnow.com got its brand into a new market with zero costs. Just because you're 25 and don't have five zeroes at the end of your salary doesn't mean that your idea isn't good or that large companies won't want to hear it. Just make sure you protect your ideas!

Creating a Flowchart

I needed to lay out the process, or flow, for how people would interact with my application. What is the first view a user will see? Should all of the information appear on one view, or should a teaser list lead to an expanded view? What happens when a user clicks the *Info* button? Will it be a subview, or will the entire screen animate to a new view altogether? All of these questions are answered by flowcharts. A flowchart is a great, quick way to decide how an application will behave moving from state to state. I like to use Illustrator to create these charts, but any type of design or layout software will work, even doing them on paper.

To create the flowchart, start with the home screen, as shown in Figure 10-3.

Home

Figure 10-3. *The home screen is the starting point for the application design flowchart.*

Next, branch out. Each one of these branches is an action that a user can take that will lead to a new view within Snow Reports. This keeps going on and on until you have a completed flowchart, like the one shown in Figure 10-4.

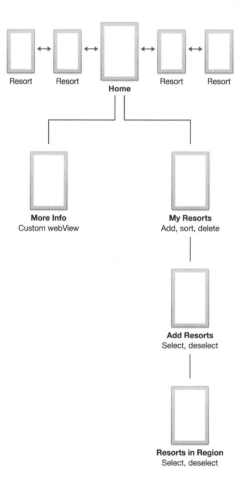

Figure 10-4. *The completed flowchart for Snow Reports*

Now, I don't get into much detail on these charts. I just want to know the views I'll need and to have them linked up. This way, I can make major decisions, like the hierarchy of views, without having to move sixty Photoshop layers around.

> **TIP:** As you may have guessed, I found a lot of help simply by looking at the native Weather application. In fact, that application was part of the inspiration for mine. Since it's a pattern that most people are used to, why reinvent the wheel?

Creating Wireframes

Next, I needed to take a closer look at each one of the views in my flowchart and design some wireframes. Wireframes provide the layout of all the objects within a view, without having to deal with the specifics of stylization, much like blueprints for a home.

I always like to start my wireframes in a sketchbook (see Figure 10-5). Sketching wireframes by hand before I move into Photoshop saves a lot of time. It's easier to sketch down 10 layouts on a piece of paper than to build them in Photoshop. On the flip side, it's *way* easier to decide on the color of a button in Photoshop than on paper. For me, the paper wireframes are all about getting the bad ideas out, so I can clear room in my head for the good ones.

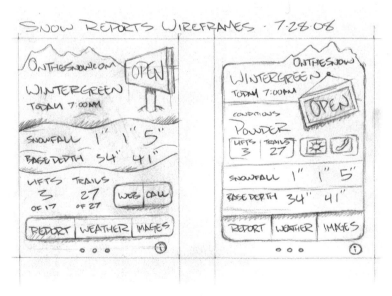

Figure 10-5. *Sketched wireframe concepts*

Try to avoid making major style decisions in these wireframe; they're just a lot of information architecture work. As Figure 10-5 shows, I do try to have some fun with my sketches (because wireframe work can get a little boring) but nothing's too detailed, just some doodling to keep myself entertained.

These are the questions I tried to work out in the Snow Reports wireframes: How will I organize all of the snowfall measurements? Should all the buttons be together, or can they be broken up into smaller groups? Where does the *Open* or *Closed* sign go? Sometimes, if very detailed work is necessary (or if it's for a larger project like a web site), I'll move from here to Illustrator to create more exact wireframes, but for Snow Reports, the real estate and number of views was so small that sketches worked just fine.

Skinning the Design

Now, I was able to get to the really fun part, designing the final interface. Why is that part so much fun? Well, I'm a designer, so it's kind of my thing, but also because it's all creative stylization at this point; most of the planning is done. I completed the flowchart (I knew all the views and how they related), and I knocked out some wireframes (I knew what should go into the interfaces and where), so now I just needed to make the application look sharp. Since I believe that all of the previous steps fall into the design of the UI, I really think this step should be called stylization or skinning.

I'll dive a bit deeper into the decisions I made with the design in the "Details of the UI" section, but for now, take a look at the final results in Figure 10-6.

Figure 10-6. *The final UI design*

But wait—shouldn't I prototype the application before I design it? There are many schools of thought on the need to prototype before you design, and for large-scale projects, I think developing a prototype first is a must. But for small projects like Snow Reports, I design before I develop. Another iPhone development company, TapTapTap wrote a really good article on the subject (http://www.taptaptap.com/blog/the-design-session/), but here are my thoughts on designing small projects before creating a prototype:

- Benefits

- When I get a really strong design solution going, it keeps me inspired.

- I can skin as I develop, instead of making extra work by skinning afterward.

- I have fewer decisions to make when developing; I already know dimensions and coordinates of everything.

- Drawbacks

- Making UI interaction decisions in Photoshop is hard.

- I may need to redesign a few small aspects to reflect discoveries made once I had a beta version to touch and feel.

When it comes to small projects, you're not going to lose out going either way; just figure out whatever keeps you motivated, and go with that!

Developing and Programming

How did I learn to program for the iPhone? Did I pay for night courses? Did I read a bunch of books? Neither—I learned under trial by fire.

Have you ever taken a clock or some other electronic device apart to see how it works? I bet you were able to put it back together with a morsel of confidence once you knew *why* everything was where it was. It's the same with programming to some extent. Breaking apart an existing program and looking at the code is the best way to learn, if you ask me. Maybe you like how-to books, but they always seem to put me to sleep. I like tutorials and example files. Sitting in a class does me no good either: it's all in one ear and out the other.

The iPhone developer community was almost nonexistent at the time, since the NDA was still alive and kicking, so there were only a handful of blog-posted tutorials and one unofficial forum. Luckily, Apple was kind enough to publish a library of sample code files; little how-to articles that were perfect for learning specific techniques. Programming Snow Reports as a whole was a very daunting task for me, so I decided instead to break my application down into numerous miniature applications. These little applications were easier to tackle, and this way, I had a good milestone system to keep me going:

- I needed two main views: one to view resort data and the other for managing the resorts I wanted to track. I also wanted these two views to flip, just like the native Weather application. For this, I used the Xcode utility template as a starting point.

- To view tracked resorts I needed a scroll view that handled multiple subviews, and luckily, Apple provided a sample PageControl application that did just this.

- I need to connect to a web service, which after a good bit of Googling, I found a great code sample for on a random blog.

- I needed to store data on the phone, holding a list of IDs for the resorts a user would want to track. This also came from a great code sample on a random blog.

At this point, I had four simple little applications, each one of them did one thing well. I used the first application as my primary one and just started bringing in code from the other miniature applications until everything was together in one: hook this up to that; plug that into this, and *voilà*!

Now, hooking these together took a bit of tinkering and didn't always go so smoothly, but doing it this way got me not only a complete application quickly but some real experience with code, not just with a book, giving me the confidence to code the rest on my own.

> **TIP:** Version control will save your life one day, so I recommend you start using it now. I know for a fact that one or two weeks of backtracking and shouting "why doesn't this work today!" would have occurred if I didn't have good version control in place for Snow Reports.
>
> I've used Subversion before when working with a larger agency, and I have never been pleased with it, so I roll with Git. Git is super lightweight, easy for a designer to understand, and doesn't require a complex server-repository thingy to use, unless you have multiple people working on your application at the same time.
>
> Once you install Git, using it is as easy as initializing a Git repository right in your projects directory, adding any files you create to the repository, and making commits whenever you want to log a point that you might need to come back to.
>
> Version control really will save you, so please look into it, or have a friend who knows it help you with it.

Testing and Deploying

I won't spend long explaining testing and deployment, as other higher minds could speak more about this than I, but I will make a few points.

Beta Testing

When testing your application, don't simply send it out to ten people and ask them to let you know what they think. Send it to the people who would be potential customers. For example, I sent Snow Reports to people I knew were into winter sports, people who would understand the point of the application and have incentive to test it. Simply sending your application to someone who has no frame of reference is just asking for all kinds of misleading results. For example, I would give horrible reviews for an application that tracks football statistics, since I know next to nothing about the sport and don't watch it at all. So why would I test a football application?

If you do have to send your application to people who are not potential users, at least give them a few use cases. For anyone that I sent Snow Reports to who wasn't into winter sports, I usually put a disclaimer in the e-mail such as, "Pretend you are a snowboarder living in Virginia and want to track all Virginia resorts, and maybe those in some surrounding states." You don't want to lead your beta testers, but at the same time, you have to give uninformed users some direction.

Deploying Your Application

If you know anyone who has successfully submitted an application to the App Store, offer them a few pints in exchange for some hand-holding when you submit your application. If you don't get deployment right, it will turn into your worst nightmare because once you submit, you don't get a response from Apple for a few days or weeks. You don't want to wait all that time only to find that your provisioning file wasn't right or some other tiny text value wasn't filled in correctly. Find a friend or associate and have them give your project the once over before you send it off.

Details of the UI

Now that we've gone through the process I used to develop Snow Reports, let's take a closer look at the UI and some of the decisions I made there, for better or for worse.

The Shape of Things

Since the main interface allows users to swipe from resort to resort, I wanted each one to have a self-contained feel. I decided to go with the floating box, as I like to call it, much like the default Weather application or any Dashboard application, for each resort's view. The OnTheSnow.com logo definitely had to be in there, and it fit *very* well, using the shape of the background mountain artwork, when I attached it to the top of the frame.

Colors

The background has a rough snow and ice feel but nothing too detailed or with too much contrast. I want it to support, not compete with, the data that sits on top. I didn't want to go for photo-realistic, just an artistic texture that fit the theme.

For text colors, I used two tones of blue-grey, a darker tone for data values and a lighter tone for labels. For buttons or other interface element that a user could touch, I decided to go with the maroon link color from OnTheSnow.com. Most other colors are darker or lighter shades of what was used in the background, so they do not stand out so much. It's a limited palette, but I knew I had a splash of color coming.

Sign of the Times

While I was happy with the UI so far, I think that every little interface, especially a custom-designed iPhone interface, needs a bit of flair, something small that gives it a splash of color and depth. For Snow Reports, this was the Open/Closed sign (see Figure 10-7).

OnTheSnow.com provides three states for the status of a resort: open, closed, and temporarily closed (which usually means it's closed for maintenance). I settled on green, red and yellow respectively to signify the differences to a user without having to make them read the sign (anything that can be recognized at a glance in an application is

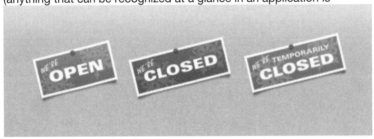

Figure 10-7. *Different status signs for a resort.*

I definitely wanted the 3-D top-lit feel shared by any good OS X icon. It needed to sit just slightly off of the interface, so I had to figure out how it should stick. Should I nail it down or hang it from some elaborate rope and hook? Call me OCD, but I decided that, since these reports move from left to right, a rope-hung sign would reveal itself for the fake that it was, as it should swing a bit when moved. I went with a single nail to hold the sign firmly in place. To further enhance the feel, I manually made the drop shadow and skewed it a bit to give the impression that the ends of the sign curl up a bit, since the nail pulls the middle tight.

Buttons

Since the *Info* button is a standard provided by the iPhone SDK, I didn't want to mess with it except to change the color. For my other buttons, however, I wanted 3-D buttons but nothing too flashy—no reflections or gloss effects, just a subtle gradient to signify a rounded shape and a bit of drop shadow to offset it from the background (see Figure 10-8). For the *Call* and *Web* buttons (the *Map* button was not implemented in the initial launch of Snow Reports), I got lucky. I had limited space, so type would have to be to small, but since both of these features are iPhone applications themselves, why not use their icons?

Figure 10-8. *The various buttons in Snow Reports*

I knew I would need a disabled state for the buttons, since not all resorts have a web site or provide weather reports. I also decided on using a highlighted state since the buttons were large enough that a full finger didn't cover them up. Also, when a processor-intensive event is fired, like loading a new view when you tap the weather button, there is a pause while the hardware chugs away at the request. The highlighted state of the button is held until that process is complete. It's a small thing, but it provides a visual confirmation to the user that "Yes, you did press me, as you can see I'm still pressed; give me a second, while I'm doing what you asked." Without this visual cue, users could easily thing that they missed the button and keep trying to tap it.

Typefaces

Since Helvetica is used through most of the Apple standard UI objects, I saw no reason to break that convention for majority of the type. I did run into space limitation for some of the labels, especially since the UI is localized and the Swedish word for *Lifts* got a little long (see Figure 10-9).

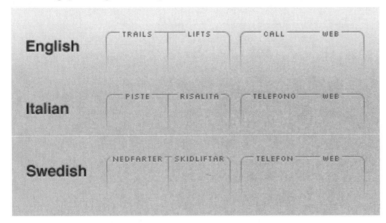

Figure 10-9. *Labels set in Silkscreen typeface*

I ended up using Silkscreen by Jason Kottke (http://kottke.org/plus/type/silkscreen/) for a few reasons (see Figure 10-10):

- Antialiased typefaces get fuzzy below 9-point, so I needed a pixel font.

- Silkscreen is about as small as you can get and remain legible. There are many other pixel fonts, but Silkscreen is the only one that has a bit of personality to it with rounded corners on the bowls, loops, and shoulders of each character.

- Most importantly, I knew that these labels wouldn't be read every time. Once users knew where the lift data was, they wouldn't need to read the label each time; they would just look at the data. Silkscreen is great when it comes to labels and small bits of text, but for general reading, pixel fonts are too small in my opinion.

- I used text shadows on pretty much every bit of text, but in the reverse sense (see Figure 10-10). I used a color lighter than the background to represent the highlighted edge at the bottom of an embossed character, enhancing the impression of the background texture.

Figure 10-10. *Close-up of text-shadow embossed technique.*

Loading vs. Splash Screen

Now, you will find many schools of thought on whether to present users with a loading screen or a splash screen. I've always found loading screens to be useful, while splash screens tend to irritate me.

What is the difference in the two screens? A loading screen (see Figure 10-11) indicates that something is going on behind the scenes, whether the application is gathering data from the server or just loading all of its assets into memory. The user isn't left wondering what is going on, the loading screen tells them via an actual loading bar, a simple activity indicator, or just a *Loading. . .* label.

Figure 10-11. *The Snow Reports loading screen*

Splash screens mostly consist of an elaborate graphic surrounding the name or logo of the application. A splash screen serves no purpose to the users; it's usually used in the belief that it will create brand awareness or something like that. Most of the time, splash screens are used as loading screens, but fail to notify the users of their purpose, resulting in the sense that the screen is an ad of sorts, being displayed before a user gets to the actual application.

In the end, I recommend that you stay away from splash screens and only use loading screens if necessary.

Reporting the Day

One final touch was the custom formatting for the date of the report. I'm a huge fan of the little human touches that Apple implements throughout its desktop, and one my favorites is the use of "Today" and "Yesterday" for e-mail dates. I decided to do the same for the report date.

Coming from a Web Design Background

As I mentioned, the majority of the design work I do is for the Web. Since both a web site and an iPhone application are based on user interaction, they share many design principles. At the same time, some differences change the game completely. I'd like to share a few key points that I've discovered and always try to keep in mind.

Apple already provides majority of the UI objects you will need for your application. Take great care in creating new design patterns for interaction; this isn't the Wild West of UI design like the Web can be sometimes. Respect the fact that your users have become familiar with the common objects in iPhone applications, and they *will* expect your application to behave the same way. A table is a table is a table, and you shouldn't go reinventing it just because you don't want to do things same as everyone else. Convention is your friend, not a hindrance to your design ego. In Snow Reports, I designed a very custom UI for reading reports, but I used the standard UI objects when it came to searching and managing tracked resorts (see Figure 10-12).

Figure 10-12. *The standard UI objects used in the resort management areas of the application*

NOTE: Apple provides the *iPhone Human Interface Guidelines* document specifically for the iPhone, and it's a great tool for anyone new to iPhone design and development. I won't reiterate what's in that document; I just recommend that you take an evening and review it.

Use cases go well beyond how a user will interact with your application: You have to take into consideration where the user will be (if you can) and how long your average use case is (I think it's safe to assume that iPhone applications have much shorter use cases than web sites). If your application uses dynamic data, you will also need to test with 2G and 3G connections to see how things perform. These are all very hard use cases to predict, so take them all with a grain of salt—but take them just the same.

Users are touching your application, not clicking with the frequency and control of a mouse. Buttons should be large enough that a user can easily tap them and maybe still see a part of what is being pressed. Spacing between buttons is key to avoid misses.

I think the fold concept applies heavily for iPhone applications, so work to keep key information above it. Just so we're all on the same page, the *fold* refers to the bottom of the screen, the point at which you can't view the rest of the content without scrolling. The term dates back to laying out a newspaper's content so the main stories were above the physical fold of the front page (I think it's about time for a new term that applies to a screen, but let's not digress).

For something like a table, scrolling is completely acceptable, and there isn't much you can do about the fold with tables. But for custom interfaces, if you have scrolling, you need to provide some indications that there is more information below the fold, because the iPhone has no constantly present scrollbar as an indicator. If your application has paging, like Snow Reports does, be sure to include a `UIPageControl`, which notifies the users of the existence of other pages.

One great thing about moving from the web to the iPhone is the controlled environment. You don't need to worry about different environments or platforms or creating browser-specific CSS, and you can use PNG files all day long. You do have to check the application when Apple updates the iPhone operating system, but this is a walk in the park compared to what I have to do for every web project.

Designing an Icon

I like to think that the icon is the logo of sorts for your application. It's the first thing that someone looks at in the App Store, and it's the representation of your application on a user's phone. I have a few guidelines that I use for icons:

- There should be one focal point; one element in your icon design gets all of the attention. If you have multiple elements, they should support this focal element by helping point the eye toward it, instead of to themselves. In rare cases, I can see the use of more than one focal point, but only if it's not possible to convey the purpose of the application with one. For example, the Maps application icon has two focal points: a red pin and a highway sign. Each one on its own *may* convey the use of the application, but together, the message is clearer.

- 57 × 57 is a tiny space, so keep things simple. I usually stay away from using photographs or text. It's an icon, not an interface. You want it to be memorable, and giving users a lot to look at doesn't make it memorable; it makes them forget most of it. If a user can't figure out what your icon is within a second or two, it's not working.

- Make it fun. Icons are fun little things to work on, so I think the content of an icon should inspire someone to use the application and be generally uplifting. This is one of the major attractions of OS X icons. If you look at most of the major titles out there, their icons seem to have a sense of humor and enjoyment.

When it came to designing the icon for Snow Reports, I was in a bit of a predicament. At the time of Snow Reports release, there were already two snow condition-reporting applications, and both of them used a snowflake for their icons. So out went that idea, and in came the decision between a snowboarder and a skier (see Figure 10-13).

Figure 10-13. *Choosing an icon design: skier versus snowboarder*

My guess (based on no major research) was that overall skiers outnumber snowboarders, but would more skiers or snowboarders have iPhones? Who do I please? Will I offend one or the other?

Instead of doing a bunch of research, I left it to the flip of a coin, and the snowboarders won. It's a little ritual I do for every version, and so far the snowboarders just seem to have the luck. I've gotten plenty of reviews that say, "Love the application but can you *please* change the icon to a skier or a snowflake?" Inevitably, two reviews later, someone says, "Great application, and keep the snowboarder icon, because we rule the slopes!" The saga continues.

One thing I was sure of was that I wanted a different look for the icon, in relation to the standard gem glossy icon. I wanted a snow texture, so I scrapped the default rendering and brought in a little bit of background noise combined with some lighting and *voilà*—a textured snow icon!

Summary

I hope you enjoyed reading this chapter, and my only wish is that you found at least one sentence that made you think, "That's a pretty good idea; maybe I'll try that next time." I definitely enjoyed writing this chapter. I don't think that anyone can call themselves an expert in the iPhone development field just yet, as I believe the App Store and even the iPhone itself are still very much in their infancy. So I can easily admit that developing for the iPhone has all been a learning experience, sometimes painfully so. A whole new medium has opened up for designers and developers. Apple has lit the way for a whole new style of mobile computing, and I can only hope that they keep the innovation coming.

Thank you for your time. I wish you the best of luck with your applications, and if we should ever meet, the first pint is on me. Cheers!

Epilogue: Reactive Music and Invisible Interfaces

Andie Nordgren, Interactive Design and Product Management RjDj

You are walking along a busy street, music player in your pocket, headphones in your ears. As you speed up your steps a bit, the deep techno drum beat in your ears speeds up with them. Noise from the street is transformed to chords as the parts of a melody fade and grow stronger again. You can't help but hum and sing as your voice is transformed into an bouncing pitch-shifted echo, cut up and synced with the beat. As you step inside the silent but echoing halls of a big bank building, the tempo drops and the music changes state into a more mellow track.

RjDj is a player for reactive music that lets you be a reality jockey - influencing and creating sound in collaboration with pre-written audio scenes that react to the environment in different ways. The user interface is not primarily the visuals on screen, but how the user moves in the world, seeking out or creating interesting sounds to feed into the RjDj scenes, or moving and interacting with the device itself. These methods of interacting with the soundscapes created by RjDj are all user interfaces - but they are invisible and carry some very different affordances and emergent patterns than the restrictions of visuals on a screen.

I won't go into the details of how RjDj works in this epilog; I'm just going to give you some food for thought that the interface is much more than the pixels on the screen.

How we got here and why we're doing it

Michael Breidenbruecker is the founder of Reality Jockey Ltd and one of the original co-founders of Last.fm; I've included a number of his insights in this section. The idea for RjDj came at a rave in Vienna in 1999 when he realised that some people find drugs can change the perception of techno beats and thought the same effect could be accomplished by altering the perception of your accoustic environment by using real-time music analysis and synthesis.

"I did the first prototype of RjDj by soldering together pieces of hardware, and the first software prototype in 2000. But at the time, the music market wasn't ready for the concept, and there was no widely distributed player hardware that could support the idea. The project rested while Last.fm took off.

"The idea of Last.fm was based on RjDj. Both platforms are based on the concept of personalized music. But Last.fm is actually personalizing playlists and not music whereas RjDj is personalizing the song itself. This only became possible because of advances in the technology sector. It took audio technology almost 10 years after my initial idea to get into shape for RjDj."

Michael places RjDj in a movement in music where the sound studio has evolved from an institution, to the home PC and now all the way to the personal mobile device. Around 2000 he saw music technology researchers shifting from mimicking real instruments to looking more and more at audio analysis - at having computers listen to, understand, and react to music and audio.

Miller Puckette, Theodore Apel, and David Zicarelli envisioned in a research paper in 1998[1] that audio could now take center stage as a control input for real-time computer music production. Using audio as an interface to control audio, along with a range of other sensors. This concept is at the core of reactive music and the idea of RjDj.

When the iPhone came out in 2008, it was a music device that could both play music and had the potential to generate it - it was a sound studio in your pocket. This triggers a lot of interesting questions, like why we are not distributing original stems och multi track material to the pocket sound studio instead of just a single recorded version of a musical composition.

"Or, the most important question, what kind of music can we create with a totally mobile sound studio which is always with you, is able to listen, is able to detect if you are moving or not, how you move and where you are on this planet, and also has a always on network connection?"

Michael thinks it will be a community effort to explore these new possibilities, and that the role of RjDj is to provide the infrastructure for that exploration.

---

[1] Miller S. Puckette, Theodore Apel and David D. Zicarelli, Real-time Audio Analysis Tools for Pd and MSP. In Proc. Int. Computer Music Conf., 1998, pp. 109--112

"We are opening our doors and invite creatives and coders out there to get wild with everything."

RjDj started in October 2008 and the mission was to build a solid foundation for reactive music.

"We did not just want to build yet another iPhone app, our goal was to build a framework for artists, producers and consumers."

Today RjDj offers a framework consisting of a composition suite, a distribution platform for RjDj scenes, the RjDj player, recording support, and an RjDj portal centered around user recordings and scenes.

Using sensors as reactive music interfaces

RjDj as an application is just a runtime environment for reactive music - it presents the scenes in a standard Cocoa interface. The scenes themselves carry the interesting interfaces by generating music that reacts to user interactions in one way or another.

When listening to reactive music with RjDj, most of the time users are not even looking at the screen. They are looking at the world around them, or thinking about what sounds could be created to enhance their experience. The interface is pervasive in the sense that the whole world can be used as input, and unexpected sounds and movements incorporated in a way that neither we as makers of RjDj or the creator of the scene could have anticipated. The recording feature of RjDj allows the user to capture these moments of unexpected or trippy delights.

Sensors of all sorts can be incorporated into the invisible user interface - geolocation, time, and analysis of movement or sound like walk detection or recognition of different audio environments and patterns. We are creating a tool box of interfaces for scene creators to use in their musical explorations, and in the same way that the iPhone touchscreen is a potential blank slate to do anything when it comes to visual user interfaces, the use of sensor input is huge space of possibilities that often blur the line between life and interface.

Here are a couple of examples of artists using RjDj:

- Roman Haefeli uses external sounds to compose music. Roman's scene Worldquantizer is listening and sampling percussive sounds of the environment of the listener. The scene then re-arranges those samples in changing beat patterns. When you are in Worldquantizer and your environment is quiet you can't hear anything. As soon as something cracks it is sampled and brought into a repeating pattern. When you use Worldquantizer on the move it feels like memories of recent events you just passed by keep popping up in your mix.

- Amaury Hazan uses movement of the device as an interface to a track of beats and samples in his scene Strike.

For the first time, a mobile music player with a global audience has the computing power to both generate music in real time, and a powerful array of sensor possibilities. RjDj is an exploration of what happens to music when it becomes location based, reactive, context-based and never ending, when there is a sound studio in your pocket.

Index

■G

■J

■K